Palgrave Studies in Impact Finance

Series Editor
Mario La Torre
Sapienza University of Rome
Rome, Italy

The *Palgrave Studies in Impact Finance* series provides a valuable scientific 'hub' for researchers, professionals and policy makers involved in Impact finance and related topics. It includes studies in the social, political, environmental and ethical impact of finance, exploring all aspects of impact finance and socially responsible investment, including policy issues, financial instruments, markets and clients, standards, regulations and financial management, with a particular focus on impact investments and microfinance.

Titles feature the most recent empirical analysis with a theoretical approach, including up to date and innovative studies that cover issues which impact finance and society globally.

More information about this series at
http://www.springer.com/series/14621

Gianluigi Giorgioni
Editor

Development Finance

Challenges and Opportunities

Editor
Gianluigi Giorgioni
The University of Liverpool
Liverpool, United Kingdom

Palgrave Studies in Impact Finance
ISBN 978-1-137-58031-3   ISBN 978-1-137-58032-0 (eBook)
DOI 10.1057/978-1-137-58032-0

Library of Congress Control Number: 2017941280

Cover Image © Luca Tettoni, robertharding / Alamy Stock Photo

Printed on acid-free paper

This Palgrave Macmillan imprint is published by Springer Nature
The registered company is Macmillan Publishers Ltd.
The registered company address is: The Campus, 4 Crinan Street, London, N1 9XW, United Kingdom

To Julia and Isabella

Acknowledgments

The editor would like to thank DRIVE (Development Research Initiative) Knowledge Platform of the University of Liverpool Management School (ULMS) for the funding received for the organisation of the workshop on "Development Finance: Issues and Challenges" held in Liverpool on Friday 3 July 2015. The workshop has provided an excellent platform to discuss ideas for this book.

Contents

List of Contributors

Paul Alagidede University of the Witwatersrand Business School, Johannesburg, South Africa

Rashmi Arora University of Bradford, Bradford, UK

Gideon Boako University of the Witwatersrand Business School, Johannesburg, South Africa

Ralitza Dimova University of Manchester, Sheffield, UK

Supriya Garikipati University of Liverpool Management School, Liverpool, UK

Gianluigi Giorgioni University of Liverpool Management School, Liverpool, UK

Paul Mosley University of Sheffield, Sheffield, UK

Rajneesh Narula Henley Business School, University of Reading, Reading, UK

André Pineli Applied Economic Research, University of Reading, Reading, UK

List of Abbreviations

AEC	African Economic Community
AIIB	Asia Infrastructure Investment Bank
ARDL	Autoregressive Distributed Lags
ASEA	African Securities Exchanges Association
BNDES	Brazil development Bank
BP	Balance of Payments
BRAC	Bangladesh Rural Advancement Committee
BRICS	Brazil, Russia, India, China and South Africa
COMESA	Common Markets for Eastern and Southern Africa
DAC	Development Assistance Committee
DfID	Department for International Development
ENADID	National Demographic Dynamics Surveys
ESAFs	Enhanced Structural Adjustment Facilities
FDI	Foreign Direct Investment
FPE	Factor Price Equalisation
GATT	General Agreement on Tariffs and Trade
GDP	Gross Domestic Product
GFC	Global Financial Crisis
GMM	Generalised Method of Moments
GSE	Ghana Stock Exchange
H-O	Heckscher-Ohlin
ICRG	International Country Risk Guide
IDP	Investment Development Path

IMF	International Monetary Fund
IPCC	Inter-governmental Panel on Climate Change
IPO	Initial Public Offering
ISI	Import-substituting Industrialisation
JB	Jarque-Bera (test for Normality)
JSE	Johannesburg Stock Exchange
LDCs	Less Developed Countries
MDGs	Multilateral (later Millennium) Development Goals
MFI	Micro Finance Institutions
MMP	Mexican Migration project
MNEs	Multinational Enterprises
NGOs	Non-Governmental Organisations
ODA	Overseas Development assistance
OECD	Organisation for Economic Cooperation and Development
OLS	Ordinary Least squares
PRSP	Poverty Reduction Strategy Papers
PRSs	Poverty Reduction Strategies
R&D	Research and Development
RCTs	Random Controls Trials
SADC	Southern African Development Community
SD	Standard Deviation
SIC	Standard Industry Classification
SNA	System of National Accounts
SSA	Sub-Saharan Africa
TFPs	Total Factors Productivities
UNCTAD	United Nations Conference on Trade and Development
UNHCR	United Nations High Commissioner for Refugees
WAMU	West African Monetary Union
WFE	World Federation of Exchanges
WTO	World Trade Organisation

List of Figures

List of Tables

1

Introduction

Gianluigi Giorgioni

1.1 Introduction

This book is being published at a very interesting juncture for both mainstream finance as well as development finance and should be of interest to academics, practitioners and policy makers. The recent (and possibly still ongoing) financial crisis has clearly put finance at the forefront of academic and political debate, given the important consequences in terms of lost output, income and jobs that it has caused.

Development finance is a very broad area encompassing, in no specific order, overseas development assistance (ODA), foreign direct investment (FDI), remittances from migrants as well as microfinance. Development finance should also focus on the way capital is being allocated (banks and/or stock markets) and the way individuals access financial institutions in terms of financial inclusion and financial literacy.

G. Giorgioni (✉)
Economics and Finance, University of Liverpool Management School, Liverpool, UK
e-mail: G.Giorgioni@liverpool.ac.uk

© The Author(s) 2017
G. Giorgioni (ed.), *Development Finance*, Palgrave Studies in Impact Finance, DOI 10.1057/978-1-137-58032-0_1

In all these areas there have been very interesting developments with important consequences for academics, practitioners and policy makers. Very clearly, the area of microfinance, an area that has attracted a lot of attention as a possible solution to the plight of poor people in developing countries over the last 20–30 years, has now reached a critical stage of reflection. The financial crisis has prompted a re-assessment of the role of the state in development and, more specifically, in finance. Political events related to globalisation, in general, and to migration, in particular, may force a re-assessment on the role of remittances. Given that private portfolio funds (loans, bonds and equity investment) still do not play an important role for very poor countries, other sources like FDI and ODA can compensate. In both areas the international landscape is changing with new emerging actors like China playing a very important role in both FDI and ODA, while foreign aid is now being offered not only by developed countries (typically organised in the DAC group) and multilateral bodies like the IMF and the World Bank, but also by non-governmental organisations (NGOs), private sector philanthropy as well as 'non-DAC countries' such as China and Saudi Arabia.

On the academic front, one could start from the 2015 presidential address by Luigi Zingales on whether finance (broadly defined as to include banks but also the equity market, the junk bond market, the option and future markets, interest rate swaps or over-the-counter derivatives) really does benefit society alongside the increasing evidence that there might be 'too much finance'. Although Zingales had the United States in mind, it is reasonable to take inspiration from his analysis and apply it to the settings of developing countries.

Zingales (2015) effectively makes *five* important points that will provide the backdrop for this book and can be summarised as follows:

1. There is no theoretical reason or empirical evidence to support the notion that all growth in the financial sector over the last 40 years has been beneficial to society (Zingales 2015, p. 1328).
2. 'The dog that didn't bark' principle or in other words the observation that papers showing a significant and positive impact on society by the junk bond market, the option and future markets, interest rate swaps

or over-the-counter derivatives have not been published despite the incentives to write papers documenting the benefit of these markets were very high and the data were readily available.

3. Use academic research and teaching to curb the rent-seeking dimension of finance (or as Zingales puts it 'act as watchdogs, not lapdogs').
4. Get more involved in (theory-based) policy.
5. Do more from an educational point of view.

This book will not necessarily attempt to act, directly, on all the five points, but will attempt to provide some tentative contributions to all five points indirectly. The book will review the theoretical and, specifically, the empirical literature on the topics of the relationship between finance and growth, the role of the state in finance, the role of remittances and foreign aid, FDI and stock markets (the spirit of points 1 and 2).

The remaining three points (3–5) will be indirectly covered by the ethos and target audience for this book. The idea of this book is to target an audience of researchers, PhD students and possibly MSc students drafting their dissertation. And the focus is on the challenges and opportunities related to development finance. Therefore, the positioning of this book is different from a textbook (the reader could access the excellent books by Spratt 2009 and Hudson 2015) and will, unlike publications of special issues focused on narrowly defined topics, include in-depth comprehensive critical reviews of developments in the literature, in a broad range of topics all related to development finance. The chapters have specifically been written with a focus on the empirical literature and in a non-technical language to be also accessible to an audience of non-specialist readers. Admittedly, the broad approach might come at the price of some lack of depth, but this was a conscious choice and the reader should benefit from the 'bird's eye' (broad) view offered by the book.

The book will also provide evidence for the need of integrating development finance into mainstream finance both in terms of teaching (especially undergraduate programmes and non-specialist finance programme) and research as the evidence is that in most finance degrees development finance is simply not present and that there is relatively limited cross-referencing between papers in development finance (predominantly published in development-oriented journals) and in mainstream finance.

The book will distinguish between actual sources of finance for development (FDI, access to capital markets, remittances and foreign aid) whose relative importance and efficacy is clearly evolving and present opportunities and challenges for the future, from the actual mechanism of allocation of resources that should be an important role of the financial sector.

It is clear that there are two strands of research that for numerous reasons do not reach out to each other. On the one hand, there is the 'macro- or country-level' analysis that provides theoretical foundations and empirical support to the role of finance for economic growth, with the empirical evidence predominantly based on econometric analysis. On the other hand, there is a micro-level approach of finance predominantly based on evidence collected on a more experimental basis through randomised control trials [RCTs].

One would find very hard to come across any cross-referencing between the two strands, although it would probably be more useful if the two were seen as complementary (or mutually reinforcing).

All these issues will be touched upon in the book. In terms of resources foreign aid will be covered by Paul Mosley, while remittances will be covered by Ralitza Dimova.

The issue of the allocation mechanisms will be covered by Gianluigi Giorgioni and by Gideon Boako and Paul Alagidede in terms of stock markets. The role of governments is covered by Rashmi Arora.

Last but not least Supriya Garikipati will cover opportunities and challenges in microfinance in terms of its impact upon poverty.

1.2   Issues and Challenges: An Assessment of the Empirical Evidence

The chapter by Giorgioni will examine the literature on finance and growth and the topics of misallocation, the impact of interventions to reduce financial illiteracy and the role of legal titles. At the macro level a link between financial development (very broadly defined and even measured) and economic growth has been empirically established in numerous papers, a finding reiterated in recent comprehensive meta-analyses that have established the relationship as a true one and not a statistical artefact. However, this conclusion must be qualified and must take into account two important findings that really stand out and clearly require some attention: the relatively negative role played by banks (the so-called too much finance or more precisely 'too much credit'), in particular once the stock of credit over GDP moves beyond a threshold set at around 90% of GDP (see for instance Arcand et al. (2015), Cecchetti and Kharroubi 2012 and Law and Singh 2014) and the relatively more benign role of stock markets.

The reasons for the clear diminishing return on bank credit are due to repeated bank crises and the distribution of loans (specifically mortgages). Basically, it is not necessarily the quantity of finance as such that prompts the relationship between finance and growth to be non-monotonic, but the type of finance, with credit to households, specifically in the form of mortgages, being one of the main culprits. Moreover, the literature appears to indicate that stock markets might have a stronger impact.

The reasons for the latter are less clear, also in light of weaker evidence from more micro- or country-focused research on the role of stock markets in developing countries that usually are very illiquid, with very few companies, and lower degrees of disclosure and transparency. However, the relative 'strength' of stock markets could also indicate a role for more project-based finance (where collateral, i.e. existing wealth is less of an issue).

Both types of financing (bank-based or stock markets-based) should also help a country overcome the misallocation issue envisaged in the literature and considered as one of the main manifestations for the lack of development (Banerjee and Duflo 2005, Banerjee and Moll 2010). However, the empirical literature has been unable to provide strong support to the role of misallocations and more specifically to the role played by frictions in financial markets as the main culprit for under-development and has indicated that the small size of firms plays a much more important role in developing countries (see Midrigan and Xu 2014, Buera et al. 2011 and Hsieh and Olken 2014). The sub-optimal size of firms in developing countries should become an important target for policy makers and has been highlighted in the recent criticisms to the microcredit practice that argue that micro-loans may not help economic activities achieve a sufficient economic dimension (see Bateman, M. and Chang, H.J. 2012 and Banerjie et al. 2015). The chapter by Giorgioni links up very nicely with the chapters by Rashmi Arora on government intervention and financial sector and the chapter by Supriya Garikipati on microfinance and poverty, while dovetailing the chapters on foreign aid and remittances.

1.3   Government Intervention and Financial Sector Development

The chapter by Rashmi Arora focuses on the complex role played by the state in the financial sector, in particular in the banking sector. A recent surge in the number of studies that have been published in the post-2008 financial crisis period provides evidence that there has been a renewed interest on the question of the role played by the government in the financial sector (see Andrianova 2012, Panizza 2012, Lin et al. 2015, Leony and Romeu 2011, Cull and Martinez-Peria 2013, De Haas et al. 2015, Brei and Schclarek 2013, Bertay et al. 2015 and Coleman and Feler 2015). The justification for a pro-active role and direct involvement – the so-called development view – is based on the idea that countries, especially poor developing countries at the early stages of development, suffer from scarcity of (long-term) capital relative to the (large) lumpiness of the investment projects required in that initial stage of development (see for instance Gerschenkron 1962). Market failures, relative scarcity of capital to fund socially valuable projects and an overall under-developed financial sector coupled with significant disparity in income distribution among different areas and regions of a country provide the justification for the government interventions.

These interventions can take the form of direct ownership of banks and the setting up of development banks aimed at funding socially valuable projects or projects in under-developed areas or in sectors/firms/industries neglected or overlooked by the private sector or in interventions in the operations of private sector banks in the form of financial repression, with both lending and saving rates not being set at appropriate market levels.

This benign view of the intervention of the state is not unanimously shared on the basis that governments may actually interfere with the workings of financial institutions and markets leading to misallocation of resources, non-performing loans and lower financial develop due to decisions being taken on the basis of political objectives. In the early 1970s publications by McKinnon (1973) and Shaw (1973) argued against the distortionary role played by interventions of governments on the activities of banks in developing countries and argued instead in favour of measures aimed at liberalising the banking and financial markets, for instance by allowing deposit rates to be set at market levels.

Finally, a third strand of the literature emphasises the role of the state as regulator of the banking and financial sector, including protecting creditor rights, regulatory practices and consumer protection and envisaging a role in the long-term, infrastructural, investment (see for instance Demirguc-Kunt 2014).

1.4   Overseas Aid as an Instrument of Development Finance

The chapter by Paul Mosley critically evaluates the literature focused on the evolution and the effectiveness of overseas aid. The identity of the donors has changed, now featuring non-DAC countries such as China which were once aid-recipient poor countries, as well as a vast array of international NGOs as well as philanthropic organisations like the Melissa and Bill Gates Foundation.

Aid has also changed its objective and its fundamental character and these changes have influenced its effectiveness, moving from having multiple objectives like trying to promote donors' exports and political influence, boost global growth, wipe out poverty and stop civil war, to focus, under the Millennium Development Goals, on the single objective of eliminating global poverty and from being a provider of hardware (capital equipment and infrastructure in various forms) to the governments of developing countries, to being a provider of technical support and ideas to the whole economy, including the private, informal and voluntary sectors as well as the government.

While aid projects have typically had a high social rate of return, the estimated impact at macro level has changed over the year, raising the issue of a 'micro-macro paradox'. The reasons for this lack of effectiveness at macro level have been ascribed to various reasons like 'fungibility' of aid flows (Heller 1975) or replacement of savings by aid (Griffiths 1970). Other explanations focused on the impact aid flows could have on the private sector in terms of the cost of labour and the competitiveness of exports ('Dutch disease', see Rajan and Subramanian 2009) and the negative long-term effects of aid on governance, for instance on the tax effort (see Bräutigam and Knack 2004).

The estimate of the impact of aid measured at macro level by means of cross-sectional analysis has oscillated considerably over the last 40 years from being positive (as in Papanek 1972, 1973), insignificant if not negative in the 1980s, positive again (at least for the short-term impact) in the early years of the new millennium (Burnside-Dollar 2000 and Hansen and Tarp 2001), negative Rajan and Subramanian (2008, 2009) and positive again (Mosley 2015, Clemens et al. 2012, Arndt et al. 2015). These inconsistent results have been influenced by the sample of countries, by the horizon of the impact (short- or long-term) and by the type of aid flow being examined.

Clemens et al. (2012) conclude that aid has made a modest but significant contribution to development. This now seems something like an equilibrium view. It may be that this at times rather turbulent field of development has now achieved maturity.

1.5   Migrant Remittances and Beyond: The Development Implications of Human Capital Mobility and Accompanying Financial Flows

The chapter by Ralitza Dimova offers a nuanced and complex analysis of the impact of remittances, correctly identified as a counter-cyclical source of finance that has grown to become a larger, more dependable, less volatile and more resilient, even after large shocks, such as natural disasters, macroeconomic and financial crises and armed conflicts, source of funds especially for poorer countries than the flows of ODA, private debt and portfolio investments (Clarke and Wallsten 2004; World Bank 2006; Weiss-Fagen and Bump 2005; Yang 2007).

Recent studies have broadened the research and policy agenda seeing remittances as integral part of the complex dynamics of both international migration and other types of cross-border capital flows moving beyond the analysis of the motivations (of out-migration), although establishing the motivations for out-migration remains a vital component for the understanding of the potential impact of remittances.

Moreover, the literature has encompassed an understanding of both the potentially negative implications of outmigration in the form of loss of human capital for either a less developed economy or an individual household and the corresponding positive implications of subsequent remittances (Bhagwati and Rodriguez 1975), with the potential for a brain gain, mostly due to greater acquisition of education by migrants' compatriots left behind in expectation of migration (see Stark et al. 1997, Stark and Wang 2002, Mountford 1997). Typically countries with low levels of human capital and low high-skill migration rates tend to gain, while losers are typically characterised by large high-skill migration rates, in particular if skilled migrants remit less than unskilled ones.

Finally, the motives (altruistic, strategy driven or familial arrangements) for sending remittance back to the country of origin will have an impact on important outcomes like benefiting those in greater need and the impact upon intra-household inequality (see Adams 1989, 1992, Taylor and Wyatt 1996, McKenzie and Rapoport 2007 and Dimova and Wolff 2008).

1.6 Multinational Enterprises and Economic Development in Host Countries: What We Know and What We Don't Know

The chapter by Rajneesh Narula and André Pineli focuses on the impact of multinational enterprises (MNEs) on development. MNEs can no longer be viewed as a synonym to FDI (Narula and Dunning 2010; UNCTAD 2011;

Collinson et al. 2016), because MNEs are increasingly able to control the value chain, even in the absence of ownership. The benefits of an FDI-assisted development strategy in terms of linkages and spillovers must be assessed net of the effect of displacement of local firms (see the extensive meta-analyses conducted by Havranek and Irsova 2011, 2012, Irsova and Havranek 2013 and Girma et al. 2015) and depended upon the ability of local firms to absorb foreign technology. If the technological gap is wide, the potential benefit is high (Findlay 1978). However, the literature has also observed that there must exist a minimum level of absorptive capacity for local firms to benefit from the presence of MNEs (Cohen and Levinthal 1989). Moreover, the impact of an FDI-assisted policy will also depend on the MNEs' investment strategy (distinguishing between initial and sequential investments) and on the level of autonomy and the mandate ('Competence-creating' or 'competence exploiting') of the affiliates.

1.7 The Impact of Microfinance on Poverty Alleviation: Making Sense of the Evidence

The chapter by Supriya Garikipati attempts to provide a synthesis of the existing literature with the intent to make some meaningful conclusions on the social effectiveness of microfinance, in particular on the impact of credit on poverty measured as income, consumption, expenditure, profits and assets. There are two broad approaches on the impact of microfinance. The theory of 'positive change' assumes that financially constrained individual or households cannot invest in income-generating activities. Access to microfinance should ease the financial constraints and allow the investment to proceed leading to an increase in profits, income and hence welfare (Duvendack et al. 2011). The theory of positive change is indeed supported by evidence suggesting that microfinance is effective and benefits clients (see, e.g., Morduch 1999, Khandker 2005, Rosenberg 2010, Imai and Azam 2012). The 'negative impact' theory emphasises effects on the households like the impact of the schooling of children due to the incentive to use the labour of their children. The negative linkages are also supported by a variety of studies (see, e.g., Hulme and Mosley 1996, Copestake 2002, Hoque 2005, Nghiem et al. 2012). The chapter will attempt at providing empirical evidence on the impact of microfinance on poverty.

1.8 The Stock Market Development and Economic Growth Puzzle: Empirical Evidence from Africa

The chapter by Gideon Boako and Paul Alagidede explores the impact of stock markets upon development by focusing on the case studies of several sub-Saharan African countries. As also briefly reported in Chapter 2, the literature on the nexus between finance and growth appears to indicate a potential positive role of stock markets, sometimes even stronger than the role played by banks (see Harris 1997, Levine and Zervos 1998, Mayer 1988, Beck and Levine 2002, Caporale et al. 2004, Tang 2006 and, Saci et al. 2009, Zhang et al. 2012; Bittencourt 2012), although Arestis et al. (2001) suggest that the contribution of stock markets on economic growth may tend to be exaggerated by studies that utilise cross-country growth regressions. Minier (2009) finds that countries experience higher economic growth during the first 5 years of existence of a stock exchange, although the longer-term results are more ambiguous.

In terms of the relationship between frontier stock exchanges and development, Hearn and Piesse (2010) analysed barriers to development of stock markets, but also limits to the contributions of stock exchanges to development. Hearn and Piesse focused on the cases of Swaziland and Mozambique and very briefly on Cote d'Ivoire. They identified political reasons for the failure to sustain development (effectively transfer of state-owned assets from the state to a small post-colonial elite) and practical reasons like lack of depth of markets, liquidity and transparency. These two markets are not part of the sample of countries studied in this chapter.

Cross-sectional studies that examine the link between financial development and economic growth in the context of sub-Saharan African countries provide mixed results. Agbetsiafia (2004) and Ndako (2010) find a positive influence of stock markets upon economic growth, but Atindehou et al. (2005) can only find evidence of a weak causal relationship between financial development and economic growth for a sample of 12 African countries. Quartey and Prah (2008) find evidence in support of the demand-following hypothesis (i.e. economic growth determines financial development) for Ghana and Odhiambo (2007) for Kenya and South Africa, but not for Tanzania, whose case supported the opposite supply-leading hypothesis.

References

Adams, R. (1989). Workers remittances and inequality in rural Egypt. *Economic Development and Cultural Change, 38*(10), 45–71.

Adams, R. (1992). The impact of migration and remittances on inequality in rural Pakistan. *Pakistan Development Review, 31*(4), 1189–1203.

Agbetsiafia, D. (2004). The finance growth nexus: Evidence from sub-Saharan Africa. *Savings and Development, 28*(3), 271–288.

Andrianova, S. (2012). Public banks and financial stability. *Economics Letters, 116* (2012), 86–88.

Arcand, J. L., Berkes, E., & Panizza, U. (2015). Too much finance? *Journal of Economic Growth, 20*(2), 105–148.

Arestis, P., Demetriades, P. O., & Luintel, K. B. (2001). Financial development and economic growth: The role of stock markets. *Journal of Money, Credit, and Banking, 33*, 16–41.

Arndt, C., Jones, S., & Tarp, F. (2015). Assessing foreign aid's contribution to growth and development. *World Development, 69*, 6–18.

Atindehou, R. B., Guyeie, J. P., & Amenounve, E. K. (2005). Financial intermediation and economic growth: Evidence from Western Africa. *Applied Financial Economics, 15*, 777–790.

Banerjee, A. V., & Duflo, E. (2005). Growth theory through the lens of development economics. *Handbook of Economic Growth, 1*, 473–552.

Banerjee, A. V., & Moll, B. (2010). Why does misallocation persist? *American Economic Journal: Macroeconomics, 2*(1), 189–206.

Banerjee, A., Duflo, E., Glennerster, R., & Kinnan, C. (2015). The miracle of microfinance? Evidence from a randomized evaluation. *American Economic Journal: Applied Economics*, *7*(1), 22–53.

Bateman, M., & Chang, H. J. (2012). Microfinance and the illusion of development: From hubris to nemesis in thirty years. *World Economic Review*, (1).

Beck, T., & Levine, R. (2002). Stock markets, banks, and growth: Panel evidence. (Working Paper 9082), National Bureau of Economic and Research, Cambridge, MA, 02138.

Bertay, A. C., Demirguc-Kunt, A., & Huizinga, H. (2015). Bank ownership and credit over the business cycle: Is lending by state banks less procyclical? *Journal of Banking and Finance*, *50*, 326–339.

Bhagwati, J., & Rodriguez, C. (1975). Welfare theoretic analyses of the brain drain. *Journal of Development Economics*, *2*(3), 195–221.

Bittencourt, M. (2012). Financial development and economic growth in Latin America: Is Schumpeter right? *Journal of Policy Modelling*, *34*, 341–355.

Bräutigam, D. A., & Knack, S. (2004). Foreign aid, institutions, and governance in sub-Saharan Africa. *Economic Development and Cultural Change*, *52*(2), 255–285.

Brei, M., & Schclarek, A. (2013). Public bank lending in times of crisis. *Journal of Financial Stability*, *9*, 820–830.

Buera, F. J., Kaboski, J. P., & Shin, Y. (2011). Finance and development: A tale of two sectors. *The American Economic Review*, *101*(5), 1964–2002.

Burnside, C., & Dollar, D. (2000). Aid, policies and growth. *American Economic Review*, *90*, 847–869.

Caporale, G. M., Howells, P. G., & Soliman, A. M. (2004). Stock market development and economic growth: The causal linkage. *Journal of Economic Development*, *29*(1), 33–50.

Cecchetti, S. G., & Kharroubi, E. (2012). Reassessing the impact of finance on growth, Bank for International Settlements.

Clarke, G., & Wallsten, S. (2004). *Do remittances protect households in developing countries against shocks? Evidence from a natural disaster in Jamaica.* Washington, DC: Mimeo, The World Bank.

Clemens, M., Radelet, S., Bhavnani, R., & Bazzi, S. (2012). Counting chickens when they hatch: Timing and the effects of aid on growth. *Economic Journal*, *122*, 590–618.

Cohen, W., & Levinthal, D. (1989). Innovation and learning: The two faces of R&D. *The Economic Journal*, *99*, 569–596.

Coleman, N., & Feler, L. (2015). Bank ownership, lending and local economic performance during the 2008–2010 financial crisis. *Journal of Monetary Economics, 71* (April), 50–66.

Collinson, S., Narula, R., & Rugman, A. (2016). *International business.* London: Pearson.

Copestake, J. (2002). Inequality and the polarizing impact of microcredit: Evidence from Zambia's Copperbelt. *Journal of International Development, 14*(6), 743–755.

Cull, R., & Martinez Peria, M. S. (2013). Bank ownership and lending patterns during the 2008–2009 financial crisis: Evidence from Latin America and Eastern Europe. *Journal of Banking & Finance, 37*(12), 4861–4878.

De Haas, R., Korniyenko, Y., Pivovarsky, A., & Tsankova, T. (2015). Taming the herd? Foreign banks, the Vienna initiative and crisis transmission. *Journal of Financial Intermediation, 24*(3), 325–355.

Demirguc-Kunt, A. (2014). Presidential address: Financial inclusion. *Atlantic Economic Journal (2014), 42,* 349–356. doi: 10.1007/s11293-014-9429-z

Dimova, R., & Wolff, F. C. (2008). Are private transfers poverty and inequality reducing? Household level evidence from Bulgaria. *Journal of Comparative Economics, 36*(4), 584–598.

Duvendack, M., Palmer-Jones, R., Copestake, J., Hooper, L., Loke, Y., & Rao, N. (2011). *What is the evidence of the impact of microfinance on the well-being of poor people?* London: EPPICentre.

Findlay, R. (1978). Relative backwardness, direct foreign investment, and the transfer of technology: A simple dynamic model. *Quarterly Journal of Economics, 92*(1), 1–16.

Gerschenkron, A. (1962). *Economic backwardness in historical perspective – A book of essays.* Cambridge: Harvard University Press.

Girma, S., Gong, Y., Görg, H., & Lancheros, S. (2015). Estimating direct and indirect effects of foreign direct investment on firm productivity in the presence of interactions between firms. *Journal of International Economics, 95*(1), 157–169.

Griffin, K. (1970). Foreign capital, domestic savings and economic development. *Bulletin of the Oxford University Institute of Economics and Statistics (Now Oxford Bulletin of Economics and Statistics), 32,* 99–112.

Hansen, H., & Tarp, F. (2001). Aid and growth regressions. *Journal of Development Economics, 64* (September), 547–570.

Harris, R. (1997). Stock markets and development: A re-assessment. *European Economic Review, 41,* 139–146.

Havranek, T., & Irsova, Z. (2011). Estimating vertical spillovers from FDI: Why results vary and what the true effect is. *Journal of International Economics, 85*(2), 234–244.

Havranek, T., & Irsova, Z. (2012). Publication bias in the literature on foreign direct investment spillovers. *Journal of Development Studies, 48*(10), 1375–1396.

Hearn, N. B., & Piesse, J. (2010). Barriers to the development of small stock markets: A case study of Swaziland and Mozambique. *Journal of International Development, 22*, 1018–1037.

Heller, P. (1975). A model of public fiscal behaviour in developing countries: Aid, investment and taxation. *American Economic Review, 65*, 429–445.

Hoque, S. (2005). Micro-credit and empowerment of women: Evidence from Bangladesh. *Asian Economic Review, 47*(3), 411–420.

Hsieh, C. T., & Olken, B. A. (2014). The missing 'missing middle'. *The Journal of Economic Perspectives, 28*(3), 89–108.

Hudson, D. (2015). *Global finance and development.* Abingdon: Routledge.

Hulme, D., & Mosley, P. (1996). *Finance against poverty.* London: Routledge.

Imai, K. S., & Azam, M. D. S. (2012). Does microfinance reduce poverty in Bangladesh? New evidence from household panel data. *Journal of Development Studies, 48*(5), 633–653.

Irsova, Z., & Havranek, T. (2013). Determinants of horizontal spillovers from FDI: Evidence from a large meta-analysis. *World Development, 42*, 1–15.

Khandker, S. R. (2005). Microfinance and poverty: Evidence using panel data from Bangladesh. *World Bank Economic Review, 19*(2), 263–286.

Law, S. H., & Singh, N. (2014). Does too much finance harm economic growth? *Journal of Banking & Finance, 41*, 36–44.

Leony, L., & Romeu, R. (2011). A model of bank lending in the global financial crisis and the case of Korea. *Journal of Asian Economics, 22*(4), 322–334.

Levine, R., & Zervos, S. (1998). Stock market, banks and economic growth. *American Economic Review, 88*, 537–558.

Lin, Y., Srinivasan, A., & Yamada, T. (2015). The effect of government bank lending: Evidence from the financial crisis in Japan. Available at SSRN 2544446.

Mayer, C. (1988). New issues in corporate finance. *European Economic Review, 32*, 1167–1188.

McKenzie, D., & Rapoport, H. (2007). Network effects and the dynamics of migration and inequality: Theory and evidence from Mexico. *Journal of Development Economics, 84*(1), 1–24.

McKinnon, R. I. (1973). *Money and capital in economic development.* Washington, DC: Brookings Institution.

Midrigan, V., & Xu, D. Y. (2014). Finance and misallocation: Evidence from plant-level data. *The American Economic Review, 104*(2), 422–458.

Minier, J. (2009). Opening a stock exchange. *Journal of Development Economics, 90,* 135–143.

Morduch, J. (1999). The microfinance promise. *Journal of Economic Literature, 37*(4), 1569–1614.

Mosley, P. (2015). Fiscal composition and aid-effectiveness. *World Development, 69* (May), 106–115.

Mountford, A. (1997). Can a brain drain be good for growth in the source country?. *Journal of Development Economics, 53*(2), 287–303.

Narula, R., & Dunning, J. (2010). Multinational enterprises, development and globalization: Some clarifications and a research agenda. *Oxford Development Studies, 38*(3), 263–287.

Ndako, U. B. (2010). Stock markets, banks and economic growth: Time series evidence from South Africa. *The African Finance Journal, 12*(2), 72–92.

Nghiem, S., Coelli, T., & Rao, P. (2012). Assessing the welfare effects of microfinance in Vietnam: Empirical results from a quasi-experimental survey. *Journal of Development Studies, 48*(5), 619–632.

Odhiambo, N. M. (2007). Financial development in Kenya: A dynamic test of the finance-led growth hypotheses. *Economic Issues, 13*(2), 21–36.

Panizza, U. (2012). Finance and economic development. *International Development Policy, 3,* 141–160.

Papanek, G. (1972). The effect of aid and other resource transfers on savings and growth in less developed countries. *Economic Journal, 82,* 863–874.

Papanek, G. (1973). Aid, private investment, savings and growth in less developed countries. *Journal of Political Economy, 81,* 120–131.

Quartey, P., & Prah, F. (2008). Financial development and economic growth in Ghana: Is there a causal link?. *African Finance Journal, 10*(1), 28–54.

Rajan, R., & Subramaniam, A. (2008). Aid and growth: What does the cross-section evidence really show? *Review of Economics and Statistics, 90,* 643–665.

Rajan, R., & Subramaniam, A. (2009). *Aid, Dutch disease and manufacturing growth.* Washington, DC: Center for Global Development. Working Paper 196.

Rosenberg, R. (2010). Does microcredit really help poor people? CGAP Focus Note, Number 59.

Saci, K., Giorgioni, G., & Holden, K. (2009). Does financial development affect growth? *Applied Economics, 41,* 1701–1707.

Shaw, E. S. (1973). *Financial deepening in economic development*. London: Oxford University Press.

Spratt, S. (2009). *Development finance: Debates, dogmas and new directions*. London: Routledge.

Stark, O., & Wang, Y. (2002). Inducing human capital formation: Migration as a substitute for subsidies. *Journal of Public Economics, 86*(1), 29–46.

Stark, O., Helmenstein, C., & Prskawetz, A. (1997). A brain gain with a brain drain. *Economics Letters, 55*, 227–234.

Tang, D. (2006). The effect of financial development on economic growth: Evidence from the APEC countries, 1981–2000. *Applied Economics, 38*, 1889–1904.

Taylor, J. E. & Wyatt, T. J. (1996). The shadow value of migrant remittances, income and inequality in a household-farm economy. *Journal of Development Studies, 32*(6), 899–912.

The World Bank. (2006). *Global economic prospects: Economic implications of remittances and migration*. Washington, DC: The World Bank.

UNCTAD – United Nations Conference on Trade and Development. (2011). *World investment report 2011: Non-equity modes of international production and development*. United Nations, New York and Geneva.

Weiss-Fagen, P., & Micah, B. (2005). Remittances in conflict and crises: How remittances sustain livelihoods in war, crises and transition to peace. The Security-Development Nexus Program Policy Paper, International Peace Academy, New York.

Yang, D. (2007). *Coping with disaster: The impact of hurricanes on international financial flows, 1970–2002*. Ann-Harbor: Mimeo, Department of Economics, University of Michigan.

Zhang, J., Wang, L., & Wang, S. (2012). Financial development and economic growth: Recent evidence from China. *Journal of Comparative Economics, 40*, 393–412.

Zingales, L. (2015). Presidential address: Does finance benefit society?. *The Journal of Finance, 70*(4), 1327–1363.

Gianluigi Giorgioni is a lecturer in economics and finance at University of Liverpool Management School (ULMS). His research interests focus on the impact of different sources of finance upon economic growth and development, currency unions in developing countries (CFA Franc Zone) and Islamic finance.

2

Issues and Challenges: An Assessment of the Empirical Evidence

Gianluigi Giorgioni

2.1   Introduction

Luigi Zingales in his 2015 presidential address on the role of finance in society published in the most important journal in finance – *The Journal of Finance* – has identified a number of areas where finance either is not making a strong positive impact or should try to improve it.

Zingales (2015) states that the benefits of the financial sector (very broadly defined as to include banks but also the equity market, the junk bond market, the option and future markets, interest rate swaps or over-the-counter derivatives) are inflated with no theoretical reason or empirical evidence to support the notion that the financial sector could be beneficial to society. He remarks that the absence of evidence on the impact of certain areas of finance may be explained

G. Giorgioni (✉)
Economics and Finance, University of Liverpool Management School, Liverpool, UK
e-mail: G.Giorgioni@liverpool.ac.uk

© The Author(s) 2017   **19**
G. Giorgioni (ed.), *Development Finance*, Palgrave Studies in Impact Finance, DOI 10.1057/978-1-137-58032-0_2

by the principle of the 'dog that did not bark', or in other words, that since empirical evidence of the positive impact had not been found, papers reporting it could not be published. Zingales (2015) also emphasises the fact that academics in the area of finance should get more involved in (theory-based) policy and do more from an educational point of view.

Although Zingales (2015) clearly focused on the United States (or possibly developed countries), it is possible to use the premises of this reasoning and apply it to developing countries in terms of development finance. This is exactly what will be done in this chapter which includes an assessment of the empirical impact of finance upon economic growth. It is clear from the review of the relevant literature that the assertion that financial development had a positive impact upon economic growth should be clearly qualified as there is some evidence that the impact of credit wanes and actually becomes detrimental once a certain threshold is reached. Moreover, not all financial interventions have the same impact, with some evidence that project-based financing is the most impactful. In other words, credit based on collateral, and fundamentally geared towards the housing market, is less effective than lending to entrepreneurs based on the perceived viability of an investment.

On the whole, there is a body of evidence that suggests that finance does have an impact upon economic growth, although even surveys are discordant about publication bias. One clear piece of evidence is that the role of credit is waning over a certain level of GDP (90%) due to role of cheap and standardised finance directed to households, specifically in the form of mortgages (based on tangible collateral with legal title), while project-based finance does have a bigger impact as evidenced by the relative impact of stock markets.

This finding leads neatly to the issue of misallocation of resources that could be caused or exacerbated by market frictions, namely, for our own purposes, financial frictions like credit constraints. The chapter will focus on the literature on misallocation and the persistent existence of widely dispersed marginal rates of returns to capital that could be ironed out by a better allocation of financial resources, with unviable projects not being financed and finding a way of being unwound and sold, while new projects with promising returns or existing ones in need of expansion should be funded. The misallocation of financial resources could lead to persistent differences in total factors productivities (TFPs) among firms within a country and persistent differences in average TFPs among different countries. The actual evidence on the differences in average TFPs among countries is mixed, but a proxy for the persistent difference in TFPs, the size of firms, appears to be a variable with quite a robust predicative power.

On average firms in developing countries are significantly smaller than in most developed countries, probably even below the minimum efficiency level. The smallness of firms can make them inappropriate target for formal lending, because the fixed costs of monitoring and enforcing loans repayments will not be covered by the interest rate, unless it is set at prohibitive levels.

Access to the financial sector as well as the awareness of availability and impact of different financial instruments can become a crucial variable, on both the sides of a bank balance sheet (loans and deposits).

This leads to the issues of creditworthiness, possibly, but not necessarily, linked to ownership of assets that could act as collateral. To use an asset as collateral the owner requires valid legal titles. However, legal titles are not sufficient as potential borrowers must be prepared to pledge the assets as collateral (with all the risks that it would entail), while potential lenders must be interested in the assets pledged as collateral and assess their re-saleability and the costs of re-possessing the assets. Therefore, the simple establishment of a legal system might not have the miraculous effects in terms of access to finance as a way of escaping poverty as envisaged in the literature. Finally, to benefit from the various services provided by the financial sector (lending, borrowing, saving, investing) people must develop some degree of financial awareness (financial literacy). This chapter will also examine the literature on financial literacy and like in the case of the literature on legal property titles, the conclusion appears to be that financial literacy interventions have a limited impact upon decisions on saving and borrowing.

Many of the issues that will be assessed in more detail in this chapter will clearly focus on developing countries and should, therefore, quite clearly fall into the remit of 'development finance'. However, they can be easily extended to developed countries as well (in fact, admittedly, some of these issues were initially studied in the context of developed countries). The issue of whether finance has an impact upon economic growth and what type of finance is more effective is clearly applicable to both the context of developed and developing countries. The same applies to access to finance, in particular for firms of smaller sizes, financial illiteracy and interventions to reduce it, and, perhaps to a lesser extent, the role of legal titles.

Therefore, finance can learn from developing finance and the challenges faced by development finance. From this it could follow that one possible recommendation is that development finance should be taught alongside mainstream finance. There is some evidence that development finance is rarely taught at undergraduate level, although it is definitely an integral part of the curriculum at postgraduate level, but in many cases in more specialist Masters programmes. This integration could be mirrored in academic research where there is some evidence that research is segmented in journals with little cross-referencing among them.

Finally, the empirical literature is based on two broad approaches: econometric methods and experimental ones (randomised control trials or RCTs) with both mainstream and development finance confronting the issue of endogeneity and the issue of omitted variables (in this chapter there are plenty of examples of papers facing the issues of endogeneity and omitted variables in the literature on financial literacy and in the literature on the impact of legal titles). Again, a recommendation is to emphasise these issues, while at the same time training researchers to be proficient in both methods.

The rest of the chapter is organised in the following way. Section 2.2 will review the literature on impact of finance upon economic growth. This is typically more macro-oriented (aggregate economies) and uses more econometric-based methods. Section 2.3 will focus on the issue of misallocations, inclusive of an assessment of the impact of microcredit, while Section 2.4 will be divided into two sub-sections examining the literature on the role of legal titles and the role of financial illiteracy and an evaluation of intervention aimed at reducing it. Finally, Section 2.5 will conclude the chapter.

2.2   Evidence from Impact of Finance upon Economic Growth

The impact of finance upon the economy, specifically upon economic growth, has been extensively analysed both in theoretical papers and books and in more recent years, in many empirical papers. A detailed overview of the theoretical foundations would be beyond the scope of this chapter (for a clear, exhaustive and yet accessible overview I would direct the reader to the excellent first chapter of Hudson 2015).

Very briefly, according to Hudson (2015) there are different approaches to finance. Neo-liberal and liberal institutionalism (to use Hudson classification) view the impact of finance as a positive force able to enhance economic growth and economic welfare. In the case of the neo-liberal approach, the economy is seen as being populated by putative entrepreneurial or established productive organisations whose development is hindered by a large number of 'market frictions', normally artificially introduced by government interventions. In the case of frictions focused on finance, we have credit constraints and all sorts of restrictions placed on the activities of banks and financial markets. One of the alleged, and strongest, pieces of evidence of the consequences of these frictions are the persistent dispersion of marginal rates of returns to capital among firms in most developing countries and in comparison to firms in developed countries.

This persistent dispersion of marginal returns to capital appears to suggest that there exists a high degree of misallocation of capital. Banerjee and Moll (2010) distinguish between misallocation on the 'intensive margin' that should be interpreted as misallocation in a more conventional sense based on the empirical evidence on differences in marginal returns to capital across countries or across existing firms within a country and misallocation in the 'extensive' sense that refers to the fact that potential (talented) entrepreneurs do not have the necessary capital to set up and invest in their own potentially successful projects.

Misallocation at the intensive margin tends to be easier to be observed and measured and may disappear in the long run, even when the one at extensive margin may not.

In the more neo-liberal approach, the persistent misallocation that could be extended to include misallocation among different sectors of the economy is predominantly attributable to market 'frictions' such as credit constraints. The elimination of these credit constraints will lead to the unleashing of market and entrepreneurial forces.

A more nuanced position is supported by the 'liberal institutionalism'. Here there is a recognition that markets as institutions do not arise spontaneously and that 'market failures' may hinder the creation, expansion or survival of markets. The role of governments is more nuanced and it is perceived that governments do have a role to play in establishing legal and institutional frameworks like property rights. At the more negative end of the spectrum, 'critical reformists' emphasise the fact that finance itself can consume resources adding to the misallocation, that finance can include elements of speculation and that in general finance should accompany the development of industry rather than leading it. Moreover, although market failures are recognised as playing a role, the inevitable degree in uncertainty over future outcomes can lead to recurrent financial crises that in turn may lead to poverty, unemployment and inequality. The policy prescription is for governments to regulate finance quite extensively and for the state to intervene directly in the economy. Finally, a more radical position sees finance, in particular global finance, as an essential part of capitalism playing an important role in causing and perpetuating the perceived inequities linked to a capitalist society.

Valickova et al. (2015) and Arestis et al. (2015) have recently published, in very quick succession, two meta-analyses based on large and quite similar samples of the papers published on the topic of the nexus between economic growth and finance. Valickova et al. (2015) manage to provide evidence of an 'authentic', significant, link between financial development and economic growth. Authentic should be interpreted as being free of publication selection bias. This conclusion, however, has to be qualified, because the relationship is dependent upon the structure of the economy (the effect appears to be stronger in developed countries than in developing ones), the structure of the financial sector itself, with stock market-oriented systems providing stronger effects than more bank-oriented ones and, finally, dependent upon the time period, as the effect of the financial sector appears to become weaker in more recent times. However, Arestis et al. (2015) find evidence of a 'positive' publication bias in the literature on a sample of papers not too dissimilar from the sample of papers used by Valickova et al. (2015).

The literature on finance and economic growth has empirically established that although both banks and stock markets may be important for economic growth (King and Levine 1993a, b; Levine 1997, 2005; Levine and Zervos 1998; Levine et al. 2000), the impact of stock markets appears to be relatively stronger, while the impact of the banking sector could even be detrimental (Beck and Levine 2004; Rioja and Valev 2004; Levine and Zervos 1998; Levine 2002; Chakraborty and Ray 2006; Loayza and Ranciere 2006; Shen and Lee 2006; Deidda and Fattouh 2008 and Saci et al. 2009; Demirgüç-Kunt et al. 2012; Rioja and Valev 2014; Luintel et al. 2016). Very early contributors in the 1990s like Atje and Jovanovic (1993) found that stock markets had a positive and significant influence on economic growth, whereas banks had a negative impact, while De Gregorio and Guidotti (1995) provided early evidence of a negative impact of bank lending on economic growth in Latin America and explained this finding by citing cycles of credit booms and busts (i.e. an over-expansion of credit was followed by a credit crunch).

A further paper highlighting a negative view of banking and financial crises was contributed by Jordà et al. (2013). They take quite a long-term, historical perspective and provide evidence that over the long period 1870–2008 successive financial crises have become increasingly more expensive in terms of lost GDP potential than crises caused by mainly non-financial causes. Moreover, more credit-intensive expansions tend to be followed by deeper recession and slower recoveries. Büyükkarabacak and Valev (2010) use a new dataset from developed and developing countries that decompose private credit into household credit and enterprise credit and find that household credit expansions have been a statistically and economically significant predictor of banking crises. Enterprise credit expansions are also associated with banking crises but their effect is weaker and less robust.

As previously mentioned, there is no unanimity on the impact of financial development upon economic growth. Robinson (1952) clearly stated that 'finance followed industry' and not vice versa, while Lucas

(1988) doubted that finance really had an important role to play in economic development. The issue of whether financial development preceded economic development was highlighted by Driffil (2003) and Trew (2006), while Bagehot (1906), Schumpeter (1934), Gurley and Shaw (1955), Goldsmith (1969), McKinnon (1973) and Shaw (1973) supported the notion that financial development preceded economic development and provided a theoretical framework.

To appropriately appreciate the contributions of the empirical literature, it is useful to remind ourselves of the many channels through which finance can affect economic development. First of all, the impact could manifest itself through enhanced accumulation of physical capital and/or enhanced productivity of the existing stock of capital. In terms of the channels, the financial sector could help mobilising savings, contribute to the allocation of funds to capital investment, provide monitoring and supervision, hence improving corporate governance, by allowing ways to manage risk (for instance trough portfolio diversification) and facilitate trade.

To perform these functions, the financial sector must handle the issues that inevitably arise from an asymmetrical distribution of information between the principal and the agents, in this specific case between providers of funds and borrowers. Since the minimisation of the impact of information asymmetry inevitably involves costly actions in terms of monitoring, supervision and enforcement, and these costs are not very sensitive to the size of loans (or deposits), these actions could effectively be treated as a 'fixed cost' making the handling of small loans or deposits economically unviable. This is clearly a universal issue especially confronted by financial institutions in developing countries, but that could be easily extended to more developed and financially sophisticated countries.

In addition to the five functions highlighted in the previous paragraphs, stock markets might specifically offer an exit option for start-up entrepreneurs and venture capitalists through IPOs, act as attractors for domestic and foreign capital inflows, provide liquidity and provide market signals and information regarding the quality of potential investment projects.

The relative effect of stock markets is particularly strong in the case of firms operating in high-tech industries with a higher degree of external finance dependency. Hsu et al. (2014) provide evidence of a positive effect of stock markets on innovation of firms operating in high-tech industries with a higher degree of external finance dependency, while credit markets appear to discourage innovation. The reasons for this are that equity markets do not require a tangible collateral, while intangible collateral embodied in R&D and human capital is difficult to accept for banks. Stock markets can process and transmit information on innovative processing and share the upside of an investment with shareholders, while for banks the unstable and limited amounts of internally generated funds to service debt are a problem.

In recent developments, Arcand et al. (2015) (see also related paper reaching very similar conclusions such as Arcand et al. 2012, Cecchetti and Kharroubi 2012 and Law and Singh 2014) show that the effect of private credit upon economic growth becomes insignificant, if not negative, once the stock of credit reaches a certain threshold (identified as being 90% of GDP). Their finding provides further evidence that the relationship between finance (more correctly banking credit) and economic growth is not monotonic. They also provide evidence that not including this non-monotonicity will lead to a (growing) downward (negative) bias in the estimate of the parameter of the variable total credit explaining the other recently discovered effect of the 'vanishing effect'(i.e. the observation that the effect of finance was stronger in the 1980s than in subsequent decades). Arcand et al. (2015) also distinguish between credit to firms and credit to households and despite the fact that their sample is significantly smaller both in terms of countries and period (and highly sensitive even to the omission of one country – Switzerland) they show that credit to households can explain a significant proportion of the non-monotonicity.

Cecchetti and Kharroubi (2013) offer a theoretical explanation of the threshold by showing in a model that further (exogenous increases in) finance, if directed to high collateral and low-productivity projects (typically mortgages), reduces total factor productivity (TFP) growth. Moreover, in a model with skilled workers and endogenous financial sector growth, there is the possibility of multiple equilibria. However, in the equilibrium where skilled labour works in finance, the financial sector grows more quickly at the expense of the real economy. Finally, they show that financial growth disproportionately harms financially dependent and R&D-intensive industries. Clearly one channel of transmission is the exogenous increase in credit directed to the housing market and this could provide a policy-oriented suggestion for the existence of the threshold. Law et al. (2013) provide evidence that the impact of finance upon economic growth depends on the level of institutional development of a country, for instance in areas like the rule of law, reducing the incidence of corruption, improving government efficiency and transparency. Beck et al. (2012) observe that the level of financial development is uneven among a sample of countries and more importantly that the distribution of credit between enterprise and households varies among different countries and might have different impacts upon the economy.

The second channel is through the bidding up of resources, primarily skilled workers, away from other productive areas into finance. Philippon and Reshef (2013) look at the historical development of the financial sector in an international perspective and show that the share of income (i.e. GDP) taken by finance was in 2012 the highest for the entire period covered in the paper (i.e. 1860–2012) and provide a number of possible explanation for this behaviour, while Philippon (2015) provides evidence that the unit cost of intermediation of the financial sector in the United States does not seem to have decreased significantly, or even at all, in recent years, despite the recent advances in information technology, in financial innovation and despite changes in the organisation of the finance industry.

In this section a number of issues have been discussed. The relative role of the banking sector that appears to be causing financial crises as a consequence of financial surges and whose effectiveness wanes after a certain threshold is reached. Moreover, the impact of the banking sector is conditional on the type of credit: credit to the private sector in the shape of loans to firms appears to be more effective, while credit to households, specifically as mortgages, appears to have a negative impact. Also project-lending, based on intangible assets and possibly affected by high levels of information asymmetry, appears to be more effective and this role is more appropriately carried out by stock markets.

In the next sections, the chapter will focus in more detail on the issue of misallocation, financial illiteracy and the role of property title in enhancing the efficacy of finance.

2.3   Misallocation

One observed difference between developed and developing countries is the persistent differential TFPs. One conclusion from the relevant literature is that misallocation of resources is a much more important source of differential TFPs between developed and developing countries rather than simple lack of capital (see Banerjie and Moll 2010). For instance, Restuccia and Rogerson (2013, p. 1) observe that from previous established work in economics, the dominant source of differences in output per worker is differences in TFP as opposed to either the amount of physical or human capital per worker, while Hsieh and Klenov (2009) observe that only 50% of the variation of TFP across countries can be explained by either physical capital or human capital.

Misallocation is empirically measured as persistent and large dispersions in the marginal products of resources, in particular capital. An economy is relatively more efficient at allocating resources if a highly productive firm (or plant) can acquire additional capital to expand. If there are frictions, highly productive firms cannot acquire the extra capital, and different rates of return to capital will persist.

Misallocations can be on the intensive or extensive margins. According to Banerjee and Moll (2010) misallocation on the intensive margin is misallocation in the conventional sense or in other words it describes how (or whether) inputs are allocated away from low-productivity units to high(er)-productivity units. Misallocation at the extensive sense could be due to the inability of talented entrepreneurs to fund their own ideas and therefore be excluded. Misallocation at the intensive margin tends to disappear in the long run, even when the one at extensive margin may not.

Regarding the magnitude of resource misallocation, Banerjee and Duflo (2005) present suggestive evidence that India's low TFP in manufacturing relative to the United States could reflect misallocation of capital across plants. Hsieh and Klenow (2009) compare the marginal return to capital of firms (at 4-digit SIC) in China, India and the United States with the United States used as the benchmark in terms of possessing an 'efficient' financial sector. Considering the somewhat critical stance expressed by Zingales (2015) and Arcand et al. (2015) is reasonable to express doubts on the desirability of using the United States as a benchmark (frontier) for optimal financial system.

Hsieh and Klenow (2009) provide evidence of a much wider dispersion in the marginal products of capital and labour in China and India than in the United States and argue that if this higher dispersion in marginal returns to capital and labour in both China and India were brought in line with those of the United States, the TFPs of both China and India could increase by between one-third or half. Hsieh and Klenow (2009) also observe that the size of firms, especially in India once formal and informal firms are included, is particularly small, with the majority of plants in Indian manufacturing have 5 or fewer workers, whereas most US plants have more than 40 workers.

Banerjie and Duflo (2005) provide empirical evidence from a variety of sources (observation, randomised experiments, natural experiments) of this dispersion (for instance small firms in developing countries borrow – and crucially repay – loans at very high interest rates, suggesting that their marginal returns to capital are high).

However, on aggregate, the difference between developed and developing countries disappears altogether or is substantially reduced in line with the observed finding that 'capital does not flow to developing countries' as observed by Lucas (1990).

Therefore, although the mean return to capital may not be that much different, the standard deviation (dispersion) in developing countries is significantly higher than in developed countries – and persistent.

And if the focus is shifted on misallocation, institutional barriers and frictions can explain the misallocation, with financial frictions identified as an important source for these misallocations. Restuccia and Rogerson (2013) identify a direct approach in estimating the effect of factors such as institutional barriers to firms' growth, trade barriers, regulations taxation and costs imposed to the firms operating in the formal sectors. One explanation for the misallocation of resources (and its persistence) is pinned on the (formal) market for assets (for instance the market for land) with successful firms unable to acquire the assets they need to expand, while at the same time failed firms survive as downsizing and investing in the asset markets is not an attractive proposition.

Restuccia and Rogerson (2013) emphasise the role of credit imperfections. Credit imperfections may lead to selection effects regarding the quality of entrepreneurs (rich entrepreneurs without bright ideas versus poorer but more promising entrepreneurs) and misallocation of financial resources. However, the actual impact of credit imperfections is relatively small as acknowledged by Restuccia and Rogerson (2013) who conclude by surveying the literature that credit imperfections (financial frictions) play a relatively small role in explaining low TFPs. This low dispersion contradicts the findings by Hsieh and Klenov (2009) about China and India. It must be noted that Midrigan and Xu (2014) focused on misallocation on the intensive margin and condition the TFPs' dispersion on firm's growth (they do find high unconditional variability), whereas Hsieh and Klenov (2009) found large unconditional variability.

Misallocation can also affect the distribution of resources across different economic sectors (agriculture, industry and service sector). Buera and Kaboski (2012) look at structural change, namely at sectoral reallocations, movements of production from home to market, and increases in establishments size. The central finding is that scale technologies are the driving force of the three phenomena.

A slightly more indirect approach is through firm size. Buera et al. (2011) document that size can explain the difference in TFPs across countries and across industries (defined as tradable and non-tradable sectors with the former being characterised by firms of a larger size).

Buera et al. (2011) provide evidence that financial frictions, together with the resulting higher relative price of tradables and lower wages in the equilibrium, lead to too many entrepreneurs with too small establishments in the non-tradables sector, and too few entrepreneurs with too large establishments in the tradables sector. More broadly speaking, the observed distribution of the size of firms in developing countries has led to the conclusion that the distribution is bimodal (many very small and few large firms) and that there is a 'missing middle'. Hsieh and Olken (2014) show that the distribution of firms – inclusive of both formal and informal enterprises in the manufacturing sector of India, Indonesia and Mexico – by size is distinctively unimodal with the overwhelming majority of firms in the small size category (with small size typically defined as below 10 employees), although the distribution by share of employment resembles more closely a bimodal distribution with a missing middle, a point reinforced by Tybout (2014). Hsieh and Olken (2014) observe that small firms tend to have a low(er) marginal return to capital than larger firms and conclude that there seems to be an inability for firms, including larger ones, to grow (the 'larger firms are constrained too' view). They question the wisdom to reduce the constraints for small firms only or focus efforts to provide credit specifically to small firms, as microcredit institutions tend to do, as this would exacerbate the situation by further increasing the incentive to stay small. Bateman and Chiang (2012) make this point, while more recent evidence from Banerjee et al. (2015) suggests that microcredit interventions fail to create viable businesses.

Re-allocation can happen both at unit level but also at sectoral level and indeed this has been one of the six stylised facts of development of economic development envisaged by Kuznets (1973). However, there is evidence that the process of structural transformation, or the re-allocation of resources across sectors that accompanies development, is not entirely replicated in many developing countries. The standard process starts from agriculture that will steadily decline while manufacturing will first rise and then decline, and services always increase. Structural change typically takes place when countries grow. This particular path/process has been followed by developed countries and some of the newly developed ones such as Korea, Japan and China.

Bah (2007) empirically examined the validity of the development path for a sample of developed and developing countries. Bah (2007) provides evidence that developing countries do not follow this path in the different level of shares of each sector for a given level of GDP per capita and for the relationship between changes in GDP per capita and changes in the structure of the economy. Also, many developing counties appear to undertake structural change in periods of economic stagnation or even decline, rather than in periods of growth as it would have been predicted theoretically.

However, sub-Saharan Africa countries tend to have lower shares of agriculture and higher shares of service at low levels of GDP per capita and appear to experience shift in the sectoral distribution of economic activity during periods of stagnation.

Therefore, the challenge appears to be to support firms with viable projects taking also care of the sector where they operate.

2.3.1 Removal of Financial Frictions: The Case of Microcredit

This section will provide an overview of several case studies focused on the impact of microcredit.

Microcredit should enable poor people in particular poor women to escape poverty by means of business creation. There are effectively three stages of the process. The first stage is allowing access to capital for individual/households and businesses that otherwise could not borrow from more mainstream financial organisations like banks due to their lack of collateral, lack of legal documents proving ownership of assets that could be pledged as collateral, lack of desirability on the part of the lenders in the assets that could be used as collateral and lack of creditworthiness – in other words, financial frictions.

From a pure financial point of view, the process through which microcredit tries to overcome the agency problems between the microcredit financial institutions (MFI) and its borrowers is joint liability, which means that small groups of borrowers become responsible, effectively act as guarantors, for the repayment of each other's loans. Every member of the group will be considered in default and denied any further loans, if one member of the group does not repay the loan. Typically, joint-liability lending will involve very regular repayment meetings, sometimes even on a weekly basis, and will also lead to strong social pressure. These characteristics may make microcredit not attractive to some potential borrowers. In some cases some MFIs have started to offer individual lending.

The second stage of the process is that once individual/households/ businesses have secured funding, they should create new businesses, strengthen and expand existing ones in terms of profitability and job creation. The final phase should translate the impact of financing business to an impact on some or all of the ultimate social targets such as eradication of poverty and hunger, universal primary education, the promotion of gender equality and empowerment of women, reduction in child mortality, and improvement in maternal health. This final phase will not be examined in this chapter as it was simply not possible to review the vast literature on microfinance and all its important facets. Unsurprisingly also the relevant literature has splintered in narrow areas of research almost solely focused on one of these objectives that hardly communicate with each other. Therefore, this section will re-examine the current empirical literature to provide evidence on the actual impact of microfinance on business creation, inclusive of job creation, profitability and financial sustainability.

By making use of recently published papers that conducted major assessments of microcredit intervention over long periods of time, this section will look closely at the first two phases of the process. Although these papers had slightly different objectives, they all have in common that they were conducted as RCTs, with a baseline survey conducted just before individual/households/villages were randomly allocated to the treatment or control group and with follow-up surveys conducted at later stages up to 36 months later. The medium- to long-term horizon of these studies is very important as the effect of different interventions like financial or training interventions may take time, while the use of RCTs should remove the problem of endogeneity and self-selection.

The section will be based on recent contributions by Banerjee et al. (2015), Crépon et al. (2015), Augsburg et al. (2012), Angelucci et al. (2015), Attanasio et al. (2011), and Tarozzi (2013).

Banerjee et al. (2015) undertook a multi-year RCT in poor neighbourhoods of Hyderabad (India) and followed 6,850 households comparing the control baseline sample in 2005 with the control households in the end line 1 (EL1) survey in 2008 and EL2 in 2010.

Crépon et al. (2015) evaluated the Al Amana's programme in rural Morocco, and Augsburg et al. (2012) use an RCT to assess the impact of microcredit, provided by a major MFI (EKI) in Bosnia to loan applicants who would have been rejected through regular screening. Angelucci et al. (2015) evaluated the impact of a Compartamos's programme in Mexico, implemented in both urban and rural areas in the state of Sonora, with a baseline survey in the first half of 2010 and follow-up surveys during 2011 and 2012, while Attanasio et al. (2011) evaluated the impact of two types of microcredit (group loans or individual loans; neither the group nor the individual-lending programmes include mandatory public repayment meetings and are thus relatively flexible forms of microcredit) intended to finance business creation offered by XacBank's MFI programme, by means of a randomised field experiment among 1,148 poor women in 40 villages across rural Mongolia. The evaluation of the results is conducted at baseline in April 2008 before the start of loans and a follow-up survey in September 2009.

Finally, Tarozzi et al. (2013) use information on the impact of 1-year group lending offered to 6,000 households originally part of Family Health International aimed at family planning programmes (FPP) in Ethiopia. The baseline survey was conducted in 2003 baseline with a follow-up survey in 2006 EL1.

Most papers report that at the level of the baseline survey, the individuals/households/villages involved in their projects already borrow, although they might not be borrowing from MFIs.

Banerjee in India and Tarozzi et al. (2013) in Ethiopia report an increase in borrowing. However, Crepon et al. (2012) in Morocco, Angelucci et al. (2015) in Bosnia and Attanasio et al. (2011) in Mongolia provide a more mixed picture. Crepon et al. find an overall low take-up of microcredit (17% in the treatment area and zero in control) at the time of their EL survey. The low take-up is difficult to explain in light of a 'back-of-the-envelope' profit estimates that imply an average return to microcredit capital in terms of business profit of around 140%.

Angelucci et al. (2015) find that the mean take-up is 18.9% during the study period, with a mean number of loans per borrower among treatment group members around 4 and with a sizable majority of borrowers (70%) borrowing more than once. They observe that typically women who had prior businesses, those with primary or secondary education only and middle-aged respondents were more likely to borrow.

Attanasio et al. (2011) find that all women who had signed up and expressed an initial interest in borrowing were visited by a loan officer and received a first loan after a successful screening. At EL (after 18 months) 54% of all treatment respondents had borrowed from XacBank: 57% in the group-lending villages and 50% in the individual-lending villages, a significant increase in borrowing.

In terms of impact, the general findings are that microloans led to minimal jobs creation. For instance Banerjee et al. (2015) report that only 10% of all businesses had an employee by the time of the second follow-up survey (EL2), while Angelucci et al. (2013) show that only existing business and only business that already had at least 3 employees were able to increase the number of employees, although they find that microloans had led to business creation. The latter was also reported by Banerjee et al. (2015) who state that the funding did increase the proportion of households with at least one business from 24% to 42% at EL2, with 43% of these businesses primarily operated by a woman.

Augsburg et al. (2012) show that the impact on self-employment and business creation was mainly driven by the highly educated, with very important differences in terms of the sector of the business activity. Those with not more than primary education were more likely to start up agricultural activities. In contrast, those with a higher education level were more likely to start up an enterprise in the significantly more profitable services sector.

Although microloans had an impact on revenues and expenditure, profitability was less affected and the impact was typically concentrated at the higher percentiles. Banerjee et al. (2015) observe that the increase in the average profits was concentrated in businesses above the 85th percentile. Also Crepon et al. (2015) find very heterogeneous effects with higher profits concentrated in higher quantiles and Angelucci et al. (2015) find that increases in revenues, expenses and profits are significant only from the 80th percentile.

However, Crépon et al. (2015) observe that profitability turned negative at the lower quantiles, with 25% of the compliers in the treatment groups registering negative profits, while almost no one in the control group does. It might be reasonable to conclude that given this risk level, individuals may be reluctant to borrow.

Another important finding is that the new businesses tend to be created in the already predominant economic sectors (for instance agriculture and animal husbandry in case of Tarozzi) and that the increase in self-employment income is offset by a decrease in employment income, which comes from a drop in labour supplied outside the farm or household business (Augsburg et al. 2011 and Attanasio et al. 2011).

On average, Attanasio et al. (2011) provide evidence to support a 50% increase in asset holding, sales and profits only for villages that had access to microcredit for longer periods of time, regardless of the type of loan. In terms of results, Attanasio et al. (2011) find that both group-loans and individual loans equally use to fund expenditure focused on the business and the household. Business creation is only observed for women offered group loans and in increase in profits.

Overall these studies lead their authors to revise downwards the role of microcredit as an engine of escape from poverty through small business growth. All the papers surveyed in this section find that access to micro-finance is associated with (some) business creation, but exclusively at the intensive margin (i.e. it enables existing businesses to expand through investment or households investing in more than one business at the same time and leads to an improvement in the profits for the already most profitable of those businesses), rather than because new households are induced to start an activity. Therefore, the business creation does not happen at the extensive margin in terms of expanding entrepreneurship.

The overall evidence is mixed with limited impact on profitability, job creation and business expansion. Bateman and Chang (2012) argue that the emphasis of microcredit institutions on entrepreneurship per se coupled with the high interest rates and short maturities demanded by most MFIs will lead to an increase in the number of simple and unsophisticated micro-enterprises, typically small production-based operations or very simple trading, retail and service operations that can service a microloan.

The size of these firms may not reach even the minimum efficient size and the creation of new micro-enterprises, if it is not accompanied by an adequate increase in demand, will lead to an increase in competition and lead to the displacement of incumbent firms.

The emphasis on lending to micro-enterprises, unable to grow, may exacerbate the penury of medium-sized and large enterprises (the so-called missing middle) that is usually evidence of lack of development exacerbating the misallocation problem, inclusive of misallocation at sectoral level to the detriment of manufacturing but in favour of commerce and subsistence agriculture.

2.4   The Unbanked: The Role of Legal Titles and the Role of Financial Illiteracy

The poor have savings and assets and appear to be able to juggle quite complex portfolios of assets and liabilities (Rutherford 2000; Collins et al. 2009). For example, as Banerjie et al. (2015) noted, in their sample of households in the area of Hyderabad in India, two thirds of households had at least one outstanding loan, borrowed mostly from moneylenders (50%), while other sources of loans were friends or neighbours (25%) and family members (13%). However, loans from commercial banks were very rare (3%) and initially there was almost no borrowing from MFIs in the sample areas at baseline. Galiani and Sharddroski (2010) reach a similar conclusion when surveying squatters given legal titles to a parcel of land in Buenos Aires. Those households tended to access credit from informal sources such as relatives, colleagues, neighbours and friends, and credit from the stores in which they perform their daily purchases.

Therefore, households appear to be unbanked (i.e. without access to loans from banks or formal financial institutions). Johnston and Morduch (2008) examine the issue of unbanked households. Some households or individuals may be unbanked because they are not creditworthy. Others may be unbanked because it is rational for them not to take loans or indeed save, including the fact that they do belong to a kinship network.

Kinnan and Towsend (2012) provide evidence for a sample of 531 households in 16 villages in Thailand that being connected to a network led to a significantly lower sensitivity of current consumption to changes in current income (1 baht change led to 0.1645 change in consumption for those without a network against a sensitivity close to zero for those with access to a network). However, the gain of being part of a network was significantly more pronounced for investment decisions, in particular for larger investment decisions (1 baht change led to 0.6370 change in investment for those without a network against a sensitivity significantly reduced to 0.1314 for those with access to a network).

However, a third group could be creditworthy, but not voluntarily excluded from borrowing. The latter group is the one predominantly targeted by microfinance institutions and will be the focus of the next section on the role of legal titles.

2.4.1 The Role of Legal Titles

As previously mentioned, some households (or individuals) could be creditworthy, but still excluded from borrowing. This group has been the target of microcredit with the idea that lending to credit-rationed borrowers would unleash a wave of entrepreneurship. Johnston and Morduch (2008) examined data for 1,438 households in Indonesia and found that, although 40% of them had been assessed as being creditworthy – even without possessing an asset to be used as collateral – by professional loan officers of the microcredit arm of a large state-owned bank, only 10% actually borrowed any money. The households that actually borrowed any money spent it to finance non-business-related expenditures such as school fees, medical treatment, home repair or expansion, consumption and social and holiday expenses. The main driver for the difference in creditworthiness was income with twice as many households well over the poverty line being classified as creditworthy as those below the poverty line. Therefore, lack of creditworthiness is not due to either lack of tangible collateral or lack of legal title to those assets as theoretically predicted by Stiglitz and Weiss (1981) and elaborated by De Soto (2000) when he argued that lack of legal titles to proving the ownership of assets, including their own house, prevented poor people to borrow and invest.

However, the unbanked required loans were significantly smaller and very uneconomical to provide even for microcredit institutions.

A similar conclusion was reached by Galiani and Shargrodsky (2010) who surveyed squatters given legal titles to a parcel of land in Buenos Aires. They found that families with formal titles of ownership substantially increased housing investment, reduced household size and enhanced the education of their children relative to the control group of households without legal titles. These effects, however, did not take place through improvements in access to credit. Therefore, Galiani and Schargrodsky (2010) concluded that, although land titling can be an important tool for poverty reduction, the channel of transmission is not through enhanced access to credit (including mortgages), but through the channel of increased investment in both physical and human capital. This very limited, if not inexistent, impact of legal titles upon credit had also been found in other papers such as Place and Migot-Adholla (1998) in Kenya, Besley (1995) for Ghanaian farmers, Braselle et al. (2002) for household farms in Burkina Faso and Field (2005) and Field and Torero (2008) for urban squatters in Lima.

However, Karas et al. (2015) show that private land rights facilitate access to external finance and promote more investment among large and well-established urban industrial enterprises in a context like Russia, – the so-called de Soto effect – where actors face fewer difficulties in accessing credit for reasons not directly related the security of land tenure, like for instance scale and location, than in rural areas of sub-Saharan Africa or Latin American slums.

Another possible reason not directly related to land titles is suggested by Galiani and Schargrodsky (2010) as they observe that real estate possession does not seem to be a sufficient condition to qualify for formal credit. A more important variable to obtain credit from formal institutions, at least in the context of Argentina, is a formal contract of work and the requirements of minimum tenure in the job and high wages. Another possible reason for the lack of collateralisation of land is that lenders may be discouraged by the combination of the limited desirability and low probability of re-possessing the land in case of default and legal costs that could exceed the actual value of the land.

2.4.2   Financial Literacy

In a recent review aimed at establishing a possible research agenda on the motivations for under-savings by poor people, Karlan et al. (2014) identify information and knowledge gaps as one of the main motives for under-saving alongside transaction costs, lack of trust and regulatory barriers, social constraints and behavioural biases.

In this section the focus will be on information and knowledge gaps. Information and knowledge gaps, also labelled as financial illiteracy, have attracted a substantial amount of research.

Remund (2010, p. 284) defines financial literacy as:

> Financial literacy is a measure of the degree to which one understands key financial concepts and possesses the ability and confidence to manage personal finances through appropriate, short-term decision-making and sound, long-range financial planning, while mindful of life events and changing economic conditions.

Karlan et al. (2014) observe that there is clear evidence that financial literacy is low, even in developed countries. However, they find that the evidence that financial illiteracy causes low savings is mixed, while on the whole, there is negative evidence that interventions to increase financial literacy actually work, in particular if the costs of these interventions are included in a cost-benefit analysis. These conclusion are reinforced by Fernandes et al. (2014) who find that interventions to improve financial literacy explains only 0.1% of the variance in financial behaviour with weaker effects in low-income samples.

However, Lusardi and Mitchell (2014) observe that acquiring financial literacy is an addition to human capital and should be treated as an economic choice. In other words, some people may consciously decide not to invest in financial literacy or consciously change their financial behaviour as a result of their improved financial literacy. Therefore, the apparent lack of impact of interventions to mitigate financial illiteracy should not lead to overtly negative conclusions about the effectiveness of these interventions. Moreover, Lusardi and Mitchell (2014) make the point that avoiding the costly consequences of 'financial mistakes' should also be included in any cost-benefit analysis. Therefore, theoretically the rate of return of financial literacy interventions is potentially high. Cole et al. (2011) document low level of financial literacy in households in India and Indonesia and provide evidence of impact of a two-hour financial literacy training session in India and Indonesia on the take-up of bank accounts. They use an RCT and find some evidence of impact specifically on a sub-sample of uneducated and less financially literate households. However, the impact is less strong than the impact of a monetary incentive.

Sayinzoga et al. (2015) organised a randomised field experiment in rural Rwanda partnering with an international NGO that provides financial training to the members of a village bank. These village banks belong to larger agricultural savings and credit cooperatives. Each village bank would send a representative, who would be trained and instructed to share the information with his/her peers to measure the extent, if any, of any possible spillover effects.

Sayinzoga et al. (2015) find that a test for the equality of means between treated (i.e. having access to financial literacy interventions) and control groups (no access to financial literacy interventions) does not provide any evidence of a difference in terms of increased savings, borrowing and probability of starting an income-generating activity. However, they find that financial training does have an impact upon financial knowledge as measured with the standard questionnaire developed by Lusardi and Mitchell (2007). Sayinzoga et al. (2015) also utilise regression analysis and find some evidence of an effect of the financial literacy intervention, although they do not find any positive spillover effect jeopardising the overall cost effectiveness of the intervention. Drexler et al. (2014) conducted an RCT in the Dominican Republic to evaluate the impact of financial interventions and provide some evidence of a negative spillover effect in terms of diminished revenue if a firm in a neighbouring area has undergone treatment.

However, both Karlan et al. (2014) and Fernandes et al. (2014) find that highly focused and targeted literacy interventions, even if based on basic heuristics and just-in time interventions, appear to be more effective than general interventions. Comparatively speaking, financial literacy interventions appear to be significantly less effective in increasing financial knowledge than other types of interventions aimed at boosting knowledge of maths and science, work setting interventions and creative thinking and career counselling. Cole et al. (2014) and Cole et al. (2016) (in the United States find that mathematical training is more beneficial than financial training as such by using changes in state-level high schools requirements.

States mandate requiring high school students to take personal finance courses do not have a discernible impact on saving or investment behaviour, while an additional high school math course increases the propensity to accumulate assets (savings and for retirement), while reducing the probability of being delinquent on credit card debt, the probability of declaring bankruptcy or experiencing foreclosure.

Drexler et al. (2014) provide some evidence on the effectiveness of focused, ad hoc interventions. They conducted an RCT in the Dominican Republic and compared the effect of two financial interventions: a standard accounting training (double-entry accounting, working capital management and investment decisions) and a simplified, rule-of-thumb, training teaching basic financial heuristics or routines on micro-entrepreneurs such as very practical rules on how to keep personal money separated from the money accrued by the business. Those trained with the latter approach significantly improved the way they managed their finances, the accuracy and internal consistency of the reported numbers, and the quality of the accounting records. They were also better at keeping personal and business finance separate. However, the difference only applied to entrepreneurs with initial lower skills and poorer financial practices.

Moreover, Karlan et al. (2014) argue that the literature on financial illiteracy and its impact are plagued by issues like reverse causality (for instance the very act of saving may actually increase financial literacy) and the possibility that financial illiteracy is highly correlated with some other variables omitted in the analysis. On the latter problem, Fernandes et al. (2014) find that econometric studies that predicted financial behaviour based on measured financial literacy would find a much stronger effect than experimental studies based on financial interventions, with the discrepancy mainly due to the effect of omitted variables, namely controls for psychological traits, although Lusardi and Mitchell (2014) focus on the issue of endogeneity and state that papers that have tried to solve the issue of endogeneity by using instrumental variables regressions have found stronger effects of financial literacy than papers that have simply used ordinary least squares (OLS). However, Lusardi and Mitchell (2014) do not compare these papers based on econometrics with papers using RCTs, unlike Miller et al. (2015) who notice that the evidence of an effect of financial literacy upon financial decisions is less strong in case the studies used RCTs.

2.5   Conclusions

This chapter has conducted an assessment of four interlinked issues in development finance: the impact of finance upon economic growth, misallocation of resources and financial frictions (inclusive of an assessment of the impact of microcredit), the role of legal titles and financial illiteracy. It is clear from the review of the relevant empirical literature, including meta-analyses, that the nexus between financial development and economic growth is quite complex and depends upon the type of finance and the size of the financial sector. Moreover, the literature appears to indicate that a project-based financing is the most impactful, unlike credit directed to the housing market.

The literature appears also to indicate a stronger role for stock markets than for banks. The issue of the impact of stock markets will be discussed in another chapter of this book.

The chapter has also looked at the issue of misallocation in light of the perceived disparity in TFPs between developed and developing countries and the wider dispersions of marginal rates of returns to capital in developing countries. These disparities could be caused or exacerbated by market frictions, namely credit constraints. Therefore, the removal of these financial restrictions should lead to a reduction in the misallocation of resources. However, the evidence that financial restrictions per se affect misallocation is not very strong.

The literature, however, has clearly managed to put in the right focus the issue of the size of firms in countries with the largest disparity of TFPs. Most firms in countries like India are very small indicating an inability to grow, for which the financial sector could be a contributor.

Therefore, although the topic of misallocation and financial frictions was clearly initiated in the neo-classical approach, at a pragmatic level, the issue of structural small size of firms should receive the attention it deserves. In this sense, the role of the state in the financial sector can become important and will be discussed in another chapter of this book on government intervention and financial sector development, while overview of the interventions by microcredit institutions provided in this chapter indicates that they may not be the provider of a quick solution.

As previously mentioned, an informed access to the financial sector, of both the sides of a bank balance sheet (loans and deposits) as well as the awareness of availability and impact of different financial instruments, is clearly an important variable. This was discussed in the section on financial illiteracy and the interventions to alleviate it. The section has clearly indicated some consensus on the type of intervention that can lead to more reliable and effective impacts. However, the literature has also indicated that actions to alleviate financial illiteracy might not have the desired impact and, methodologically, that a more rigorous assessment is needed as issues of endogeneity and omitted variables might affect the results of some of the empirical papers.

The chapter has also examined the literature on legal titles. Legal titles on their own do not appear to lead to more access to finance or significantly different outcomes in terms of economic welfare, although they do tend to impact on investment in the property and in human capital, probably as a consequence of the stability brought about by the legal title of ownership.

The chapter also makes the point that development finance should not exclusively be confined to the area of development, both in terms of teaching and research, but should be an integral part of a curriculum and research agenda in finance and, although many of the issues assessed in this chapter were clearly focused on developing countries, they could be easily extended to developed countries as well (not only access to finance and financial illiteracy, but also methodological issues like how to deal with endogeneity and omitted variables).

References

Angelucci, M., Karlan, D., & Zinman, J. (2015). Microcredit impacts: Evidence from a randomized microcredit program placement experiment by Compartamos Banco. *American Economic Journal: Applied Economics*, 7(1), 151–182.

Arcand, J. L., Berkes, E., & Panizza, U. (2012). Too much finance?, International Monetary Fund.

Arcand, J. L., Berkes, E., & Panizza, U. (2015). Too much finance? *Journal of Economic Growth, 20*(2), 105–148.

Arestis, P., Chortareas, G., & Magkonis, G. (2015). The financial development and growth nexus: A meta-analysis. *Journal of Economic Surveys, 29*(3), 549–565.

Atje, R., & Jovanovic, B. (1993). Stock markets and development. *European Economic Review, 37*(2), 632–640.

Attanasio, O., Augsburg, B., De Haas, R., Fitzsimons, E., & Harmgart, H. (2011). Group lending or individual lending? Evidence from a randomised field experiment in Mongolia (Working Paper 11/20). Institute for Fiscal Studies.

Augsburg, B., De Haas, R., Harmgart, H., & Meghir, C. (2012). Microfinance at the margin: Experimental evidence from Bosnia and Herzegovina. European Bank for Reconstruction and Development.

Bagehot, W. (1906). *Lombard Street (1873)*. London: Kegan Paul.

Bah, E. H. M. (2007). Structural transformation in developed and developing countries.

Banerjee, A., Duflo, E., Glennerster, R., & Kinnan, C. (2015). The miracle of microfinance? Evidence from a randomized evaluation. *American Economic Journal: Applied Economics, 7*(1), 22–53.

Banerjee, A. V., & Duflo, E. (2005). Growth theory through the lens of development economics. *Handbook of Economic Growth, 1*, 473–552.

Banerjee, A. V., & Moll, B. (2010). Why does misallocation persist? *American Economic Journal: Macroeconomics, 2*(1), 189–206.

Bateman, M., & Chang, H. J. (2012). Microfinance and the illusion of development: From hubris to nemesis in thirty years. *World Economic Review*, (1), 13–36.

Beck, T., & Levine, R. (2004). Stock markets, banks and growth: Panel evidence. *Journal of Banking and Finance, 28*, 423–442.

Beck, T., Büyükkarabacak, B., Rioja, F. K., & Valev, N. T. (2012). Who gets the credit? And does it matter? Household vs. firm lending across countries. *The BE Journal of Macroeconomics, 12*(1), 1–46.

Besley, T., (1995). Property rights and investment incentives: Theory and evidence from Ghana. *Journal of Political Economy 103*(5), 903–937.

Braselle, A.-S., Gaspart, F., & Platteau, J.-P. (2002). Land tenure security and investment incentives: Puzzling evidence from Burkina Faso. *Journal of Development Economics, 67*, 373–418.

Buera, F. J., & Kaboski, J. P. (2012). Scale and the origins of structural change. *Journal of Economic Theory, 147*(2), 684–712.

Buera, F. J., Kaboski, J. P., & Shin, Y. (2011). Finance and development: A tale of two sectors. *The American Economic Review, 101*(5), 1964–2002.

Büyükkarabacak, B., & Valev, N. T. (2010). The role of household and business credit in banking crises. *Journal of Banking & Finance, 34*(6), 1247–1256.

Cecchetti, S. G., & Kharroubi, E. (2012). Reassessing the impact of finance on growth, bank for international settlements.

Cecchetti, G., & Kharroubi, E. (2013). Why does financial sector growth crowd out real economic growth? Finance and the wealth of nations workshop, Federal Reserve Bank of San Francisco & The Institute of New Economic Thinking.

Chakraborty, S., & Ray, T. (2006). Bank-based versus market-based financial systems: A growth-theoretic analysis. *Journal of Monetary Economics, 53*(2), 329–350.

Cole, S., Sampson, T., & Zia, B. (2011). Prices or knowledge? What drives demand for financial services in emerging markets? *The Journal of Finance, 66*(6), 1933–1967.

Cole, S., Paulson, A., & Shastry, G. K. (2014). Smart money? The effect of education on financial outcomes. *Review of Financial Studies, 27*(7), 2022–2051.

Cole, S., Paulson, A., & Shastry, G. K. (2016). High school curriculum and financial outcomes: The impact of mandated personal finance and mathematics courses. *Journal of Human Resources, 51*(3), 656–698.

Collins, D., Morduch, J., Rutherford, S., & Ruthven, O. (2009). *Portfolios of the poor: How the world's poor live on $2 a day*. Priceton (New Jersey): Princeton University Press.

Crépon, B., Devoto, F., Duflo, E., & Parienté, W. (2015). Estimating the impact of microcredit on those who take it up: Evidence from a randomized experiment in Morocco. *American Economic Journal: Applied Economics, 7*(1), 123–150.

De Gregorio, J., & Guidotti, P. E. (1995). Financial development and economic growth. *World Development, 23*(3), 433–448.

De Soto, H. D. (2000). *The mystery of capital: Why capitalism triumphs in the west and fails everywhere else*. New York: Basic Books.

Deidda, L., & Fattouh, B. (2008). Banks, financial markets and growth. *Journal of Financial Intermediation, 17*, 6–36.

Demirgüç-Kunt, A., Feyen, E., & Levine, R. (2012). The evolving importance of banks and securities markets. *The World Bank Economic Review*, p.lhs022.

Drexler, A., Fischer, G., & Schoar, A. (2014). Keeping it simple: Financial literacy and rules of thumb. *American Economic Journal: Applied Economics*, 6(2), 1–31.

Driffill, J. (2003). Growth and finance. *The Manchester School, 71*(4), 363–380.

Fernandes, D., Lynch Jr, J. G., & Netemeyer, R. G. (2014). Financial literacy, financial education, and downstream financial behaviors. *Management Science, 60*(8), 1861–1883.

Field, E. (2005). Property rights and investment in urban slums. *Journal of the European Economic Association, 3*, 279–290.

Field, E., & Torero, M. (2008). *Do property titles increase credit access among the urban poor? evidence from a nationwide titling program.* Unpublished manuscript. Durham, NC: Duke University, Department of Economics.

Galiani, S., & Schargrodsky, E. (2010). Property rights for the poor: Effects of land titling. *Journal of Public Economics, 94*(9), 700–729.

Goldsmith, R. W. (1969). *Financial structure and development.* New Haven, CT: Yale U.

Gurley, J. G., & Shaw, E. S. (1955). Financial aspects of economic development. *The American Economic Review 45*(4), 515–538.

Hsieh, C. T., & Klenow, P. J. (2009). Misallocation and manufacturing TFP in China and India. *The Quarterly Journal of Economics, 124*(4), 1403–1448.

Hsieh, C. T., & Olken, B. A. (2014). The missing 'missing middle'. *The Journal of Economic Perspectives, 28*(3), 89–108.

Hsu, P. H., Tian, X., & Xu, Y. (2014). Financial development and innovation: Cross-country evidence. *Journal of Financial Economics, 112*(1), 116–135.

Hudson, D. (2015). *Global finance and development.* London: Routledge.

Johnston, D., & Morduch, J. (2008). The unbanked: Evidence from Indonesia. *The World Bank Economic Review, 22*(3), 517–537.

Jordà, Ò., Schularick, M., & Taylor, A. M. (2013). When credit bites back. *Journal of Money, Credit and Banking, 45*(s2), 3–28.

Karas, A., Pyle, W., & Schoors, K. (2015). A 'de Soto effect' in industry? Evidence from the Russian Federation. *Journal of Law and Economics, 58*(2), 451–480.

Karlan, D., Ratan, A. L., & Zinman, J. (2014). Savings by and for the poor: A research review and agenda. *Review of Income and Wealth, 60*(1), 36–78.

King, R. G., & Levine, R. (1993a). Finance, entrepreneurship and growth. *Journal of Monetary Economics, 32*(3), 513–542.

King, R. G., & Levine, R. (1993b). Finance and growth: Schumpeter might be right. *The Quarterly Journal of Economics, 108*(3), 717–737.

Kinnan, C., & Townsend, R. (2012). Kinship and financial networks, formal financial access, and risk reduction. *The American Economic Review, 102*(3), 289–293.

Kuznets, S. (1973). Modern economic growth: Findings and reflections. *The American Economic Review, 63*(3), 247–258.

Law, S. H., & Singh, N. (2014). Does too much finance harm economic growth? *Journal of Banking & Finance, 41*, 36–44.

Law, S. H., Azman-Saini, W. N. W., & Ibrahim, M. H. (2013). Institutional quality thresholds and the finance – growth nexus. *Journal of Banking & Finance, 37*(12), 5373–5381.

Levine, R. (1997). Financial development and economic growth: Views and agenda. *Journal of Economic Literature, 35*(2), 688–726.

Levine, R. (2002). Bank-based or market-based financial systems: Which is better? *Journal of Financial Intermediation, 11*(4), 398–428.

Levine, R. (2005). Finance and growth: Theory and evidence. *Handbook of Economic Growth, 1*, 865–934.

Levine, R., & Zervos, S. (1998). Stock markets, banks, and economic growth. *American Economic Review, 88*(3), 537–558.

Levine, R., Loayza, N., & Beck, T. (2000). Financial intermediation and growth: Causality and causes. *Journal of Monetary Economics, 46*(1), 31–77.

Loayza, N. V., & Ranciere, R. (2006, June). Financial development, financial fragility, and growth. *Journal of Money, Credit and Banking, 38*(4), 1051–1076.

Lucas, R. (1988). On the mechanics of development planning. *Journal of Monetary Economics, 22*(1), 3–42.

Lucas, R. (1990). Why doesn't capital flow from rich to poor countries? *The American Economic Review, 90*(2), 92–96.

Luintel, K. B., Khan, M., Leon-Gonzalez, R., & Li, G. (2016). Financial development, structure and growth: New data, method and results. *Journal of International Financial Markets, Institutions and Money, 43*, 95–112.

Lusardi, A., & Mitchelli, O. (2007). Financial literacy and retirement preparedness: Evidence and implications for financial education. *Business Economics, 42*(1), 35–44.

Lusardi, A., & Mitchell, O. S. (2014). The economic importance of financial literacy: Theory and evidence. *Journal of Economic Literature, 52*(1), 5–44.

McKinnon, R. I. (1973). *Money and capital in economic development.* Washington, DC: Brookings Institution Press.

Midrigan, V., & Xu, D. Y. (2014). Finance and misallocation: Evidence from plant-level data. *The American Economic Review, 104*(2), 422–458.

Miller, M., Reichelstein, J., Salas, C., & Zia, B. (2015). Can you help someone become financially capable? A meta-analysis of the literature. *The World Bank Research Observer, 30*(2), 220–246.

Philippon, T. (2015). Has the US finance industry become less efficient? On the theory and measurement of financial intermediation. *The American Economic Review, 105*(4), 1408–1438.

Philippon, T., & Reshef, A. (2013). An international look at the growth of modern finance. *The Journal of Economic Perspectives, 27*(2), 73–96.

Place, F., & Migot-Adholla, S. (1998). The economic effects of land registration for smallholder farms in Kenya: Evidence from Nyeri and Kakamega districts. *Land Economics, 74*(3), 360–373.

Remund, D. L. (2010). Financial literacy explicated: The case for a clearer definition in an increasingly complex economy. *Journal of Consumer Affairs, 44*(2), 276–295.

Restuccia, D., & Rogerson, R. (2013). Misallocation and productivity. *Review of Economic Dynamics, 16*(1), 1–10.

Rioja, F., & Valev, N. (2004). Does one size fit all?: A reexamination of the finance and growth relationship. *Journal of Development Economics, 74*(2), 429–447.

Rioja, F., & Valev, N. (2014). Stock markets, banks and the sources of economic growth in low and high income countries. *Journal of Economics and Finance, 38*(2), 302–320.

Robinson, J. (1952). *The generalization of the general theory, in: The rate of interest and other essays.* London: MacMillan.

Rutherford, S. (2000). *The poor and their money* (pp. 6–7). New Delhi: Oxford University Press.

Saci, K., Giorgioni, G., & Holden, K. (2009). Does financial development affect growth? *Applied Economics, 41*(13), 1701–1707.

Sayinzoga, A., Bulte, E. H., & Lensink, R. (2015). Financial literacy and financial behaviour: Experimental evidence from rural Rwanda. *The Economic Journal, 126*(594), 1571–1599.

Schumpeter, J. A. (1934). The theory of economic development: An inquiry into profits, capital, credit, interest, and the business cycle, Transaction publishers.

Shaw, E. S. (1973). *Financial deepening in economic development, 1973*. New York: Oxford University Press.

Shen, C. H., & Lee, C. C. (2006). Same financial development yet different economic growth: Why? *Journal of Money, Credit and Banking, 38*(7), 1907–1944.

Stiglitz, J. E., & Weiss, A. (1981). Credit rationing in markets with imperfect information. *The American Economic Review, 71*(3), 393–410.

Tarozzi, A., Desai, J., & Johnson, K. (2013). On the impact of microcredit: Evidence from a randomized intervention in rural Ethiopia.

Trew, A. (2006). Finance and growth: A critical survey*. *Economic Record, 82*(259), 481–490.

Tybout, J. (2014). The missing middle revisited. *Journal of Economic Perspectives, 28*(4), 235–236.

Valickova, P., Havranek, T., & Horvath, R. (2015). Financial development and economic growth: A meta-analysis. *Journal of Economic Surveys, 29*(3), 506–526.

Zingales, L. (2015). Presidential address: Does finance benefit society? *The Journal of Finance, 70*(4), 1327–1363.

Gianluigi Giorgioni is a lecturer in economics and finance at University of Liverpool Management School (ULMS). His research interests focus on the impact of different sources of finance upon economic growth and development, currency unions in developing countries (CFA Franc Zone) and Islamic finance.

3

Government Intervention and Financial Sector Development

Rashmi Arora

3.1 Introduction

The contribution of finance to economic growth has been well established in the literature (King and Levine 1993a, b; Levine 1997). However, in the recent literature doubts have emerged on the strength and limits of the contribution of financial development to economic growth (Arcand et al. 2015; Law and Singh 2014; Beck et al. 2014a). The role of governments and markets in the financial sector has remained contentious as well and despite a voluminous literature on the subject, questions still persist on what should be the role of government in the financial sector. On the one hand, lending activities of government-owned banks tend to be countercyclical, focus on long-term lending, target sectors or firms or industries typically neglected or overlooked by the private sector, enhance banking habit and promote financial inclusion. On the other hand, lending activities of government-owned banks may lead to non-performing loans, low quality of lending, and

R. Arora (✉)
Lecturer in Development Economics, University of Bradford, Bradford, UK
e-mail: r.arora6@bradford.ac.uk

© The Author(s) 2017   **53**
G. Giorgioni (ed.), *Development Finance*, Palgrave Studies
in Impact Finance, DOI 10.1057/978-1-137-58032-0_3

lending to cronies and political allies. Since the financial crisis there has been a renewed interest on the question of the role played by the government in the financial sector. A significant number of studies have emerged in the post-crisis period. However, despite a plethora of studies on the subject the issue on whether government interventions in the financial sector lead to positive or negative outcomes still remains controversial, although there is some consensus on the countercyclical role of public banks.

Three strands of literature exist on the issue of government intervention in the financial sector. The first is the so-called development view, according to which the government should intervene and develop financial institutions, especially in the early stages of a country's economic development. For instance during the 1950s and 1960s, a number of developing countries adopted a supply-side oriented approach to finance in order to catch up with developed countries. Other reasons to justify the intervention by the state were the very large size and lumpiness of infrastructural and investment projects and scarcity of private sector capital to finance them (Gerschenkron 1962). With the supply-leading approach to financial institutions pursued in many developing countries, the policymakers perceived that the government could step in and jump-start financial and economic development (La Porta et al. 2002). Those against government interventions (also known as political view) have argued that they may lead to misallocation of resources, political interference, inefficiencies and lower financial development. There is a third strand of literature that argues that government interventions in the financial sector are fine so long as they confine themselves to building financial infrastructure, carrying out institutional and regulatory reforms and improving competition.

This chapter presents evidence from the literature highlighting different views on the role played by the government in financial development. The chapter is organised as follows. Section 3.2 examines the arguments in favour of government interventions. The next section looks closely at the literature that argues against state interventions in the financial sector.

Section 3.4 examines the third strand that argues that the role of governments is in the regulation of the financial sector. Section 3.5 concludes the chapter by presenting a balanced view of the three main arguments.

3.2   Governments Should Intervene in the Financial Sector

The rationale for government interventions in the financial sector has been based on the grounds of market failure, to enhance the safety and soundness of the banking system, to finance socially valuable projects and provide access to financial services to rural areas and less developed regions (Yeyati et al. 2005). In India, for instance, the objective of the nationalisation of the major banks, which took place in two phases in 1969 and 1980, was to enhance credit to selected sectors such as agriculture, promote balanced regional development and support rural areas. The Narasimham Committee Report on financial sector reforms (Narasimham 1991) summarised the objectives of nationalisation as follows:

> Nationalisation was recognition of the potential of the banking system to promote broader economic objectives such as growth, better regional balance of economic activity and the diffusion of economic power. It was designed to make the system reach out to the small man and the rural and semi-urban areas and to extend credit coverage to sectors hitherto, neglected by the banking system and through positive affirmative action provide for such expansion of credit to agriculture and small industry in place of what was regarded as a somewhat oligopolistic situation where the system served mainly the urban and industrial sectors and where the grant of credit was seen to be an act of patronage and receiving it an act of privilege. (Narasimham 1991, p. 9)

Stiglitz (1989, 1994) argued that financial markets are different from other markets and government intervention is required as market failures are pervasive in the financial sector. The major market failures that could justify market interventions, according to Stiglitz, are monitoring failure, the externalities of monitoring and selection, the impact of the failure of a financial institution for the whole economy, missing and incomplete markets, imperfect competition; the difference between private returns and social returns of financial activities and, finally, the existence of uninformed or less informed investors. Besley (1994) argued that government interventions are justified in the rural credit markets as they are characterised by constraints like poor availability of secure collateral (mainly due to poverty and less developed institutions), low institutional development, risks involved in lending to agriculture and segmented credit markets. Spratt (2009) maintained that government intervention in the financial sector is required for the 'production of public goods' that the private sector is not interested to produce due to its inability to appropriate externalities.

Panizza (2012) suggested that the choice between market-based or government-based financial systems or a combination of both will depend on a country's stages of economic development. State-owned banks may play a useful role in supporting and developing the financial sector in the early stages of economic development when institutional quality is low and socially profitable investments may not be taken up due to market imperfections (Panizza 2012). Also, the private sector may not have the incentives to establish financial institutions and the only other alternative source of finance could be informal financial sector (Yeyati et al. 2007; Micco and Panizza 2006; Detragiache et al. 2005). Furthermore, in the early stages of a country's economic development, arm's-length relationships as in market-led financial development may not be preferred. Relationship banking in contrast is able to overcome informational barriers through regular interactions between the bank and the borrowers, through the constant monitoring that banks are able to provide borrowers and through the ability to offer long-term credit especially at the time of crisis (Beck et al. 2014).

Direct ownership of banks by governments also helps build the trust of people in the banking sector and helps develop the banking habit of the population (Gerschenkron 1962; Andrianova et al. 2008). The rapid spread of bank branches in developing countries during 1950s and 1960s stemmed from the belief that the development of banking habit (i.e. the practice of going to the banks, and performing banking transactions) may precede, or itself promote, the real growth of the economy (Porter 1966). Porter (1966) noted that the development of the habit of banking would lead to increased savings and investment, improve the efficiency of the allocation of capital and increase the ability of monetary authorities to stabilise the economy. Lewis (1955) also had argued:

> Experience shows that the amount of saving depends partly on how widespread these facilities (i.e. savings institutions) are: if they are pushed right under the individual's nose – people save more than if the nearest saving institution is some distance away. (Lewis 1955, p. 229)

In the Indian context, for instance, a beneficial effect of massive expansion of bank branches was the inculcation of banking habits, which spread among the population, rural and urban alike, and led to increased savings. Among the few studies on the impact of bank branches and sub-national economic development, Burgess and Pande (2005) examined the expansion of branches of commercial banks in India which was implemented in 1977 and discontinued in 1990s and was based on the so-called rule of 1:4. The rule allowed banks to open a new branch in a location with one or more bank branches, only if they had opened four branches in locations with no existing bank branches. Between 1977 and 1990, this rule encouraged commercial banks to open rural branches in states with initial lower financial development. Burgess and Pande (2005) identified the impact of opening a new rural branch on poverty and output, and their results suggested that a 1 per cent increase in the number of rural banked locations reduced rural poverty by 0.36 per cent and increased total output by 0.55 per cent. The rural bank branch expansion also increased non-primary sector output and non-agricultural employment.

A more recent literature suggests that public banks contribute to and provide lending support during periods of financial instability and economic recessions thus leading to financial stability; avoid extreme moral hazard problems associated with the private sector banks; encourage constrained behaviour often accompanied with the development objectives and promote economic growth (Andrianova et al. 2009; Andrianova 2012; Cole 2009; Bertay et al. 2015; Coleman and Feler 2015; Panizza 2012; Yeyati et al. 2007; Micco and Panizza 2006).

Credit by state banks is less pro-cyclical and less responsive to macro-economic shocks than credit through private banks. For example, during the 2008 financial crisis, state-owned banks continued to provide funds to the real economy in contrast to the withdrawal by private and foreign banks (Coleman and Feler 2015). Micco and Panizza (2006) examined the lending behaviour of public banks during the business cycles. They conjecture that public banks may play a positive role in restoring stability due to their mandate to support development and through the enhanced trust by the public for being safer than private banks. Public banks also appear to offer fewer incentives to bank managers to respond aggressively to cyclical fluctuations even during economic downturns, although political factors could also influence lending. Micco and Panizza (2006) show that state-owned banks play an important role in 'credit smoothing' and contribute to financial stability. Other studies that have observed low responsiveness of public banks to cyclical fluctuations compared to the private banks are Cull and Martinez-Peria (2013) and De Haas et al. (2015). Brei and Schclarek (2013) empirically examined the lending pattern of public and private banks in Latin American countries over the period 1994–2009. They find evidence that government-owned banks play a countercyclical role during the time of crisis. The authors conjecture that lending by public banks grows more slowly during normal times (that is, a crisis-free period), but grows faster during periods of economic downturns unlike private banks which are more cautious and risk averse.[1] Based on their empirical findings, Brei and Schclarek (2013) propose an active role for government in the financial sector especially during the downturns. Some country-specific studies also observed positive role of government-owned banks during crises period (Coleman and Feler 2015; Foos 2009; Lin et al. 2015; Leony and Romeu 2011).

In another study, Brei and Schclarek (2015) theoretically modelled differential lending responses of public and private banks. In an overlapping intergenerational model the stakeholders – depositors, firms and

---

[1] In their paper, the word 'normal' appears 31 times, yet the authors however have not defined it clearly.

private and public banks – interact together. Their model focused on the portfolio allocation decisions of the banks and considered risks involved in such decisions. They show that the responses of public banks and private banks differ as, unlike private banks that reduce lending in crisis times, public banks continue to provide credit to the rest of the economy. The rationale for such a behaviour is based on three grounds: public banks have developmental objectives; public banks are also required to promote stability and support economy recovery after a crisis; higher degree of trust in public banks by the public leads to lower withdrawals of deposits, with consequent lower probability of a run on the banks and higher probability of recapitalisation of public banks in times of crisis.

Easy availability of funds and government guarantees may also make public banks less risk averse enabling them to provide more credit (Ivashina and Scharfstein 2010; Coleman and Feler 2015). On the role of government guarantees and trust in the financial system, Chabot and Moul (2014) examined the consequences of failed government guarantees in the state of Indiana in the US. They concluded that the loss of trust in the regulatory regime had negative long-run consequences on the financial depth of the state. Government ownership may be beneficial in the absence of well-developed institutions, high corruption and lack of property rights as it may increase trust of the population in financial system (Panizza 2012). Regulatory constraints and thus low institutional development may lead the government to opt for state-owned banks (Panizza 2012).

Again, state intervention in the financial sector may be justified if infrastructure and public goods financing is required. This may also be necessary when large projects exist with lumpiness of investments and if the private financial markets underfund such investments.

3.2.1 Historical Evidence on Government Intervention

Political and historical factors have gained importance, in the recent literature, as reasons to explain the evolution of financial development and the role played by government and markets. Ang (2013) argued that the early role played by the state in promoting the development of the financial sector has not been considered by the existing literature. In his model, Ang (2013) incorporated a financial development indicator as the dependent variable (average ratio of private credit to GDP over the period 2000–2009), a state antiquity index and a set of control factors as explanatory variables. To measure state antiquity index, Ang (2013) employs the Putterman's (2004) dataset on the presence of government covering a period of 39 centuries from 1 AD to 1950 AD for 151 countries. The state antiquity index score ranges from 0 to 50 including indicators such as rule by the government instead of tribal rule, foreign or national government, and territorial boundaries of the government. The author finds that the countries where governments had intervened and developed institutions (for instance bureaucracy) have higher financial development. He argues that historical accumulation of state experience is important in explaining levels of financial development.

Andrianova et al. (2011) traced the role of governments in developing major financial centres around the world such as London, Amsterdam and Hong Kong. The authors examine the development of these centres in an historical context and highlight the role played by the government in igniting financial development. Other studies which have emphasised a positive role of government in financial development in an historical context are Sylla (1999), Rousseau and Sylla (2003) and Sylla et al. (1999). These studies show a close association of trading companies and government and the supportive role of governments in financial development. Dehejia and Lleras-Muney (2007) studied the effect of state-level banking regulations on financial development and economic growth in the US from 1900 to 1940. Their study showed impact of different state-level interventions. They argue that the expansion of bank branches promoted agricultural mechanisation and manufacturing sector development. However, the introduction of state deposit insurance had a negative impact due to inefficient bank lending especially during economic upturns.

The rapid rise of the East Asian economies since the 1960s also provides an historical evidence on the positive impact of interventionist policies followed by government in the financial sector and in the economy at large (Wade 1990). Citing the nurturing role played by the financial sector in the East Asian countries leading to their successful economic development, Stiglitz and Uy (1996) cautioned that the key to success was that both government and market acted complementary to each other. Page (1994) too confirmed,

> Much of East Asia's dramatic growth is due to superior accumulation of physical and human capital. But these economies were also better able than most to allocate these resources to highly productive investments. They did this with combinations of policies, always including market-oriented 'fundamentals', but sometimes relying on tailored government interventions. (Page 1994, p. 2)

Vittas and Cho (1994) observed that well-coordinated and focused government intervention in the financial sector was one of the crucial factors in the high growth rates achieved by the so-called Asian tiger countries. Some of the features of the financial sector intervention were: close coordination with the private sector, close and effective monitoring focused on the achievement of export targets by firms, with firms that achieved their targets were rewarded with further credit, while credit was reduced for those not able to achieve their targets. Monitoring, for instance, was through detailed appraisal of projects and firms' history of repayment of loans. Vittas and Cho (1994) state,

> Policymakers and economists have long believed that attempts to direct the allocation of credit would not be successful. Yet the experiences of Japan and the Republic of Korea suggest that directed credit programs can increase investment provided countries have a strong institutional capacity for designing projects and appraising and monitoring performance. (Vittas and Cho 1994, p. 10)

3.2.2 Role of Development Banks

More recently, since the financial crisis, the role of development banks has come into prominence again. De Luna-Martinez and Vicente (2012) defined development bank 'as a bank or financial institution with at least 30 per cent state-owned equity that has been given an explicit legal mandate to reach socioeconomic goals in a region, sector or particular market segment'. The authors surveyed 90 development banks based in 61 countries.[2] The development banks, according to them, provide 'long term credit, loan guarantees, and other financial services in the infrastructure, housing and agriculture sectors'. Their survey showed the existence of development banks both in the developed and developing countries providing credit to different sectors such as services, industry, agribusiness, construction and energy. Some of the recent lending by development banks in the area of energy has been for activities like clean energy, biotechnology and environmental projects. The survey also noted that development banks are heterogeneous in nature and differ in respect of ownership, policy mandates, deposit taking versus non-deposit taking institutions, targets, lending models, pricing strategies, regulatory regimes and transparency standards. Yet despite these heterogeneities, a common factor among them is their useful role in enhancing financial inclusion. Nonetheless, some of the factors impacting the performance of development banks globally are high subsidies, lower or lighter regulation compared to the private banking sector, poor governance and high non-performing loans in some countries.

Development banks in a number of developing countries played countercyclical role during the recent financial crisis and provided credit to selective sectors. Gutierrez et al. (2011) highlight the useful and significant role played by development banks during the crisis. The authors suggest that long-term developmental role and the countercyclical role played by development banks should be aligned with each other. According to Gutierrez et al. (2011) development banks also performed the useful role of increasing access to finance such as to small and medium enterprises. Culpeper (2012) suggests that two major reasons why G20 countries incorporated financial inclusion as a major objective were to reduce the dependence on informal sector and to achieve macroeconomic targets of increased investment, employment and economic growth. National development banks can help achieve

---

[2] Some of the limitations of their survey are: there are unconfirmed data; the survey does not explore effectiveness of development banks; distinction between commercial bank and development bank is not very clear in many countries; and finally the survey does not take into account multilateral, regional and sub-regional development banks.

both these objectives by providing financial services to small and medium enterprises and enhancing financial inclusion.

As the survey by De Luna-Martinez and Vicente (2012) also noted, development banks exist both in the developing countries and developed countries, although not much is known about the ones operating in the developed countries. In the context of Norway, Rasmussen (2010) finds that government ownership of banks is well supported by the existence of good institutions and corporate governance standards and this is reflected in the performance of the state-owned banks.

Several other authors highlighted the useful role played by the development banks (Hanson 2004; Rudolph 2009; Schmit et al. 2011). For instance, Brazil Development Bank (BNDES) in Brazil has played a very developmental and useful role especially during the crisis (Hochstetler and Montero 2013). BNDES has lent funds to large as well as small enterprises in all economic sectors, including energy-related projects, and has supported innovation and technological development through the support of R&D expenditure, including pharmaceutical research. Although a large proportion of the loans were directed to large established firms in the form of 'leader firms' and 'national champions', substantial loans via rural cooperatives and microcredit were also offered to small enterprises (Hochstetler and Montero 2013).

In contrast to the strategy followed by many countries in promoting and establishing development banks and using them as a countercyclical tool during the crisis, in India several development banks were closed down or merged with their parent institution during the 1990s. This policy deprived the industrial sector, and manufacturing in particular, of a useful source of finance (Nayyar 2015; Chandrasekhar 2016; Ray 2015).

In 2014 a multilateral development bank – New Development Bank – was set up by the so-called BRICS countries (Brazil, Russia, India, China and South Africa) as an alternative to the IMF and the World Bank. The bank was established to promote economic cooperation and mobilise resources for infrastructure and sustainable development projects in BRICS, other emerging economies and developing countries. Another multilateral development bank set up by the developing countries is the Asia Infrastructure Investment Bank (AIIB) with the objectives of 'development of infrastructure and other productive sectors in Asia, including energy and power, transportation and telecommunications, rural infrastructure and agriculture development, water supply and sanitation, environmental protection, urban development and logistics'. As these banks have been established very recently, not much is known about their performance.

Some studies have, however, challenged the role played by development banks. Among them Lazzarini et al. (2015) argued that BNDES lends to large established profitable firms that also are politically well connected instead of directing credit to firms in need. Similarly, Bonomo et al. (2015) between the years 2004 and 2012 found that public banks (primarily BNDES) had continued to provide low cost credit even after the financial crisis was over and that most of this credit had gone to large established firms.

3.2.3 Role of Government in Financial Regulation

Barth et al. (1999) focus on the regulation and supervision of the banking sector and examine the relationship between regulatory restrictions, government quality, efficiency of the banking sector and banking fragility. Using a World Bank database covering 45 countries, the authors try to provide evidence on whether countries with weak government/bureaucratic systems have stricter regulations on banks; whether countries with these stricter regulatory controls have low levels of banking development and finally, whether countries with highly controlled and regulated systems have a lower probability of suffering banking crisis. The authors find that countries with weak governments or bureaucratic systems have stricter regulatory regimes for the banks, while countries with better government quality (those with lesser bureaucratic controls or red tape, lower corruption level and strong rule of law) have less restrictive regulations especially on real estate and non-financial firm ownership. However, Cihak et al. (2012) showed that banks operating in countries with lower restrictions and regulatory controls and banks that operated in activities such as real estate lending and other non-financial activities were more affected by the financial crisis.

Furthermore, Barth et al. (1999) found mixed evidence on the question of whether countries with stricter regulatory regime have low levels of banking efficiency and development. They also noted that countries with highly regulatory and stricter regimes face a higher probability of crisis. This result especially holds true for the countries where banks are not allowed to diversify their activities. Barth et al. (1999) suggest that to improve regulation and avoid banking crisis countries should improve legal systems, increase transparency and information disclosure, set limits on credit to certain sectors such as real estate and diversify loan portfolios. They, however, cautioned that the adoption of these measures would depend on the country's stage of economic development.

In another study Barth et al. (2004) examined the relationship between regulatory and supervisory practices in 107 countries and found that direct government supervision and regulation may not be the best strategy to enhance the stability of the banking system. They rather emphasise that high degrees of information disclosure and privatisation of banks would lead to achieving banking development and stability.

3.3   Government Should Not Intervene

Several studies have, however, failed to find any evidence of a positive impact of government interventions in the financial sector. While evidence against interventionist policies had been building up over the years, the turning point against government intervention in the financial sector was provided by the publication of two books on 'financial repression' by McKinnon (1973) and Shaw (1973).[3]

The literature on 'financial repression', a concept introduced by McKinnon (1973) and Shaw (1973), questioned the distortionary role played by state-owned banks and interventions of the governments in

---

[3] An exception to this was the positive experience of four Asian tigers (South Korea, Singapore, Taiwan and Hong Kong). Among the various factors responsible for high growth rates experienced by these countries are: state interventionist policies including those in the financial sector.

the financial sector in developing countries and argued, instead, in favour of financial liberalisation. According to McKinnon (1973) and Shaw (1973), loan rate ceilings distorted the economy in four ways: (i) reduction in savings; (ii) low yielding projects; (iii) emphasis on capital-intensive projects, and (iv) poor-quality projects. McKinnon (1973) argued that money holdings and capital accumulation were complementary in the development process. Because of the lumpiness of investment, and reliance on self-financing, savings were needed and high and positive rates of interest could play a major part in the mobilisation of savings. Shaw (1973) emphasised the importance of financial liberalisation for financial deepening and the beneficial effect of high interest rates on savings and investment.

Therefore, during the early 1970s, there was an increasing criticism of the interventionist policies of governments, while emphasis was put on the role of markets, prices and incentives in the efficient allocation of resources (see for instance Meier and Rauch 2000). Cole and Slade (1991), for example, remarked: 'The policies deriving from these theories have failed to take account of the complex nature of finance and its multidimensional role in the economy. Instead they have led to distortion and misuse of finance' (Cole and Slade 1991, p. 316).

In a highly cited study La Porta et al. (2002), arguing against the government ownership of banks, indicated that government ownership of banks leads to misallocation of resources and hurts financial development and economic growth. Andrianova et al. (2009), however, showed that if other variables such as institutional quality and governance quality were included, La Porta's (2002) results would not hold. They concluded, 'widely publicised negative effect of government ownership of banks was clearly the result of omitted variable bias, rather than the true effect of government owned banks on the long-run average growth rate'.

Among other studies critical of government ownership are Barth et al. (1999) and Caprio and Peria (2002) who argued that government ownership of banks may lead to banking crisis, while Dinc (2005) provided evidence that government-owned bank lending was politically motivated compared to the lending of private banks. Sapienza (2004) finds that state-owned banks charged lower interest rates than private banks. Khwaja and Mian (2005) found evidence of high politically connected lending by government-owned banks in Pakistan in particular to the party in government. Cornett et al. (2010) examined difference in the performance between state-owned and private banks in 16 countries in the Far East for the period 1989–2004. They found a negative relationship between government ownership and bank performance, mainly due to the incentive structure of the bank managers and politicians. Their results also showed that in the post-Asian crisis period 1997–2000, the deterioration in the quality of credit provided by the government-owned banks was greater than that of the private banks. More recently, Carvalho (2014) provided evidence on politically motivated lending and employment for Brazil. Iannotta et al. (2013) examining a sample of 210 large Western European banks during the period 2000–2009 also confirmed the presence of political factors in influencing lending outcomes. Yeyati et al. (2005) argued that, although public banks performed some useful functions such as building trust among the public and performing development functions, the evidence regarding their performance is rather mixed.

Some studies highlighted the negative influence of regulated policies in the banking sector. Demetriades and Luintel (1996) examined the effects of repressive banking sector policies (such as interest rate controls, reserve and liquidity requirements, directed credit programmes) on financial deepening in the pre-reform period in India. Their results suggest that these policies had a negative influence on financial development. Ketkar and Ketkar (1992) concluded that credit allocation schemes had a negative effect on deposit mobilisation and capital accumulation. They observed this result based on the hypothesis that enhanced and easy access to external credit reduced the need to generate internal finance, thereby depressing financial savings. Meyer and Nagarajan (2000) noted that the evolution of the financial system in India was a consequence of constant governmental intervention over the decades since independence. The study observed that while aggressive expansion of bank branch did lead to a decline in the average population per bank branch, other policies such as directed credit, loan waivers, subsidies and bailing out of non-performing institutions have contributed to a weakening of the banking sector. These studies however, did not take into account the positive contribution made by the banks in India in terms of creating awareness for financial products, sources of finance, and as outlet for savings (Joshi and Little 1996). This is particularly noteworthy in view of the inadequate development of a market-based financial system in the country, where the only other source of finance is the informal market.

Xiao and Zhao (2012) use a World Bank survey data covering 28,000 firms in 46 countries and find that while development of stock markets has a positive effect on firms' innovation, banking sector development, especially of public banks, has a negative effect on firms' innovation. This result is found significantly stronger for smaller firms. Bertrand et al. (2007) examined the effects of banking reforms on industrial structure in France and argued that deregulation of the banking sector and a reduction of the role of the government have led to increased competition and more efficient allocation of resources.

Herring (2010) analysed the role of various policies which actually contributed to the crisis and the role of principal-agent problems in the public as well as the private sector. This also resulted in large number of bailouts organised by the governments funded by taxpayer money. The author suggests that market discipline by the stakeholders is the key to dealing with the crisis. Dell'Ariccia et al. (2008) do not find evidence that government interventions such as guarantees and bank recapitalisations can mitigate the effects of the crisis. Claessens et al. (2005) also indicated that government interventions to reduce the impact of financial crisis on total output have not been effective. Klingebiel et al. (2001) arrive at a similar conclusion as they observed that stock market responses to bank restructuring policies and public interventions in banks were largely ineffective. Farhi and Tirole (2012) observed that bailouts by the government resulted in increased leverage of private institutions and also high social costs. Giannetti and Simonov (2013) examined the impact of Japan's recapitalisation of banks during the 1990s crisis on the performance of firms. They concluded that while large recapitalisations have benefitted the firms and increased investments, smaller recapitalisations have not been effective in providing bank credit.

3.4   Conditional Interventions

In between the two stances of intervention and no-intervention is the third middle stance of conditional interventions. This literature argued that government can intervene in the financial sector but only for specific objectives. Cho (2010) argued that the role of state interventions is for the prevention, containment and resolution of financial crises that in the case of developing countries could mean currency and financial crisis. Drawing from the experience of South Korea, Cho (2010) suggests that government interventions should aim to build quality information on financial institutions and should be supported by strong political commitment leading to prompt action and regulatory balance. Beck (2013) outlined the role of government in terms of three sets of policies. The first set of policies should focus on market development and include policies such as promoting macroeconomic stability and strengthening information frameworks like credit information bureaus. The second set of policies is market-enabling policies. These policies should include regulatory reforms, reform of tax policies, and should aim at increasing competition. Finally, the third set of policies should aim at stabilising markets by means of regulation and supervision, increasing financial literacy and consumer protection.

Laeven and Valencia (2013) examined the impact of government recapitalisation of financial institutions in response to the recent financial crisis on the performance of firms dependent on external finance located in 50 developed and developing economies. The results of their study show that the recapitalisation of banks significantly influenced the growth performance of financially dependent firms through increases in the supply of credit. The authors also found that countercyclical fiscal policy was more helpful for these firms than monetary policy in dealing with the crisis, once again highlighting a positive role for governments.

Freixas and Mayer (2011) arrive at similar conclusion when they suggest that the state should play crucial role in five major areas related to the financial sector. Freixas and Mayer (2011) indicate corporate governance in the private financial institutions (or micro-prudential regulation) as one area where the government could play an important role. They also highlight macro-prudential regulations covering capital adequacy and liquidity requirements, the introduction of a deposit insurance scheme. Like Laeven and Valencia (2013), they also mention the importance of promoting of competition and finally the role of governments in the restructuring and recapitalising of failing financial institutions.

Gulde and Wolf (2005) critically examine the academic debate on the role of public sector banks in the financial sector. They find important motives for the existence of state-owned banks, in terms of their prioritising social over private returns to kick-start economic development and in their ability to develop the trust of public in banking system. Public sector banks can also help increase access to financial services and stimulate savings in rural areas thus contributing to financial depth. Furthermore, they can smoothen the provision of funds by increasing access to credit in times of crisis and promote financial stability. However, state-owned banks are quite heterogenous and important factors need to be taken into account when comparing their performance across different countries. For instance, some governments may influence more extensively the lending decisions of banks. Gulde and Wolf (2005) also provide arguments against government ownership of banks. They indicate political capture of banks by the government for its own vested interests as a clear drawback. Public banks may crowd out private financial development and might enhance the chances of the occurrence of financial crises if the quality of public bank loans is poor leading to non-performing loans. The authors conclude that on balance, the evidence against public banks is mixed and suggest that these banks may be successful provided there is absence of political pressure, and good governance standards are followed to achieve clear performance criteria, with a focus on clearly specified lending areas.

Demirguc-Kunt (2014) states that governments do have an important role to play in building the financial infrastructure of a country. Demirguc-Kunt (2014) specifically refers to protecting creditor rights, regulatory practices and consumer protection. However, the development of such mature institutions depends upon the level of economic development of a country. The latter observation is also made by Luo and Wen (2015) who contend that institutions are a consequence of economic development and will only develop after a country embarks on the process of industrialisation.

3.5   Conclusion

Despite a voluminous literature on the relationship between the development of the financial sector and economic growth, the role played by governments in financial sector has remained contentious. Historically, government interventions in the financial sector have been prominent from the 1950s until the early 1990s. Criticisms against financial repression and poor performance of public banks in several countries, however, turned the tide against government interventions. As a result, the 1990s saw the introduction of financial sector reforms in several developing countries with the objectives of improving allocative efficiency of the financial institutions and financial markets. The recent global financial crisis and its deleterious consequences have, however, once again stirred up debates on the government's role in the financial sector.

In this chapter we examined, through the lenses of the existing literature, whether the government should intervene in the financial sector. The findings remain inconclusive although the positive role played by the public sector banks during the financial crisis has been acknowledged in the recent literature. This stance is in stark contrast to the earlier literature on public banks according to which 'state ownership tends to stunt financial sector development, thereby contributing to slower growth' (World Bank 2001). Nonetheless, the findings of the emerging literature especially on the positive countercyclical role played by the public banks during crises times and not so positive role in normal times raises contradictory messages for the policymakers. To conclude, despite the mixed opinions on role of government in the financial sector, there is a consensus that governments still have a useful role in supervision and regulation, building financial infrastructure and promoting macroeconomic stability. It is also clear from the experience of the so-called Asian tigers countries that governments can lend an effective helping hand to the financial sector and to the economy and can move it in the desired directions especially in the early stages of economic development, provided their objectives are clear and are accompanied by strong political commitment.

References

Andrianova, S. (2012). Public banks and financial stability. *Economics Letters, 116*(2012), 86–88.

Andrianova, S., Demetriades, P., & Shortland, A. (2008). Government ownership of banks, institutions, and financial development. *Journal of Development Economics, Elsevier, 85*(1–2), (February), 218–252.

Andrianova, S., Demetriades, P. O., & Shortland, A. (2009). Is government ownership of banks really harmful to growth? (Economics and Finance Working Paper Series). London, Brunel University.

Andrianova, S., Demetriades, P., & Xu, C. (2011). Political economy origins of financial markets in Europe and Asia. *World Development, 39*(5), 686–699.

Ang, J. B. (2013). Are modern financial systems shaped by state antiquity? *Journal of Banking & Finance, 37*, 4038–4058.

Arcand, J. L., Berkes, E., & Panizza, U. (2015). Too much finance? *Journal of Economic Growth, 20*(2), 105–148.

Barth, J. R., Caprio Jr., G., & Levine, R. (1999). Financial regulation and performance: Cross-country evidence (World Bank Policy Research Working Paper No. 2037). Santa Monica, Calif.: Milken Institute.

Barth, J. R., Caprio, G., & Levine, R. (2004). Bank regulation and supervision: What works best? *Journal of Financial Intermediation, 13*(2), 205–248.

Beck, T. (2013). Finance, growth and fragility: The role of government. *International Journal Banking, Accounting and Finance, 5*(1/2), 49–77.

Beck, T., Degryse, H., & Kneer, C. (2014a). Is more finance better? Disentangling intermediation and size effect of financial system. *Journal of Financial Stability, 10*, 50–64.

Beck, T., Degryse, H., De Haas, R., & Van Horen, N. (2014b). When arm's length is too far: Relationship banking over the business cycle (Working Paper 169, European Bank for Reconstruction and Development).

Bertay, A. C., Demirguc-Kunt, A., & Huizinga, H. (2015). Bank ownership and credit over the business cycle: Is lending by state banks less procyclical? *Journal of Banking and Finance, 50*, 326–339.

Bertrand, M., Schoar, A., & Thesmar, D. (2007). Banking deregulation and industry structure: Evidence from the French banking reforms of 1985. *The Journal of Finance, 62*(2), 597–628.

Besley, T. (1994). How do market failures justify intervention in rural credit markets? *World Bank Research Observer, 9*(1), 27–48.

Bonomo, M., Brito, R. D., & Martins, B. (2015). The after crisis government-driven credit expansion in Brazil: A firm level analysis. *Journal of International Money and Finance*, *55*, 111–134.

Brei, M., & Schclarek, A. (2013). Public bank lending in times of crisis. *Journal of Financial Stability*, *9*, 820–830.

Brei, M., & Schclarek, A. (2015). A theoretical model of bank lending: Does ownership matter in times of crisis? *Journal of Banking and Finance*, *50*, 298–307.

Burgess, R., & Pande, R. (2005). Do rural banks matter? Evidence from the Indian social banking experiment. *American Economic Review*, *95*(3), 780–795.

Caprio, G., & Peria, M. S. M. (2002). Avoiding disaster: Policies to reduce the risk of banking crises. Chapter 7 In E. Cardoso & A. Galal (Eds.), *Monetary policy and exchange rate regimes: Options for the Middle East* (pp. 193–230). Cairo, Egypt: The Egyptian Centre for Economic Studies.

Carvalho, D. R. (2014). The real effects of government owned banks: Evidence from an emerging market. *Journal of Finance*, *69*, 577–609.

Chabot, B., & Moul, C. C. (2014). Bank panics, government guarantees, and the long-run size of the financial sector: Evidence from free-banking America. *Journal of Money, Credit and Banking*, *46*(5), 961–997.

Chandrasekhar, C. P. (2016). National development banks in a comparative perspective. In A. Calcagno, S. Dullien, A. Márquez-Velázquez, N. Maystre, & J. Priewe (Eds.), *Rethinking development strategies after the financial crisis: Volume II: Country studies and international comparisons* (pp. 21–30). New York and Geneva: United Nations.

Cho, Y. J. (2010). Crisis resolution, policies, and institutions: Empirical evidence. In P. Honohan & L. Laeven (Eds.), *Systemic financial distress: Containment and resolution* (pp. 169–196). Cambridge: Cambridge University Press.

Čihák, M., Demirgüç-Kunt, A., Martínez Pería, M. S., & Mohseni-Cheraghlou, A. (2012). Bank regulation and supervision around the world: A crisis update (World Bank Policy Research Working Paper (6286)).

Claessens, S., Klingebiel, D., & Laeven, L. (2005). Crisis resolution, policies, and institutions: Empirical evidence. In Patrick Honohan and Luc Laeven (Eds.), *Systemic financial distress: Containment and resolution* (pp. 169–96). Cambridge, UK: Cambridge University Press.

Cole, D., & Slade, B. (1991). Reform of financial systems. In D. H. Perkins & M. Roemer (Eds.), *Reforming economic systems in developing countries* (pp. 313–340). Harvard University, Harvard Institute for International Development.

Cole, S. (2009). Financial development, bank ownership, and growth: Or, does quantity imply quality? *The Review of Economics and Statistics*, February 2009, *91*(1), 33–51.

Coleman, N., & Feler, L. (2015). Bank ownership, lending and local economic performance during the 2008–2010 financial crisis. *Journal of Monetary Economics*, *71* (April), 50–66.

Cornett, M. M., Guo, L., Khaksari, S., & Tehranian, H. (2010). The impact of state ownership on performance differences in privately-owned versus state-owned banks: An international comparison. *Journal of Financial Intermediation*, *19*(1), 74–94.

Cull, R., & Martinez Peria, M. S. (2013). Bank ownership and lending patterns during the 2008–2009 financial crisis: Evidence from Latin America and Eastern Europe. *Journal of Banking and Finance*, *37*(12), 4861–4878.

Culpeper, R. (2012). Financial sector policy and development in the wake of the global crisis: The role of national development banks. *Third World Quarterly*, *33*(3), 383–403. doi: 10.1080/01436597.2012.657470.

De Haas, R., Korniyenko, Y., Pivovarsky, A., & Tsankova, T. (2015). Taming the herd? Foreign banks, the Vienna initiative and crisis transmission. *Journal of Financial Intermediation*, *24*(3), 325–355.

De Luna-Martinez, J., & Vicente, C. L. (2012). Global survey of development banks. (World Bank Policy Research Working Paper, Vol. 5969).

Dehejia, R., & Lleras-Muney, A. (2007). Financial development and pathways of growth: State branching and deposit insurance laws in the United States, 1900–1940. *Journal of Law and Economics*, *50*(2), 239–271.

Dell'Ariccia, G., Detragiache, E., & Rajan, R. (2008). The real effects of banking crises. *Journal of Financial Intermediation*, *17*, 89–112.

Demetriades, P., & Luintel, K. (1996). Financial development, economic growth and banker sector controls: Evidence from India. *Economic Journal*, *106*(435), 359–374.

Demirguc-Kunt, A. (2014). Presidential address: Financial inclusion. *The Atlantic Economic Journal (2014)*, *42*, 349–356. doi: 10.1007/s11293-014-9429-z.

Detragiache, E., Gupta, P., & Tressel, T. (2005). Finance in lower-income countries: An empirical exploration (Working Paper 05/167). Washington: International Monetary Fund.

Dinc, S. (2005). Politicians and banks: political influences on government-owned banks in emerging markets. *Journal of Financial Economics, 77*(2), 453–479.

Farhi, E., & Tirole, J. (2012). Collective moral hazard, maturity mismatch, and systemic bailouts. *American Economic Review, 120*, 60–93.

Foos, D. (2009). Lending conditions, macroeconomic fluctuations and the impact of bank ownership. Retrieved April 1, 2016, from https://www.wiwi.uni-muenster.de/fcm/downloads/forschen/ifk_bankenworkshop/Foos_LendingMacroOwnership_200904.pdf.

Freixas, X., & Mayer, C. (2011). Banking, finance, and the role of the state. *Oxford Review of Economic Policy, 27*(3), 397–410.

Gerschenkron, A. (1962). *Economic backwardness in historical perspective – A book of essays*. Cambridge: Harvard University Press.

Giannetti, M., & Simonov, A. (2013). On the real effects of bank bailouts: Micro evidence from Japan. *American Economic Journal: Macroeconomics, 5*(1), 135–167.

Gulde, A.-M., & Wolf, H. (2005). Publicly owned banks in the development process. In M. Frenkel & H.-R. Hemmer (Eds.), *Finanzmarkt – und Währungsprobleme von Schwellen – und Transformationsländern* (pp. 115–130). Entwicklungsökonomisches Seminar vom 19.-22. Januar 2005 im Hotel "Kaiserin Augusta" in Weimar.

Gutierrez, E., Rudolph, H., Homa, T., & Beneit, E. B. (2011). Development banks: Role and mechanisms to increase their efficiency. World Bank Policy Research Working Paper Series, Vol. 5729.

Hanson, J. A. (2004). The transformation of state-owned banks. In G. Caprio, L. Fiechter, R. Litan, & M. Pormeleano (Eds.), *The future of state-owned financial institutions*. Washington, DC: Brookings Institutions Press.

Herring, R. J. (2010). How financial oversight failed & what it may portend for the future of regulation. *Atlantic Economic Journal, 38*, 265–282.

Hochstetler, K., & Montero, A. P. (2013). The renewed developmental state: The national development bank and the Brazil model. *The Journal of Development Studies, 49*(11), 1484–1499. 10.1080/00220388.2013.807503.

Iannotta, G., Nocera, G., & Sironi, A. (2013). The impact of government ownership on bank risk. *Journal of Financial Intermediation, 22*(2), 152–176.

Ivashina, V., & Scharfstein, D. (2010). Bank lending during the financial crisis of 2008. *Journal of Financial Economics, 97*(3), 319–338.

Joshi, V., & Little, I. (1996). *India's economic reforms, 1991–2001*. New Delhi: Oxford University Press.

Ketkar, K. W., & Ketkar, S. L. (1992). Bank nationalisation, financial savings, and economic development – a case study of India. *The Journal of Developing Areas, 27* (October), 69–84.

Khwaja, A., & Mian, A. (2005). Do lenders favor politically connected firms? Rent provision in an emerging financial market. *Quarterly Journal of Economics, 120*(4), 1371–1411.

King, R. G., & Levine, R. (1993a). Finance, entrepreneurship and growth. *Journal of Monetary Economics, 32*(3), 513–542.

King, R. G., & Levine, R. (1993b). Finance and growth: Schumpeter might be right. *Quarterly Journal of Economics, 108*(3), 717–738.

Klingebiel, D., Kroszner, R., & Laeven, L. (2001) Stock market responses to bank restructuring policies during the East Asian crisis. (World Bank Policy Research Working Paper No. 2571).

La Porta, R., Lopez-de-Silanes, F., & Shleifer, A. (2002). Government ownership of banks. *The Journal of Finance, 57*(1), 265–301.

Laeven, L., & Valencia, F. (2013). The real effects of financial sector interventions during crises. *Journal of Money, Credit and Banking, 45*(1), 147–177.

Law, S. H., & Singh, N. (2014). Does too much finance harm economic growth? *Journal of Banking & Finance, 41*, 36–44.

Lazzarini, S. G., Musacchio, A., Bandiera-De-Mello, R., & Marcon, R. (2015). What do state-owned development banks do? Evidence from Brazil, 2002–2009. *World Development, 66*, 237–253.

Leony, L., & Romeu, R. (2011). A model of bank lending in the global financial crisis and the case of Korea. *Journal of Asian Economics, 22*(4), 322–334.

Levine, R. (1997). Financial development and economic growth: Views and agenda. *Journal of Economic Literature, 35*(2), 688–726.

Lewis, W. A. (1955). *The theory of economic growth*. George Allen and Unwin.

Lin, Y., Srinivasan, A., & Yamada, T. (2015). The effect of government bank lending: Evidence from the financial crisis in Japan. Available at SSRN 2544446.

Luo, J., & Wen, Y. (2015). Institutions do not rule: Reassessing the driving forces of economic development (Working Paper 2015–001A) http://research.stlouisfed.org/wp/2015/2015-001.pdf. Federal Reserve Bank of St. Louis, St. Louis, MO, 63166.

McKinnon, R. I. (1973). *Money and capital in economic development*. Washington, DC: Brookings Institution.

Meier, G. M., & Rauch, J. E. (2000). *Leading issues in economic development*. New York: Oxford University Press.

Meyer, R. L., & Nagarajan, G. (2000). Rural financial markets in Asia: Policies, paradigms, and performance. A Study of Rural Asia, Oxford University Press.

Micco, A., & Panizza, U. (2006). Bank ownership and lending behaviour (Working Paper No. 67), Department of Public Policy and Public Choice – Polis, Universita' Del Piemonte Orientale 'Amedeo Avogadro' Alessandria.

Narasimham, M. (1991). Report of the committee on the financial system. New Delhi, Ministry of Finance, Government of India.

Nayyar, D. (2015). Birth, life and death of development finance institutions in India. *Economic & Political Weekly, L*(33), 51–60.

Page, J. (1994). The East Asian miracle: Building a basis for growth. *Finance & Development, 31*(1), 2–5.

Panizza, U. (2012). Finance and economic development. *International Development Policy, 3*, 141–160.

Porter, R. C. (1966). The promotion of the banking habit and economic development. *Journal of Development Studies, 2*(4), 346–366.

Putterman, L. (2004). State antiquity index (statehist) Version 3.

Rasmussen, A. J. A. (2010). State ownership in banking – theory applied to a case study of the Norwegian government's ownership in DnB NOR. Bergen, våren 2010, Norges Handelshøyskole. Masters Thesis Master Degree in Economics and Business Administration.

Ray, P. (2015). Rise and fall of industrial finance in India. *Economic and Political Weekly, 50*(5), January 31.

Rousseau, P. L., & Sylla, R. (2003). Financial systems, economic growth, and globalization. In M. D. Bordo, A. M. Taylor, & J. G. Williamson (Eds.), *Globalization in historical perspective* (pp. 373–415). Chicago and London: The University of Chicago Press.

Rudolph, H. P. (2009). State financial institutions: Mandates, governance and beyond. (Policy Research Working Paper Series, 5141). The World Bank.

Sapienza, P. (2004). The effects of government ownership of bank lending. *Journal of Financial Economics, 72*(2), 357–384.

Schmit, M., Gheeraert, L., Denuit, T., & Warny, C. (2011). Public financial institutions in Europe. European Association of Public Banks.

Shaw, E. S. (1973). *Financial deepening in economic development.* London: Oxford University Press.

Spratt, S. (2009). *Development Finance: Debates, Dogmas and New Directions.* Milton Keynes, UK: Routledge.

Stiglitz, J. (1989). *Markets and development* (pp. 1–20). Cambridge: National Bureau of Economic Research.

Stiglitz, J. (1994). The role of the state in financial markets. In M. Bruno & B. Pleskovic (Eds.), *Annual conference on development economics* (pp. 19–52). Washington, DC: World Bank.

Stiglitz, J. E., & Uy, M. (1996). Financial markets, public policy, and the East Asian miracle. *World Bank Research Observer, 11*(2), 249–276.

Sylla, R. (1999). Shaping the US financial system, 1690–1913. In R. Sylla, R. Tilly, & G. Tortella (Eds.), *The state, the financial system and economic modernization* (pp. 249–270). Cambridge: Cambridge University Press.

Sylla, R., Tilly, R., & Tortella, G. (1999). Introduction: Comparative historical perspectives. In R. Sylla, R. Tilly, & G. Tortella (Eds.), *The state, the financial system and economic modernization* (pp. 1–19). Cambridge: Cambridge University Press.

Vittas, D., & Cho, Y. J. (1994). The role of credit policies in Japan and Korea. *Finance & Development, 31*(1), 10–12.

Wade, R. (1990). *Governing the market: Economic theory and the role of government in East Asian industrialization.* Princeton, NJ: Princeton University Press.

World Bank. (2001). *Finance for growth: Policy choices in a volatile world.* Washington, DC: World Bank.

Xiao, S., & Zhao, S. (2012). Financial development, government ownership of banks and firm innovation. *Journal of International Money and Finance, 31*(4), 880–906.

Yeyati, E., Micco, A., & Panizza, U. (2005). February. State-owned banks: Do they promote or depress financial development and economic growth?. In *Conference on Public Banks in Latin America: Myths and reality.* Inter-American Development Bank.

Yeyati, E., Micco, A., & Panizza, U. (2007). A reappraisal of state-owned banks. *Economia, 7*(2), 209–247.

Rashmi Arora is currently working as a lecturer in development economics at University of Bradford, United Kingdom. She has worked earlier as a research fellow in the Department of Accounting, Finance and Economics, Griffith Business School, Griffith University, Australia. In 2007 she was a postdoctoral research fellow at the Centre for Asia Pacific Social Transformation Studies, University of Wollongong, Australia. She has also worked as Assistant Adviser and Research Officer in the Reserve Bank of India (India's central bank) in its economic policy department for several years.

4

Overseas Aid as an Instrument of Development Finance

Paul Mosley

4.1 Background to the Aid Debate

4.1.1 Introduction

What we now call overseas aid is the product of the post-World War II international political settlement. The 'Bretton Woods system', consisting at the time of the World Bank, the International Monetary Fund (IMF) and the General Agreement on Tariffs and Trade (GATT; now the World Trade Organisation, WTO) was jointly designed in 1944–1945 by the victorious powers with a view to restoring the world economy to growth in place of the instability and recession that had characterised the interwar period. The newly formed World Bank and private overseas investors, at this time, played the principal role in transferring capital, then seen as the main driver of development, to developing countries; however, some developing countries, especially in

P. Mosley (✉)
Department of Economics, University of Sheffield, Sheffield, UK
e-mail: p.mosley@sheffield.ac.uk

© The Author(s) 2017   **79**
G. Giorgioni (ed.), *Development Finance*, Palgrave Studies
in Impact Finance, DOI 10.1057/978-1-137-58032-0_4

Africa and South Asia, were at this time so poor that few private investors were willing to accept the risk of lending to or investing in them. The only authorities at this time willing to consider providing money as a gift or on concessional terms – 'overseas aid', as it has come to be known – were the governments of industrialised countries, who in many cases had been involved in colonial relationships with the poorest countries since the nineteenth century and earlier, but who were now, in the case of India, Indonesia and Pakistan, actively engaged in giving them independence and, in the case of most African and Caribbean countries, attempting to lay an economic and political base for it to happen shortly. Overseas aid as we now know it was thus in most cases an accompaniment to political independence, which was expected to lead quite rapidly to the achievement of economic autonomy, even for these very poor developing countries.

As we now know, things turned out very differently: 70 years on from that time, many African countries, and quite a few in Asia, still depend on aid donors to finance their capital spending, and in some cases parts of their recurrent budgets as well. The identity of the donors has changed, now featuring countries such as China which were once aid-recipient poor countries, as well as a vast array of international NGOs. But the inequality of wealth between the global North and the global South remains, and for many poor countries is still increasing, in spite of the persistence of aid flows which were intended to help them reduce it. A majority of poor countries are still exporters of primary commodities, and importers of manufactures, just as they were in colonial times. This looks like a sorry performance on the part of aid donors, and this inevitably puts the spotlight on the effectiveness of aid flows, and how that can be increased, which is the theme of this chapter. Over the 70 years since overseas aid began in its modern form, we trace three kinds of evolution. Its objective has changed from trying to do everything – promote donors' exports and political influence, boost global growth, wipe out poverty and stop civil war – to focus, under the Millennium Development Goals, on the single objective of eliminating global poverty. (The Millenium Development Goals have evolved from 2015 into the Sustainable Development Goals, to be discussed below.) Its fundamental character has changed also, from being a provider of hardware (capital equipment and infrastructure in various forms) to the governments of developing countries, to being a provider of technical support and ideas to the whole economy, including the private, informal and voluntary sectors as well as the government. And finally, and also related to these changes in purpose and method, there have been variations over time in aid effectiveness too. But the nature of these last is highly disputed, as well it might be, as everyone has their own method of calculating the effectiveness of aid and many of these methods are suspect, often because they try to 'sell a story', intending either to defend an aid programme against its many enemies or possibly to do the opposite and attack what they see as an unnecessary drag on the (donor) economy.

In this chapter, we review these various transformations in the overseas aid instrument, with a focus on the last of them, the effectiveness of aid flows. It will become clear as we go along that aid, in our opinion, still has an important job to do, especially in the poorest and most politically fragile countries. However it is a political process, constantly at risk of being undermined and corrupted by those whose objectives are far away from the objective of supporting and protecting poor people. This chapter attempts to show how aid, as an instrument of development finance, can be made effective only if it can find ways of getting around these ever-present obstacles.

4.1.2 The Economics and Politics of Aid (1945–1970s)

Overseas aid, and indeed development economics as a whole, were born in a climate of hope and fear. During and immediately after World War II, there was political pressure, extreme in South Asia and more moderate in Africa, to decolonise, and generally willingness on the part of colonial powers to help them achieve this; but at the same time great fear that ever-increasing population pressure might stop those countries from growing, never mind being able to pay their way as independent countries. Given this predicament, aid flows from north to south were cast by many in the role of saviour: the source of the savings which, if productively invested, might take poor countries out of the poverty trap[1] and enable them to grow. During the 1950s, many economists used the newly minted Harrod-Domar equation ($g = s/v$, where g = the growth rate of GDP, s = savings as a proportion of GDP, and v = the incremental capital-output ratio; that is the ratio of investment to the change in GDP) to illustrate the role of aid in development in something like the following terms:

Suppose that, in a typical developing economy, the savings rate s is 6% and the incremental capital-output ratio v is 4. This gives a GDP growth rate of 1.5%; however, if the population is growing at 2% per annum (a typical figure in developing countries in those days) then the consequence of this will be an annual decline in living standards (per capita GDP) of 0.5% per annum.

However, let us now introduce an aid flow whose value as proportion of GNP (a) is 4%. If this can be sustained, and if the savings rate (s) and capital coefficient (v) remain unchanged, then the growth rate of GDP per capita rises from minus 0.5% to:

$$\text{Growth in per capita GDP} = \frac{s+a}{v}, \text{ less population growth rate}$$
$$= +0.5\,per\,cent[2]$$

By this means, aid is able to perform a rescue operation, and to take low-income economies out of poverty and dependence into sustained growth. If this vision is to materialise, of course, everything depends on the assumptions and parameters underlying this scenario being plausible. In the 1950s and 1960s, however, they were scarcely questioned, and aid allocations (Rosenstein-Rodan 1961; Chenery and Strout 1966) and development targets, such as the aid, growth and investment targets for the UN's 'Development Decade' of the 1960s,

---

[1] Poverty, leading to poor health and low income, leading to low savings and low productivity, and thence to poverty once again.

[2] This example is imaginary but corresponds well both to the savings, GDP growth and population growth rates at that time prevailing in the developing world, and also to the numbers used by Arthur Lewis in his famous statement (Lewis 1955, p. 1) that 'the fundamental problem in the theory of economic development is to understand how a country saving only 5 per cent of national income converts itself into a 12, even 15, per cent saver'.

were calculated in the confident expectation that they would yield something like the results indicated above.

Meanwhile, the international politics of the cold war had entered the landscape of policy-making. Between the capitalist west and the communist east stood a hundred or so, for the most part 'unaligned', poor developing countries, who presented a tempting target for rival offers of aid – a competition which developing countries for the most part encouraged. The risk existed, of course, that this kind of motivation might bring about aid-tying and thereby, and otherwise, undermine the objective of sourcing aid through the most economical provider. But for the most part, at this time, aid quantity objectives prevailed over quality objectives and continued to do so for another couple of decades.

The first assessments of the effectiveness of overseas aid, to our knowledge, are those conducted by Gustav Papanek (1972, 1973) in the early 1970s. This does not really indicate complacency on the part of donors: it was only at this time that the global national income data required to make such calculations became available. Papanek's research is fascinating to students of development finance not only for its pioneering nature but for its ambition: for it attempted to assess the effectiveness not only of aid but of development finance as a whole, and in particular to compare the effectiveness of concessionary international financial flows (i.e. international aid) with that of non-concessionary flows (e.g. bank loans and foreign direct investment [FDI]). His research concluded that the impact of aid (for a sample of around 50 developing countries over the period 1951–1969) was not only positive and significant, but more positive than the impact of commercial financial flows. His estimated regression equation (Papanek 1973, p. 121) is

$$\text{Growth} = 1.5^* + 0.20^{***}\text{savings} + 0.39^{***}\text{aid} + 0.17^{**}\text{foreign private investment}$$
$$\quad (2.5)\ \ (6.0) \qquad\qquad (5.8) \qquad\qquad (2.5)$$

$$+ 0.19^{**}\text{other foreign inflows}, \ r^2 = 0.37$$
$$(2.1)$$

Source: 85 observations for the 1950s and 1960s provided in Papanek, *Statistical Appendix to Economic Development Report no. 195*, Development

Research Group, Harvard University, 1971. Figures in parentheses below coefficients represent student's t-statistics; ***/**/* denote significance of a coefficient at the 1%/5%/10% level.

Commenting on the apparently superior leverage of aid over other forms of development finance, Papanek comments:

> Aid, unlike domestic savings, can fill the foreign exchange gap as well as the savings gap. Unlike foreign private investment and other foreign inflows, aid is supposed to be specifically designed to foster growth and, more important, is biased towards countries with a balance-of-payments constraint. (Papanek 1973, p. 122)

Around the same time as Papanek produced these euphoric results concerning the effectiveness of aid at the cross-country, or macro-economic, level, the World Bank's operations evaluation department was beginning to produce results from project evaluations suggesting that the social rate of return on its projects was in excess of 15% – that is higher than the rate of return on infrastructure and other investment projects financed by the private sector in the poorer developing countries.[3] Once again, aid inflows appear to be leading the field.

Later in the decade of the 1970s, however, Griffin (1970) showed that one of the fundamental assumptions of our earlier 'modified Harrod-Domar' model and of Papanek's empirical analysis, namely the idea that aid supplements savings, might be wrong, and aid recipients might use aid inflows to *replace* domestic savings rather than supplement them. Griffin's idea was based only on negative correlations between aid and savings, but Heller (1975) took the analysis further and constructed an optimising model of fiscal policy in which, depending on the preferences of the recipient government, any aid inflow, however much formally tied by the donor, can be used either for investment, for consumption, or for

---

[3] Source: World Bank, *Operations Evaluation Department, Annual Reviews of Project Performance Audit Results*, various. These data relate only to 'IDA projects', in other words projects qualifying for concessional aid from the Bank because they were located in the poorer developing countries (at the time countries with a per capita income of less than $1000). Developing countries with a higher per capita income than this borrow on market (non-concessional) terms from the Bank and so are not classified as aid recipients from this source.

a mixture of the two, since it is always possible for the aid recipient to switch budgeted expenditure to new projects and activities which donors are willing to finance in order to spend that money on activities which the donors are not willing to finance – a practice known in the aid trade as fungibility. Thus, the impact of aid is not only the impact of the individual projects which the aid budget finances, but also the impact of the overall aid inflow on the recipient's entire public finances. To complicate the matter further, there are impacts of aid on the private as well as the public sector, since new aid projects will impact on the cost of labour, the competitiveness of exports (i.e. drive the exchange rate upwards and thereby act as a form of 'Dutch disease') and other prices affecting the private sector in such a way as potentially to cause the overall micro-impact of individual projects to diverge quite a lot from the macro-impact as evidenced by the regression coefficient of aid on growth. And indeed, especially once the crisis of the 1980s hit, assessments of the macro-impact of aid on growth did present a much more pessimistic picture than either the World Bank's micro-estimates, or, more importantly, the initial macro-estimates which Papanek made using data from an earlier period. Table 4.1 compares these two kinds of results for the period up to the late 1980s, which as will be seen provide evidence of a 'micro-macro paradox': most answers to the question 'does aid work?' which derive from project evaluations tell a happy story, whereas most answers which derive from regression analyses of the Papanek type say exactly the opposite: that aid on balance, across the entire developing world, has no significant net impact at all.

4.1.3 Analytical Frameworks for Understanding Aid Effectiveness

What is going on here? To understand this, the first thing we need to do is to take proper note of the diversity of experience across developing countries. This has always been very wide. If we focus for the moment on the 1970s to which most of the data of Table 4.1 relate, and look at how aid was used at that time, the range of experiences in East Asia cover a spectrum from South Korea, which used American aid during the

Table 4.1 The 'micro-macro paradox'

Micro		Macro			
Average rates of return on World Bank-financed projects, 1968–1989 (%)		Partial regression coefficients of aid on growth, 1960s to 1990s, various investigators			
		(Panel-data analysis for period indicated; sample is all LDCs for which data available)			
Type of trade regime	Rate of return (%)	Investigator	Period	Regression coefficient of aid on GDP growth	t-value
'Closed economies'	13.2	Papanek 1973	1950s and 1960s	0.40**	5.90
'Moderate trade restrictiveness'	15.0	Voivodas 1973	1960	−0.01	0.20
'Open economies'	19.0	Mosley 1980	1960s and 1970s	0.94	1.85
Overall average	15.6	Mosley et al. 1987	1970s	−0.03	0.32
			1980–1983	0.01	0.07
		Reichel 1995	1980s	0.04	0.87
		Boone 1994	1970–1990	0.00	0.03

Source: Left-hand half of table: World Bank, Operations Evaluation Department, *Annual Review of Project Performance Audit Reports*, various; right-hand half of table: sources listed in Bibliography. **/* denote significance of a coefficient at the 1%/5% level of significance.

1950s to go from having virtually no manufacturing industries to achieving global dominance in exports of steel and shipbuilding a quarter of a century later – to the Philippines, whose President Marcos appropriated most of the American aid he received for the private use of his extended family. If we move across to Africa we can see the same sort of contrast between how aid was used in Mauritius – that is to transform the economy from being based on monocropping of sugar to being based on exports of textiles, tourism and electronic components – and how it was used in the Democratic Republic of the Congo – then and now the world's poorest country – that is for the construction of a range of private palaces in the middle of the Congolese jungle, equipped with every modern convenience from helicopter pads to gold-plated bathroom fittings from which champagne flowed if you turned the tap – at a

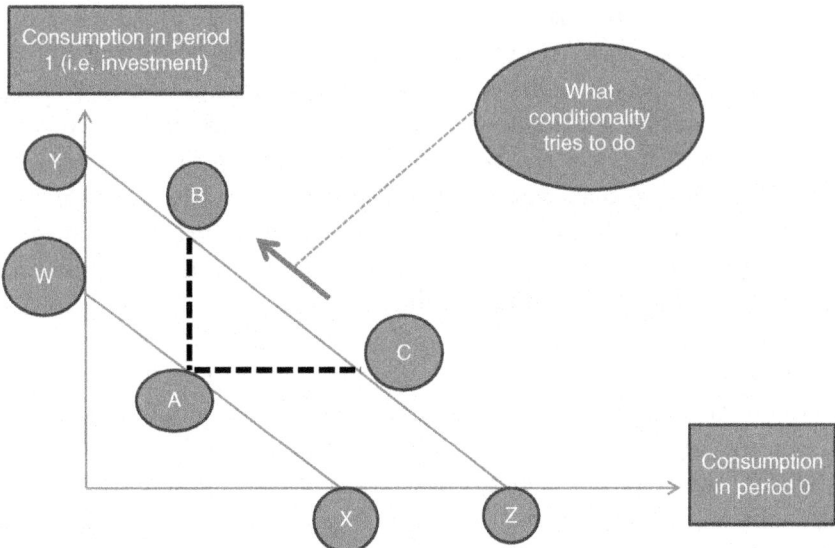

Fig. 4.1   Aid effectiveness as intertemporal choice

time when 90% of the population were hungry and had no access to clean water. We can relate this diversity of experience to standard microeconomic theory by means of Fig. 4.1, which illustrates the process of 'intertemporal choice', in other words, choice between different time periods, or the choice between consumption and investment. Let us imagine a developing country operating on a basis of self-sufficiency (like Japan before 1868, when it opened itself up to trade with the outside world). Its consumption possibilities are defined by the line WX: if it allocates all of its resources to consumption in the current period, it ends up at point X; if it elects to defer all consumption, and allocates all its resources to consumption in the future, that is to investment, it ends up at point W. Typically, it will elect to do neither of these things, but rather to balance between current and future consumption, and therefore to end up at an intermediate point such as A.

Now let us bring overseas aid into the picture, and bring the story forward into the 1970s. Let us imagine that the recipient country receives an amount of aid whose value (in terms of current consumption) is XZ, or WY if all of the aid is allocated to investment. How will it use this money? The answer to this question is the key to aid effectiveness. Of course, what its government chooses to do is constrained by where it is at present, which is point C; and it would be politically unwise, especially in a fragile state, deliberately to choose to let current consumption fall below that level. But even accepting this limitation, it can either choose to allocate all the aid inflow to investment, as donors would typically wish, and go to point B (as South Korea and Mauritius did in the example above); or to allocate all the inflow to consumption, and go to point C (as the Philippines and Congo-Kinshasa did in the example above)[4]; or it may choose somewhere in between. As we can now see, measured aid effectiveness (i.e. the regression coefficient of aid on GDP growth, holding constant all other likely influences on growth) is the average of these diverse country impacts. The evidence from virtually every regression study conducted between the mid-1970s and the millennium suggests that the country cases in which the impact of aid on growth is positive (of which there are many) are cancelled out by the country cases in which the impact of aid on growth is negative, so that the net impact is insignificantly different from zero, as in most of the studies on the right-hand side of Table 4.1. This then opens up the question of whether donors have the ability to change things so as to make aid more effective, and if so how.

We shall tackle this question in the next section below; but before that, let us resume the narrative where we left off, in the early 1970s, the time when the world economy grew faster than at any other time in

---

[4] It may be objected that if donors do their job and monitor the use of aid properly, then this kind of switching cannot happen. But it can, and does, as long as the recipient government has money left in its capital budget which can be switched to the purpose desired by the donor. Suppose the donor awards the recipient $50 million which, it insists, must be spent on a network of health centres. The recipient objects and says it wants to spend the money on a football stadium. The donor objects to this use of the aid and threatens to walk away. The recipient replies, 'OK, we give in', takes $50 million from its development budget to build the health centres, and then spends the $50 million offered by the donor to build the football stadium. This is fungibility, of a kind that has occurred thousands of times and which explains the room for manoeuvre which the recipient has between points B and C on Fig. 4.1. The only constraint on it is when the domestic development budget runs out, making switching impossible. As we relate in Section 4.2, this actually happened in a number of African countries in the 1980s and 1990s – in the process increasing the bargaining power of donors and, as a result, very possibly increasing the measured effectiveness of aid.

history. The developing countries shared in this growth, and indeed grew much faster than industrialised countries during this period. However, this was also the time when a number of observers, significantly including the World Bank chief economist, Hollis Chenery, noticed that about a third of the people in the developing world had got little or no benefit from that growth. Chenery, in association with colleagues at the World Bank and IDS, Sussex, commissioned a study of this issue (eventually published as Chenery et al. 1975) which proposed a range of initiatives in the areas of, for instance, fiscal, infrastructure, land-reform, integrated rural development, and housing policies, many of which were immediately taken up by the World Bank, its President, Robert MacNamara, and sympathetic aid donors under the banner of 'poverty focus'.[5] This is the beginning of the reorientation of aid towards a range of objectives much wider than economic growth. However, for many these reformist measures did not go far enough, because of their failure to acknowledge that global inequalities were rooted in power-structures which ran much deeper than could possibly be changed by a mere reorientation of aid flows.[6] Some writers who were aware of this, such as Hans Singer (e.g. Singer 1950) nonetheless threw their weight behind the Bank's reformist work (and indeed contributed to the *Redistribution with Growth* book). But others, notably Hayter (1971), used evidence related to power-structures in the Bank and within aid donors, and their interrelationship, to argue that aid as currently constituted was not and could not be effective, because it served the interests of donor countries at the expense of recipient countries.[7] Thus, throughout the 1970s there existed many voices, both reformist and more

---

[5] For a review of these initiatives, see Ayres (1983) and Mosley (1981).

[6] Notably the concentration of FDI in the developing world into mines and plantations owned by nationals of rich countries (especially the US) who then used their leverage in the World Bank and related institutions to make sure that rich countries captured the lion's share of such investments. Note that this aspect of multinational corporations reinforces Papanek's point (page [4] above) that there are reasons for expecting the effectiveness of concessional aid to exceed the effectiveness of FDI.

[7] This approach continues up to the present in works such as Moyo (2009).

radical, arguing that aid needed to be amended in ways which went beyond just tinkering with its impacts on prices and fiscal policy. However, all these voices were shortly to be submerged by the global economic crisis which struck the developing world at the beginning of the 1980s, which was to alter the practice of aid in a fundamental way.

4.2   Aid, Donor Pressure and Recipient Response in the Open Economy (1980 – Early 2000s)

In 1980, the world was hit by the first global crisis since the 1930s depression. Its immediate cause was the transmission of deflationary pressure from high-income economies (which in the 1970s had had to deal with 'stagflation', a combination of inflation and stagnation not previously experienced) to low-income economies. To control the inflation, the governments of the US, Germany, the UK and other high-income economies reduced aggregate monetary demand and public spending, which translated into a fall in the prices and values of Third World exports; worse, this recession then evolved into a full-scale financial crisis when the banks of the northern hemisphere separately and collectively stopped lending to the developing world. Development finance (of all kinds) provided by northern international finance institutions to southern governments fell by two-thirds, from $74 billion to $27 billion, between 1981 and 1986. In face of a crisis of this magnitude, most poor developing countries, which were in most cases overspent and suffering from unsustainable balance of payments deficits anyway, were forced to make desperate appeals for more aid. This aid was provided, but from the 1980s on in a quite different form from the way it had been provided previously. Capital aid (especially for low-income countries) was gradually phased out, and replaced by technical assistance, assistance for organisations outside central government (such as NGOs and the private sector), and eventually humanitarian and emergency assistance also (Table 4.2). These compositional changes,

Table 4.2 Compositional shifts within the budgets of international finance organisations, 1973–2014

	1973	1980	1996	2007	2013
(a) ODA/DFID					
Budget (2014) $17.5 billion (all concessional)					
Share of total budget taken *by particular forms of aid* *(% of total)* Project aid	38	17	8	3	3
Programme aid (including adjustment credits, budget support and debt relief)	0	9	7	22	14
Technical cooperation	33	42	51	40	43
Private sector(CDC) and civil society organisations	9	8	15	18	13
Emergency and humanitarian	0	2	23	15	16
Other	20	22	10	5	1
(b) World Bank group					
Total budget (2013) = $52.6 billion, of which non-concessional (IBRD and IFC) = $24.6 billion; concessional (IDA and IFC) = $28.0 billion					
Share of total budget taken *by particular forms* *of expenditure* *(% of total)* Project aid	86	82	58	48	45
Programme aid (including 'adjustment credits' and/or 'development policy lending')	0	2	15	23	35
Private sector (IFC)	5	15	16	27	16
Other	9	1	1	2	4

Source: ODM/ODA/DFID and World Bank Group, *Annual Reports*, various augmented for recent years by Currey (2014) (World Bank group) and DFID, *Statistics on International Development 2015*, https://www.gov.uk/government/uploads/attachment_data/file/482332/SID2015c.pdf.

which we now discuss, are not just relabelling: they amount to a fundamental alteration of the aid instrument, which is particularly interesting because it responds both to the evidence of macro-ineffectiveness of aid earlier presented (for example in Table 4.1) and also to changes occurring at the same time in the economics of growth.

4.2.1 Liberalisation and the 'Washington Consensus'

The new international economic order established by the Bretton Woods agreements of 1944 and 1945 established the free market as its guiding principle, seeking to learn from the damage which had been done to trade and investment by the widespread protectionism of the 1930s. The IMF in particular, as the institution primarily responsible for emergency lending and fiscal policy, tried very hard to resist the exchange controls and overvalued exchange rates which developing countries frequently used to deal with inflation and balance of payments crises. However, they were fighting the dominant development-policy ideology of the time, which was to try and break out of underdevelopment by means of import-substituting industrialisation, backed by heavy protection. In many countries of East Asia, notably South Korea and Taiwan, this approach was so successfully applied as to transcend the objective of simply building up an industrial base and grew into export-based industrialisation. But elsewhere, throughout most of Latin America and all of Africa except for Mauritius, it was wastefully applied, because government was typically in the grip of rent-seekers aiming only at protecting their livelihoods and keeping imports cheap, and these countries moved into a state of chronic budgetary crisis; this crisis became acute in the early 1980s when the banks ceased to lend.

At that point, the World Bank moved in, offering financial support, but demanding in return that recipient policies be liberalised. Its diagnosis of the global crisis (exposited in e.g. World Bank 1983) was that debtor countries (with the exception of East Asia) had surrendered to political pressure to implement 'inward-looking' policies of pegged exchange rates, taxes on primary exports and subsidies on food and fuel in preference to the 'outward-looking' policies which could achieve competitiveness on export markets – most notably, free exchange rates. The Bank therefore now offered aid of a quite different sort from the infrastructure credits which had previously dominated its lending – namely what it called 'adjustment loans', designed to push the economy away from autarchy and towards the open economy – conditioned on performance criteria designed to achieve this objective such as decontrol of exchange rates, removal of export taxes, removal of input subsidies, and sometimes also privatisation of state-owned enterprises – the approach which came to be known as the 'Washington Consensus'.[8] As Table 4.2 shows, adjustment credits of this sort – generally orchestrated by the World Bank, but often co-funded by a raft of supportive bilateral donors – rose from next to nothing in 1980 to account for one-sixth of the Bank's concessionary (aid) funding in the mid-1990s, and an only slightly lesser share of the British (ODA/DFID) aid budget. The main purpose of all this policy leverage was, of course, to take developing countries out of the state of stagnation and decline into which they had fallen and back on to a growth path. However, any policy which helped increase growth was also, potentially, good for aid effectiveness, which as Table 4.1 shows had fallen on bad times. Donors, at this time, pinned their hopes on conditionality as the lever which would make aid more effective – by preventing aid from being gobbled up by consumption, as at point C on Fig. 4.1, and redirecting it towards investment and towards higher productivity, in the direction of point B on that trade-off. This policy of leverage on recipient governments was accompanied by an auxiliary policy of reducing dependence on them as vehicles for aid flows. In the new world of the 1980s, in which right-wing governments had taken over from centre-left ones in the US, the UK, Germany and several Scandinavian countries, it had become traditional to see government as part of the problem rather than part of the solution, and these governments especially proceeded to implant this approach into their aid policies. Gone now was the poverty-focussed aid of the 1970s, which depended heavily on local administrations; gone were approaches such as government-sponsored land reform and integrated rural development; and in their place emerged policies channelling aid into the private sector of LDCs, through subsidiaries such as the World Bank's

---

[8] Typically these credits were conditional on an IMF stand-by or extended facility already being in place; indeed, through the 1990s the IMF itself, in pursuit of greater control over the adjustment process, became an aid donor in its own right, offering credits known as Enhanced Structural Adjustment Facilities or ESAFs; see Bredenkamp et al. (1999). For a full list of the conditions applied by the Bank to adjustment lending at this time, see Mosley, Harrigan and Toye (1995), especially volume 1, chapters 2, 3 and 4.

International Finance Corporation and the British government's Commonwealth Development Corporation. As Table 4.2 shows, these aid vehicles took up an increasing share of donor aid budgets from the 1980s onwards. However, it was not only private firms which benefited from this disillusion with the LDC state. As developing countries' governments, under the stress of budgetary cuts and structural adjustment, cut back their service provision in the 1980s and 1990s across the board, especially in sectors such as health, education and agricultural extension, so the burgeoning voluntary NGO sector took over their functions and their budget. By the 1990s, just one NGO in Bangladesh, BRAC (formerly the Bangladesh Rural Advancement Committee), was providing 77% of vaccinations against key diseases. This kind of budgetary reallocation in favour of NGOs provided useful ammunition to donors wishing to show that the humanitarian and redistributive objectives of aid had not, in these times of austerity and liberalisation, been abandoned.

4.2.2 The Rise of Human Capital and the 'New Poverty Agenda' as Development Solutions

In the early days of development economics (and aid) growth was seen as flowing from investment in physical capital, embodied in increasingly high-productivity technologies, as discussed above; on this view, the bigger the share of savings (and investment) in GNP, the better. However, during the 1990s, through the insight of Paul Romer (1986) our understanding of the growth process was changed. Romer's discovery was to show that 'increasingly high-productivity technologies' are not something exogenous which comes out of the sky, but something endogenous which happens if and only if new ideas and new knowledge make them happen. In 'new growth theory', therefore, growth is caused not only by increases in physical capital, as of old, but by improvements in knowledge, typically embodied in healthcare and educational systems, which make technological change possible.

This insight was quickly recognised as important by theorists, but not by development practitioners such as aid donors, nor even at first by applied economists. What eventually gave it traction within the development business was a gradual evolution of development policy away from objectives defined purely in terms of economic growth, and towards broader objectives defined in terms of human development and in particular the welfare of the poor. This evolution had begun modestly with research illustrating the social costs of adjustment (Cornia et al. 1987) and even when the World Bank showed its humanitarian credentials with a World Development Report of its own on poverty (World Bank 1990), emphasising the developmental merit of labour-intensive strategies such as those practised in the Far East, there was no expectation that it would move into the mainstream: the Bank's rhetoric at this time was still all about 'getting prices right' and 'outward-looking strategies' and not at all about poverty reduction. However, towards the mid-1990s, the mood began to change. The UN published its Multilateral (later Millennium) Development Goals (MDGs) in 1996, acknowledging poverty reduction to be not one thing but several but amongst those things privileging those measures such as health and education which provided an *asset* to the poor and thereby made poverty reduction sustainable. Third World leaders quickly saw the political merits of universalising health and education and endorsed the MDGs with enthusiasm. And, with enthusiastic support from aid donors, they embraced new strategies of social protection such as conditional cash transfers which expanded provision beyond formal-sector employees to embrace the genuinely poor, and did so moreover in a sustainable, asset-based manner. The old apparatus of conditionality was a liability rather than an asset in achieving the consensual, bipartisan approach to policy-making implicit in the MDGs,[9] and indeed was hard to apply now that donor conceptions of good policy (the Washington Consensus) had expanded far beyond openness and 'getting prices right' into any number of softer issues of governance and pro-poor

---

[9] Indeed, the language of conditionality was dropped from the millennium onwards, not only by bilateral donors such as DFID (2013) but by multilaterals; even the IMF began at this point to moderate its language.

policy, or what Rodrik (2006) was to call the 'Washington Confusion'. The 'Letters of Development Policy' which central bank governors and finance ministers of recipient countries had been commanded to write to define their acceptance of the terms of a conditional aid agreement were now rebadged as bipartisan 'Poverty Reduction Strategy Papers' (PRSPs; later Poverty Reduction Strategies or PRSs), jointly drafted by both sides.[10] By the millennium the development community was hooked on the new development strategy: pro-poor growth, incorporated into aid strategies mainly through a focus on technical assistance to education (and especially primary and non-formal education) and to health (and especially rural health centres and reproductive and peri-natal health, together with an attack on diseases mainly afflicting the poorest countries, such as malaria).[11] As may be seen from another look at Table 4.2, this was a time when technical assistance (aid for the development of human capital) expanded as aid for the provision of infrastructure and physical capital was almost wiped out – reflecting the change of emphasis taking place in economic theory at the same time. By the millennium, in fact, aid was a quite different thing from what it had been 25 years previously: consisting of transfers of services and not physical goods; the creation of institutions and relationships rather than transfers of equipment; support for the economy as a whole and not just for recipient-country government. These changes in the emphasis, even the definition, of aid need to be borne in mind by all those involved in assessing how well it works.

4.2.3 New Regression Results at the Millennium, and Their Interpretation

As might have been hoped, all of these changes in the practice and the targeting of aid did make it more effective. However, it required some econometric skill to make the data tell the right story. In the first

---

[10] For a sceptical view of this notion of bipartisanship see chapter by Stewart in Ranis et al. (2005).

[11] See Sachs (2007); the Bill and Melinda Gates Foundation have also had a strong emphasis on malaria eradication in Africa.

attempt, conducted by the World Bank economists Craig Burnside and David Dollar in the late 1990s, a simple (ordinary least squares) regression of aid on growth yielded an insignificant coefficient of aid on growth,[12] as in the results reported by earlier authors in Table 4.1. Only if aid was multiplied by a composite variable representing 'good policy' (an average of the inflation rate, the budget deficit and an index of economic openness, or avoidance of pegged exchange rates and other interferences with the market) did aid become significant, as shown in the left-hand column of Table 4.3. This result was immediately interpreted by Burnside and Dollar, and indeed by the entire World Bank and IMF group, as vindication of its structural adjustment policies, since low inflation and openness were, as we have seen, precisely the policies on which their aid was conditioned. As per the green arrow on Fig. 4.1, policy had indeed, it seems, managed to drag the developing world away from consumption now and towards investment-oriented policies.

However, the debate did not end here. The Danish economists Henrik Hansen and Finn Tarp (2001), using the state-of-the-art econometric technique GMM (Generalised Method of Moments), challenged Burnside and Dollar's interpretation of aid effectiveness, making just one amendment in the specification of Table 4.3 from the Burnside-Dollar model: the inclusion of a term in the square of aid flows, alongside aid levels and the previous controls. This was not just a statistical artifice: it is a perfectly plausible application of the law of diminishing returns, which states that increasing amounts of a variable factor of production (be it land, or capital, or in this case aid flows), all other factors of production remaining fixed, will yield gradually diminishing returns. (Or, in the context of the aid process, if gradually increasing amounts of aid, say in response to a disaster, are channelled through an airport of – in the short term – fixed capacity, then the supplies of aid will pile up at the end of the runway or be lost to corruption, and in any

---

[12] See the two left-hand columns of Table 5, page 839, in Burnside and Dollar (2000) – which estimate, by OLS and 2SLS methods respectively, that if aid as a percentage of GNP is regressed against growth of GNP, using the standard controls employed in Table 4.3 but not any other aid variable, then its measured impact on growth is insignificant, small and, for what this is worth, negative.

Table 4.3 Two aid-effectiveness regressions of the millennium period: Comparative results

Authors	Burnside and Dollar (2000)	Hansen and Tarp (2001)
Dependent variable	Per capita GDP growth	Per capita GDP growth
Sample	56 countries, 1970–1973 through 1990–1993	56 countries, 1974–1977 to 1990–1993
Estimation method	OLS	GMM
Regression coefficients (t-values in parentheses) on		
Aid (defined as a percentage of recipient GNP)	−0.013 (0.10)	0.238** (2.28)
Aid* policy[1]	0.27** (2.25)	−0.006 (2.22)
Aid squared		−0.754** (2.27)
Initial GDP per capita	−0.74 (0.80)	0.001 (0.13)
Assassinations	−0.75* (1.63)	−0.45** (1.98)
Institutional quality	0.77*** (4.05)	0.81** (4.57)
Other variables in regression	M2/GDP (lagged), sub-Saharan Africa and East Asia dummies, (aid/GDP)[1]* policy	Policy[1], budget surplus, inflation, openness, financial depth, ethnic fractionalisation,
Number of observations	189	211
R^2	0.42	Not quoted

Sources: Burnside and Dollar (2000) table 5; Hansen and Tarp (2001) table 1.

Notes: (1) 'Policy' is defined as an average of inflation rate, budget deficit and the Sachs-Warner openness index.

* 10%, ** indicates significance at the 5% level, *** indicates that the coefficient is significant at the 1% level.

case the productivity of the aid will diminish over time.) In Hansen and Tarp's specification (Table 4.3, second column) the verdict of the regression analysis changes dramatically: all of a sudden, it is not just aid to countries which obey the rules of the 'Washington Consensus', but all aid, which in the aggregate has a positive and (at the 5% level) significant impact on growth. The aid effort, under the impetus of the changes it had undergone since the pioneering days, appeared to have turned a corner.

4.3 Aid in the Twenty-First Century: Hopes Dashed and Regained

The years immediately following the millennium were quite a euphoric time. Most countries in the world, including now African countries, were growing. Growth was fairly steady, and some finance ministers, such as the UK chancellor Gordon Brown, boasted that the business cycle, active for over 200 years, had now been overcome. The IMF, whose remit is to assist countries with severe adjustment and liquidity problems, lamented in 2006 that it was expecting to have to make some staff redundant shortly because there was a lack of work for them to do. And aid donors, as we have seen, confident now that the new poverty agenda provided them with a raison d'être and encouraged by the new findings on aid effectiveness,[13] started to step up their aid budgets once again – even the US, which had been sceptical of aid for decades.

This needs to be set in the context of what was happening to global development finance, not just concessional aid. As discussed above, private (non-concessional) flows of bank lending, bond and equity finance and private direct investment had suddenly collapsed at the start of the 1980s, suddenly putting the poorer developing countries at the mercy of the aid donors and giving them the opportunity to get their act together. During the late 1980s and 1990s private financial flows did indeed revive, but the new environment of open and highly volatile short-term capital markets had embedded huge vulnerabilities into the global financial system, as the world was to discover between 1997 and

---

[13] These findings, in the new millennium when the effects of aid on growth started to be questioned (see Dollar and Kraay (2002) and the surrounding debate), came to embrace 'softer' objectives of aid such as poverty reduction, as well as aid flows (see for example Mosley et al. 2004), which shows that aid flows have a positive effect on poverty reduction as well as on growth, providing that the pattern of public expenditure is also pro-poor (and in particular is oriented towards social expenditures, in particular health and education).

2000 when first Thailand, then Indonesia, then South Korea of all countries, and finally Russia, Brazil and Argentina were hit by sudden capital flight, requiring each of them to have emergency recourse to the World Bank and IMF (see *World Development* 1997). Only a dozen or so countries were hit in this way, but the fact that this time the affected countries were in nearly all cases, quite unlike the 1980s, robust, dynamic middle-income countries with small budget deficits provoked quite reasonable fears on the part of almost every country that standard defences against capital flight (such as those provided by the IMF) were worthless and 'it could be us next'. Hence, even though the contagion affected a smaller number of countries than in the 1980s, global non-concessional financial flows in the last few years of the 1990s fell by almost as much as in the 1980s (as shown by Table 4.4). But, as it was now the millennium, it was time to celebrate, and, except in the southern cone of Latin America, most treated the East Asian crisis as a one-off, needing no more than a few tweaks in the system of supervision of regulation to set right.

As may be observed from the above figures, aid flows are normally (i.e. in a non-crisis year) much smaller than private financial flows, but they have the merit, from the point of view of a poor developing country, of being not only (as Papanek had noted) purposely designed to support the economies of developing countries, but also much more stable and dependable than private financial flows. However, they are not as stable and dependable as tax revenue; and this takes us to the next step in the argument.

During the decade of the 2000s, 'institutions' took over from human capital as the primary focus for aid donors and for the analysis of development generally. 'Institutions', of course, encompasses a multitude of aspects of local and national governance – including law and order, public administration, public finance, justice, the operation of democratic institutions, and of course the institutions of economic policy, including taxation. However, during this first decade of the new millennium it was common for donors to focus their fire, now not so much on opening up the economy as on two specific institutional indicators – the tax ratio and the level of corruption in recipient countries. Both of these were important, not only because they are

Table 4.4 Financial flows from rich to poor countries, 1981–2012 ($ billion)

	1981	1986	1993	2000	2004	2009	2010	2012
(1) Aid ('official development assistance'; DAC* countries only)	46	58	67	63	87	115	117	126
(2) Net private capital flows (total) of which:	74	27	182	74	232	112	408	383
(a) Long-term private direct investment	17	11	57	167	184	95	44	80
(b) Long-term bonds	3	5	73	17	34	9	65	74
(c) Short-term bonds	54	29	52	110	11	15	59	55
(d) Short-term flows	–	–	–	–	–	7	235	174
(3) Grants by development NGOs (estimate)	2	3	8	15	18	30	32	35
(1)+(2)+(3) Total capital flow from rich to poor countries	122	86	257	152	337	257	557	544

Source: World Bank, *Global Development Finance* and IMF, *World Economic Outlook*, various.

Notes: Shaded columns represent crisis years (note that during the first two of these, private flows fell below government-to-government aid flows).

*DAC = Development Assistance Committee of the OECD (Organisation for Economic Co-operation and Development).

clearly related with an economy's ability to develop, but also because, in the opinion of many observers, they actually tended to degenerate as aid flows increased – precisely the opposite of the effect they were intended to have. Why did this happen? Essentially because they provided a perverse political incentive: for example, the political costs associated with taking on increased aid finance are small, but the political costs associated with increasing rates of domestic taxation are large, especially in a fragile state; and this may motivate especially the poorest and most fragile countries to depend on aid flows to finance the budget, and not grasp the nettle of developing proper tax systems. Deborah Bräutigam and Stephen Knack (2004) built on this insight to argue that the proliferation of aid flows from many different donors, each with its own system of aid procurement, might have the effect of undermining domestic institutions and therefore the effectiveness of aid flows, and produced regressions which suggest a negative correlation between the size of aid flows and the ICRG index of institutional quality, which included the tax/GNP ratio as one of its components.[14] This conclusion, even if it is accepted, does not directly question the thrust of the general Burnside-Dollar–Hansen-Tarp consensus that the short-term impact of aid, with or without policy conditions attached, is positive. However, it does point out that aid might have a longer-term negative impact on institutional quality. Thus, the first seeds of post-millennium doubt were sown.

What really put the cat amongst the pigeons was the subsequent work of Arvind Subramaniam and Raghuram Rajan (at the time chief economist of the IMF, now governor of the Reserve Bank of India). Rajan and Subramaniam, dissatisfied with the tendency of the literature so far discussed to simply pick the story they wanted their listeners to hear and then to design a specification (including a set of robustness tests) consistent with that, produced the most rigorous set of variations on the standard aid-effectiveness regressions so far attempted, focussing especially on the length of the lag between the injection of aid and the measured impact. This issue had been acknowledged before; indeed in many ways it constitutes the main justification for aid, since a major reason why banks and multinational companies will not finance investments in education, health, or infrastructure is that they have a long gestation period, which prevents investors from getting their money

---

[14] Using 2SLS estimation methods, Bräutigam and Knack (2004, table 3) derived the following result:

$$\text{Value of ICRG quality of governance index} = \underset{(4.25)}{10.2^{***}} - \underset{(0.14)}{0.78^{***}} \text{initial value of ICRG index}$$

$$\underset{(1.26)}{-4.11} - \underset{(1.91)}{2.3^{*} \text{politicalviolence}} -, \underset{(2.42)}{0.08^{**} \text{aid/GNP}}, n = 32, r^2 = 0.60$$

back quickly. However, Rajan and Subramanian took the exploration of the lag between aid and growth to extremes not previously examined, estimating aid-growth equations with not only 5-year and 10-year lags, as had been normal, but now 20-, 30- and even 40-year lags also. Their conclusion (Rajan and Subramanian 2008), published at the same time as the world economy fell into recession and inducing in many development workers a similar feeling of their world having fallen apart, was that whatever specification is adopted, aid flows have no significant and measurable impact on growth.[15] In other words, we are back in the world of Table 4.1: the good work of the well-performing recipient countries is neutralised by the backsliding of the ill-performing countries. This main result is presented, in the original paper published in the *Review of Economics and Statistics*, simply as a statistical conclusion without any theoretical rationale. However, in a subsequent paper (Rajan and Subramaniam 2009) the authors do present two explanations of their negative (or rather neutral) results: first, negative long-term effects of aid on governance (as in the analysis of Bräutigam and Knack) and secondly, 'Dutch disease' effects in which large-scale aid flows have the same effect as large-scale exports of oil and minerals; in other words, they drive up the real exchange rate to a point which damages competitiveness and makes diversification impossible.

For a while, the aid world went quiet in face of this very rigorous assault, as if stunned. Was it really the case that all the transformational efforts of the 1990s and 2000s had yielded nothing?

Not quite. If nothing else, there has been progress in the econometric analysis of aid in relation to development, and whatever our point of view, we can no longer argue our case by going back to the methods of 50, or even 15, years ago. However, in various ways, it has been very recently discovered that the aid landscape is and in all probability never has been as bleak as Rajan and Subramaniam painted it. These discoveries have taken three different forms.

---

[15] See for example Rajan and Subramaniam (2008) table 8 (which divides the results according to type of aid and lag structure), 9 and 10. The method of estimation used is generally GMM (now split into two variants, difference-GMM and system-GMM).

The approach I have taken (Mosley 2015) is to deal with the classic problem of endogeneity (i.e. aid levels influence economic performance, but poor economic performance also justifies higher levels of aid, which makes aid endogenous and will produce biased estimates of aid effectiveness in equations such as those of Table 4.1 unless adequate instruments can be found.) We begin from the link in the chain found by Bräutigam and Knack to be weakest, namely the risk that aid may damage the quality of institutions and in particular tax ratios, and then trace the chain of causation from the political determinants of tax ratios, to public expenditure, to growth, which aid and public expenditure can be presumed to influence. This entire chain of causation is estimated by standard GMM methods, using population and historical GNP per capita as instruments for aid. Our finding (Mosley 2015, tables 3 and 4) is that within this framework, aid continues to be a significant influence on growth.

The second approach, by Clemens and associates, innovates by differentiating between types of aid according to the impact which they seek to achieve. In particular, they exclude '[aid] flows that are not intended or used to promote expansion in generalised productive capacity (such as humanitarian assistance or disaster relief), as well as flows whose effect on overall national growth, if it ever arrives, might come long after the time period under study (such as a vaccination campaign or school feeding project)' (Clemens et al. 2012, p. 594). Conversely, they focus on what they call 'early-impact' aid, which they characterise as budget support or programme aid, plus project aid given for infrastructure or 'immediately productive' activities, such as transport, telecommunications, energy, banking, agriculture and industry (*ibid*) – in other words excluding from the analysis long-gestation activities such as, in particular, health and education, the spearhead of the aid reform efforts of the 1990s and 2000s. They replicate the Burnside-Dollar (2000) and Rajan-Subramaniam (2008) models with the original data, and also vary those models by including the most innovative feature of the Hansen-Tarp model, namely the inclusion of the aid-squared term. The main finding is that once the definition of aid is restricted to early-impact aid, even the Rajan-Subramaniam model exhibits a positive impact of aid (thus redefined) on growth, especially once the data period is extended forward to 2005 (Clemens et al. 2012, table 9, p. 608). Thus, even without amending the model as we have done, the original story, namely that most aid does not disappear 'down the rathole',[16] still holds up.

The final and most ambitious recent attempt to rehabilitate overseas aid is that by Arndt et al. (2015), published in the same *World Development* symposium as our own paper summarised above. The authors re-estimate a similar sort of 'new growth theory' model to that estimated by Hansen and Tarp in 2001 (but, surprisingly, omit aid squared, the big novelty of that paper, from their story this time round) and find, this time using maximum likelihood rather than GMM techniques, that aid, within this formulation, has a significant impact not only on growth of GDP but also on headcount poverty, years of schooling and the infant mortality rate.

4.4 Conclusions

Aid, and for that matter development finance as a whole, have not turned out as the world expected. What the world expected in the 1950s and 1960s was that developing countries, as a mass, would emerge from poverty quite quickly, with the help of quite substantial amounts of aid, and also with substantial help from banks and private investors. Few people expected at this time that only a minority of countries would win the fight against poverty and dependence and become manufacturing exporters,[17] and that every time there was a crisis there would be panic withdrawals of bank loans and FDI, forcing developing countries back into the arms of the donors. Thus, aid flows are still a much more important feature of the developing world than they were predicted to be 70 years ago, and this is a matter for anxiety rather than for rejoicing.

Some changes in the role of aid there have been. South Korea and China, having grown rapidly over 40 years, are now no longer aid

---

[16] This was a phrase used by *The Economist* in 1997 shortly after the publication of the Boone (1996) article (see Table 4.1), provocatively suggesting that most aid was a waste of money.

[17] Maybe 9 or 10 countries in the Far East, including China; in Latin America, only Brazil and arguably Mexico; in Africa, only Mauritius; in other words, only about a dozen in total, plus Europe and North America.

recipients, and indeed alongside the Gulf states, some Eastern European countries and Venezuela have evolved from aid recipients into aid donors. This diversification of the donor world away from dependence on members of the Development Assistance Committee (DAC) of the Organisation for Economic Co-operation and Development (OECD) has come too late to be includable in our statistical review of aid effectiveness, but nonetheless is important as an illustration of how multi-polar the world has become, with many of the new donors using their new status to fashion new sub-regional trade and investment blocs within the global South to complement, maybe even remake, the existing North-South linkages (Gore 2015; Koehler 2015).

It is in the context of this multi-polar world that we have attempted to reappraise the role and effectiveness of overseas aid. Unexpectedly forced into becoming, for the poorest countries, the prop of the international financial system in times of crisis, the aid industry has also been forced to confront a series of statistical analyses, including one by ourselves, suggesting that all these efforts were, on balance, achieving nothing overall during some periods, with the achievements of the 'success' countries being effaced by the failures of the 'failure' countries. To these challenges the development community responded, in the 1980s and 1990s, with some creativity and agility, completely refashioning the architecture of aid flows and refocussing them on the hardest cases in Africa and other fragile states. Even then, hard questions have continued to be asked, in the shape of the Rajan-Subramaniam investigation; but this too has provoked creative responses, notably the paper by Clemens et al. (2012) which, as described above, eschews the Punch-and-Judy-show behaviour of many contributors to the aid debate and seeks to reconcile these different contributors rather than set them against each other once again. They warn that 'many important growth successes across the developing world have been achieved with very little foreign aid, such as in post-Mao China and post-renovation Vietnam' (Clemens et al. 2012, p. 614), but conclude (ibid) that aid has made a modest but significant contribution to development. This now seems something like an equilibrium view. It may be that this at times rather turbulent field of development has now achieved maturity.

References

Arndt, C., Jones, S., & Tarp, F. (2015). Assessing foreign aid's contribution to growth and development. *World Development, 69,* 6–18.

Ayres, R. (1983). *Focus on poverty.* Washington, DC: World Bank.

Boone, P. (1994). *The impact of Foreign aid on savings and growth.* London School of Economics Center for Economic Performance (Working Paper No. 677).

Boone, P. (1996). Politics and the effectiveness of foreign aid. *European Economic Review, 40,* 289–329.

Bräutigam, D.A. & Knack, S. (2004). Foreign aid, institutions, and governance in sub-Saharan Africa. *Economic development and cultural change, 52*(2), 255–285.

Bredenkamp, H., & Schadler, S. (1999). *Economic adjustment and reform in low income countries.* Washington, DC: International Monetary Fund.

Burnside, C., & Dollar, D. (2000). Aid, policies and growth. *American Economic Review, 90,* 847–869.

Chenery, H., & Strout, A. (1966). Foreign assistance and economic development. *American Economic Review, 56,* 679–733.

Chenery, H., Ahluwalia, M., Bell, C., Duloy, J. & Jolly, R. (1975). *Redistribution with growth.* Washington, DC: World Bank and Brighton: Institute of Development Studies at the University of Sussex.

Clemens, M., Radelet, S., Bhavnani, R., & Bazzi, S. (2012). Counting chickens when they hatch: Timing and the effects of aid on growth. *Economic Journal, 122,* 590–618.

Cornia, A., Jolly, R., & Stewart, F. (1987). *Adjustment with a human face.* Oxford: Oxford University Press.

Currey, K. (2014). *Briefing note: some evolving trends at the World Bank: Lending, funding, staffing.* www.bankinformationcentre.org/wp_content/uploads/2014/07/some-evolving-trends-at-the-World-Bank.pdf.

Department for International Development (of the UK Government) (2013, first published 2005). *Partnerships for poverty reduction: Rethinking conditionality.* https://www.gov.uk/government/publications/partnerships-for-poverty-reduction-rethinking-conditionality.

Dollar, D., & Kraay, A. (2002). Growth is good for the poor. *Journal of Economic Growth, 7,* 195–225.

Gore, C. (2015). The post-2015 moment: Towards sustainable development goals and a new global development paradigm. *Journal of International Development, 27,* 717–732.

Griffin, K. (1970). Foreign capital, domestic savings and economic development. *Bulletin of the Oxford University Institute of Economics and Statistics (Now Oxford Bulletin of Economics and Statistics), 32,* 99–112.

Hansen, H., & Tarp, F. (2001). Aid and growth regressions. *Journal of Development Economics, 64* (September), 547–570.

Hayter, T. (1971) *Aid as imperialism.* Harmondsworth: Penguin.

Heller, P. (1975). A model of public fiscal behaviour in developing countries: Aid, investment and taxation. *American Economic Review, 65,* 429–445.

Koehler, G. (2015). Seven decades of 'development', and now what? *Journal of International Development, 27,* 733–751.

Lewis, W. A. (1955). *The theory of economic growth.* London: Allen and Unwin.

Mosley, P. (1980). Aid, savings and growth revisited. *Oxford Bulletin of Economics and Statistics, 42,* 79–97.

Mosley, P. (1981). Aid for the poorest: Some early lessons of UK experience. *Journal of Development Studies, 17,* 214–226.

Mosley, P. (2015). Fiscal composition and aid-effectiveness. *World Development, 69* (May), 106–115.

Mosley, P., Harrigan, J., & Toye, J. F. (1995). *Aid and power: The World Bank and policy-based lending* (Vol. 1). London: Psychology Press.

Mosley, P., Hudson, J., & Horrell, S. (1987). Aid, the public sector and the market in less developed countries. *Economic Journal, 97,* 616–642.

Mosley, P., Hudson, J., & Verschoor, A. (2004). Aid, poverty reduction and the 'new conditionality'. *Economic Journal, 114,* 217–244.

Moyo, D. (2009). *Dead aid: Why aid is not working and why there is a better way for Africa.* London: Zed Press.

Papanek, G. (1972). The effect of aid and other resource transfers on savings and growth in less developed countries. *Economic Journal, 82,* 863–874.

Papanek, G. (1973). Aid, private investment, savings and growth in less developed countries. *Journal of Political Economy, 81,* 120–131.

Rajan, R., & Subramaniam, A. (2008). Aid and growth: What does the cross-section evidence really show? *Review of Economics and Statistics, 90,* 643–665.

Rajan, R., & Subramaniam, A. (2009). *Aid, Dutch disease and manufacturing growth.* Washington, DC: Center for Global Development (Working Paper 196).

Ranis, G., Vreeland, J., & Kosack, S. (Eds.) (2005). *Globalisation and the nation state.* London: Routledge.

Reichel, R. (1995). Development aid, savings and growth in the 1980s: A cross-section analysis/aide au développement, espargnes et croissance dans les années

1980: Une analyse en section transversale. *Savings and Development, 19,* 279–296.

Rodrik, D. (2006). Goodbye Washington consensus, hello Washington confusion? A review of the World Bank's economic growth in the 1990s: Learning from a decade of reform. *Journal of Economic Literature, 44,* 973–987.

Romer, P. (1986). Increasing returns and long-run growth. *Journal of Political Economy, 94,* 1002–1037.

Rosenstein-Rodan, P. (1961). International aid for underdeveloped countries. *Review of Economics and Statistics, 43*(1961), 107–138.

Sachs, J. (2007). *The end of poverty: How we can make it happen in our lifetime.* London: Penguin Books.

Singer, H. (1950). The distribution of gains between investing and borrowing countries. *American Economic Review, 40,* 251–273.

Voivodas, C. (1973). Exports, foreign capital and economic growth. *Journal of International Economics, 3,* 337–349.

World Bank. (1983). *World Development Report 1983: Getting Prices Right.* Washington, D.C.: World Bank.

World Bank. (1990). *World Development Report* 1990: *Poverty.*

World Development. (1997). Complete issue on the East Asian crisis. September.

Paul Mosley holds BA and PhD degrees (1968, 1980) from the University of Cambridge. He has spent most of his career in the university sector, but in his main area of specialisation, economic development, he has alternated between academic and hands-on work: he was an economist/statistician in the Ministry of Economic Planning, Kenya, in the early 1970s, worked from 1979 to 1981 as an economic adviser at the Ministry of Overseas Development (now DFID), has done much consultancy and advisory work for DFID, the World Bank and other development organisations, co-founded a pressure group, the Independent Group on British Aid, and has been a trustee of the development NGO Action Aid. He was a lecturer, then reader, at the University of Bath from 1974 to 1985, and before coming to Sheffield in 1999 held professorships at Manchester (1986–1992) and Reading (1993–1999). He has been editor of the *Journal of International Development* since 1989, and from 1998 until 2001 served as President of the Development Studies Association.

Paul's main research interests are in economic development, with related interests in economic history, in social policy and in the politics of economic policy-making. A major focus of his work has always been the reduction of poverty: in 1996 he co-authored *Finance Against Poverty*, one of the first assessments of the effectiveness of micro-finance, followed by *Out of the Poverty Trap: Overcoming Financial Exclusion in the Inner City* (Routledge, 2011) which examines the effectiveness of action against financial exclusion in Britain during the recent recession, *The Politics of Poverty Reduction* (Oxford U.P., 2012), based on a recently concluded ESRC project, which examines comparatively the political factors which determine the possibilities for global poverty reduction, and most recently, with Palgrave Macmillan (2013), a biography of the first and arguably greatest development economist, Sir Arthur Lewis (1915–1991). *Fiscal Policy and the Natural Resource Curse: Escaping from the Poverty Trap* was published by Routledge in March 2017.

5

Migrant Remittances and Beyond: The Development Implications of Human Capital Mobility and Accompanying Financial Flows

Ralitza Dimova

5.1 Introduction

A high-quality development finance course would be incomplete without the topic of migrant remittances as key component of cross-border financial flows towards less developed countries. Not only is the sheer volume of migrant remittances well in excess of that of overseas development assistance and private debt and portfolio investments – while their cyclical volatility tends to be lower than that of foreign direct investments (FDIs) (Fig. 5.1) – but also their development impact on smaller and less developed countries is disproportionately higher than that of other forms of international finance for development. The key problem with foreign direct investments and portfolio investments is that their benefits are only felt when a contry has reached a certain threshold of both financial and overall economic development. Below that threshold the probability of receiving this

R. Dimova (✉)
Global Development Institute, University of Manchester, Manchester, UK
e-mail: ralitza.dimova@manchester.ac.uk

© The Author(s) 2017   **111**
G. Giorgioni (ed.), *Development Finance*, Palgrave Studies
in Impact Finance, DOI 10.1057/978-1-137-58032-0_5

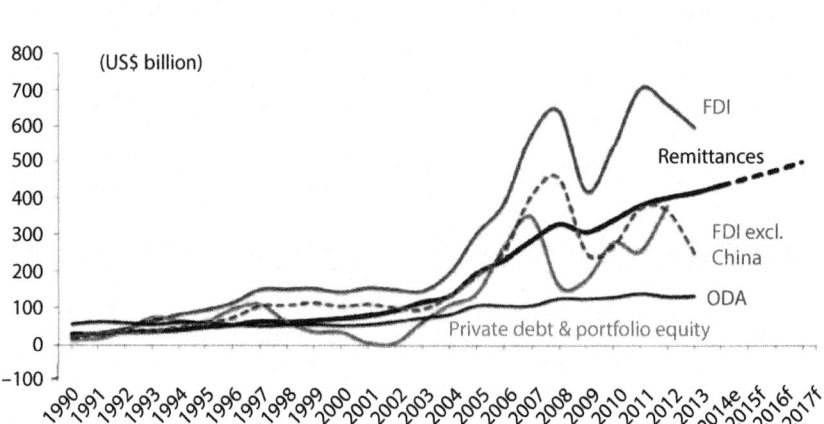

Fig. 5.1 Remittances as part of a broader range of cross-border financial flows. *Source*: The World Bank (2014). Permission granted by World Bank

types of foreign investments and reaping benefits from them is very low (Harrison and Rodriguez-Clare, 2010; Kose et al, 2010). Overseas development assistance on the other hand is often driven by political conciderations and are thus dependent on the interest of donors to allocate aid to specific destinations, which are not necessarily the poorest and most vulnerable ones in the world (Alesina and Dollar, 2000). By contrast, migrant remittances tend to benefit most some of the poorest and most vulnerable countries in the world. Specifically, both the remittances-to-GDP and remittances-to-foreign reserve ratios are highest among such countries (World Bank, 2015). Although this increases the vulnerability of poor economies and households to crises in origin countries, the counter-cyclical power of remittances compared to alternative sources of finance and insurance in crisis-ridden beneficiary countries has long been acknowledged (Mohapatra et al. 2009; Mitrut and Wolff 2014).

While the literature on remittances has traditionally focused almost exclusively on understanding the motivations behind, and consequences of, this type of international financial flow mainly in terms of growth, poverty and inequality of recipient countries and households, more recent studies have broadened the research and policy agenda towards analyses of remittances as integral part of the complex dynamics of both international migration and other types of cross-border capital flows.

Studying the complex process of international migration and its link to a range of financial flows, including remittances, is important for a proper understanding of the economic role of development finance for several reasons. To begin with, the cross-border mobility of people represents an important capital flow that deserves special attention on its own within the broader range of cross-border financial flows. While the simplest neoclassical factor mobility theoretical framework provides a starting point for the understanding of migration as a form of cross-border capital flow (typically in direction opposite to that of physical capital), most of the traditional development literature has focused on internal as opposed to international mobility of human capital as in the stylised Lewis and Harris-Todaro deviations from the simplest neoclassical model. More recently, key authors in the field of international migration have introduced interesting new nuances. Kugler and Rapoport (2007) ask the question of whether international labour and capital flows are substitutes or complements and find evidence in favour of contemporaneous substitutability and dynamic complementarity, which have important policy implications. Further developments in the literature highlight links with networking and information flow implication of migration in the context of international financial flows, emphasising the importance of labour mobility in facilitating productivity-enhancing finance for development (Kugler et al. 2013; Javorcik and Spatareanu 2011).

Secondly, stylised growth models emphasise the crucial role of human capital for a country's long-term development prospects, while microeconomic models highlight potentially negative implications of outmigration in the form of reduced child protection or education or as withdrawal of a key resource in labour constrained farm households. Hence, one has to acknowledge that migrant remittances are a result of migration and the development implications of loss of human capital for either a less developed economy or an individual household may be important and of a greater dimension than corresponding positive implications of subsequent remittances. At the very least, the development role of migrant remittances has to be evaluated as a balancing act between the cost and benefits of migration and the cost and benefits of migrant remittances.

The purpose of this chapter is to provide a comprehensive overview of both the stylised and some of the cutting edge literature on migration and remittances. The review will start by positioning human capital mobility within a broad set of cross-border capital flows and exploring the potential complementarity or substitutability of these flows, which has important policy implications for both migrant exporting and remittance receiving countries and countries that are net recipients of migrants. This will be followed by separate analyses of (i) the determinants and consequences of skilled migration and (ii) the determinants and consequences of migrant remittances, which will be brought together in a succeeding section in order to highlight a combined conceptual and empirical effect of migration and remittances on developing countries. A separate sub-section will be devoted to the special case of forced migration and related remittances. The conclusion will bring all of the preceding analyses together and highlight key recent developments of the literature.

5.2   The Economics of Labour Mobility and Related Cross-Border Financial Flows

Until recently, international trade, migration and capital mobility have typically been part of three disjoint analytical spheres, even though they are integral components of unified classical theoretical frameworks such as that of Heckscher and Ohlin. The literature on international migration tends to abstract from issues related to the movement of goods, services and capital, while the literatures on international trade and either foreign direct or portfolio investments have traditionally abstracted from issues related to labour mobility (Navaretti et al. 2007). This is an obvious shortcoming in the literature, as potential complementarities or substitutabilities between goods and factors of production, on the one hand, and between different factors of production, on the other hand, are likely to have important policy implications for both origin and destination countries. For instance, if labour and capital are substitutes and a net migrant recipient country imposes barriers to migration, that country is likely to experience a capital outflow with negative implications that can potentially well exceed any benefits of the prescribed policy. By contrast, it is essential for resource-poor developing countries to explore the development potential of any capital and labour complementarities and substitutabilities. While outflow of skilled labour from these economies is typically expected to have detrimental implications for the country's development, one needs to evaluate the costs and benefits of potential barriers to skilled migration against costs and benefits of related capital inflow in the form of not only migrant remittances, but also alternative forms of finance for development.

The Heckscher-Ohlin theoretical framework, where trade is a result of differences in factor endowments, is a useful starting point for this type of analysis. Countries export goods that are intensive in the domestically abundant factor of production and import goods that are intensive in the domestically scarce factor of production. A world of perfect mobility of goods thus leads to international Factor Price Equalization (FPE) and obviates the need of movement of people and capital from locations in which these factors are abundant to locations in which they are scarce and hence their marginal returns are higher.

Alternatively, in a neoclassical world of constrained trade opportunities, freely mobile factors of production and identical constant-returns-to-scale technologies everywhere, capital and labour are expected to move from locations where their marginal products are low to locations where their marginal products are high. Suppose that originally the world's concentration of capital is in location N (North), which makes it capital abundant and hence characterised by relatively low marginal returns to capital, while the world's concentration of labour is in location S (South), which makes it labour abundant and characterised by low relative returns to labour. In a world of free factor mobility, capital will move from N to S, while labour will move from S to N, leading to FPE and hence no further incentive for cross-border movement. In other words, within a standard neoclassical theoretical framework of goods and factor mobility, international trade, migration and FDIs are substitutes.

This theoretical postulate has apparently failed to pass the empirical test. At the most aggregate and crudely disaggregated level, evidence suggests that the dominant aggregate flows of both labour and capital tend to be in the South-North or North-North directions. Indeed, while the majority of both foreign and portfolio investments are found to originate and end in relatively more developed economies (Harrison and Rodriguez-Clare 2010; Kose et al. 2010), labour moves predominantly either across developed or from less developed towards more developed parts of the world (Hanson 2010). Hence, in the 1980s and 1990s, researchers started looking for explanations of the obvious failure of the standard neoclassical model to explain the apparent absence of substitutability (or cross-border movement in opposite directions) of labour and capital. Lucas (1990) asks the question of why capital does not flow to poor countries and finds a novel explanation in the form of productivity differences between North and South, based on external economies of human capital. Namely, higher investments in human capital in the North not only contribute to enhanced effective labour supply of the worker who made the investment, but also to higher productivity of the rest of the workers and of capital. Using factor price frontiers, Razin and Sadka (1997) follow Lucas's logic to show that North and South can have the same rental price of capital even if the wage per effective unit of labour in the South is one third of that of the North. Hence, labour has the incentive to move from South to North, even when capital does not have incentive to migrate. In other words, while classical models emphasise the substitutability in cross-border resource flows, productivity differences may lead to complementarity (cross-border movement in the same direction) of labour and capital.

More recent literature has tested the hypothesis of substitutability versus complementarity of cross-border labour and capital movements within more complex theoretical frameworks. Literature on networking effects and information asymmetries has highlighted substitutability in cross-border labour and capital mobility. In the case of FDIs, Javorcik and Spatareanu (2011) argue that migrants can stimulate FDI by enhancing the information flow and serving as a contract-enforcing mechanism. They find that US FDIs abroad are positively correlated with the presence of migrants from the host country. The relationship is especially strong for migrants with tertiary education. Kugler et al. (2013) extend this argument and find an analogical answer in the case of a wider range of cross-border investments, including not only FDI, but also international bank lending, loans, equity shares and bonds. The argument is that while

information costs prevent larger diversification of financial investments, migration alleviates information imperfections between the
host and the home country. The investment-enhancing role of migration is strongest for financial flows where information costs are most
acute and for the type of migrants that are best able to enhance the
flow of information, namely skilled migrants.

The substitutability of cross-border capital and labour flows has also
been explored in the context of outsourcing of activities by companies in
developed country. Bandyopadhyay and Wall (2005) find that immigration of skilled programmers raises the labour–capital ratio and
reduces the marginal product of labour and thus the wages of programmers. As wages decline, firms face lower incentives to outsource. Both
types of evidence indicate that more restrictive immigration policies may
encourage offshoring and those discouraging FDI/offshoring may
encourage the inflow of migrants. In either case, the substitutability
effect needs to be taken into account by policymakers in both developed
and developing countries if the would like to achieve the expected net
policy intentions.

By contrast, research on FDI in developing countries highlights the
possible complementarity in cross-border labour and capital flows. In
particular, FDI spillovers in developing countries may lead to the creation of new job opportunities, especially among higher skill workers,
thus potentially reversing the outflow of migrants and brain drain
(namely outflow of more educated migrants). Aroca and Maloney
(2005) find a negative relationship between migration and FDI, whereby
greater exposure to FDI deters outmigration from Mexico. Taken
together, this part of the literature indicates that migration represents a
conceptually important flow of resources which merits its own attention
as part of a wide range of cross-border capital flows, going well beyond
the flow of remittances from migrants towards their own families in the
country of origin. The networking and information flow-enhancing
impact of migration on other types of cross-border capital flows is
strongest among more educated migrants. Given the importance that a
large part of the empirical literature gives to skilled migration and given
the importance of the stock of human capital on the long-term development   prospects   of   developing   (typically   migrant   exporting)

economies, the next section will be devoted to the debate on migrant selectivity, brain drain and brain gain from developing countries.

5.3   The Economics of Migrant Selectivity, Brain Drain and Brain Gain

Much of the neoclassical literature that looks at migration in the framework of cross-border factor mobility – where the two factors considered are labour and capital – tends to ignore the heterogeneity of labour. Yet from the point of view of long-term economic development of labour exporting countries, it matters whether migrants belong to the lower skill or higher skill groups of the population. For instance, a simple theoretical framework, such as that of the Solow model, would tell us that even if we disregard the heterogeneity of labour, labour shortages per se would have detrimental consequences for long-term growth; this is a consequence of the fact that in steady state, the growth of the labour force should be at par with that of capital and technology. An extension of this model to take into account the heterogeneity of labour indicates that the development implications of the outflow of educated workers would exceed those of the sheer availability of workers as it would reduce the sending economy's capacity to innovate and adopt modern technologies.

Traditionally, the focus of most of the literature devoted to the study of educated migrants has focused on the negative implications of brain drain not only for economic growth, but also for the labour market. More recently, both theoretical models and empirical tests have developed along the lines of *brain gain* consequences of *brain drain* (mostly due to greater acquisition of education by migrants' compatriots left behind in expectation of migration). This section will first explore arguments on why people belonging to different sections of the skill distribution migrate and then present results from key empirical papers. It will then take a look at the consequences of educated people's migration by comparing and contrasting arguments on the link between brain drain and brain gain.

The classical model exploring the decision of individuals belonging to different skill groups to migrate is the Roy's (1951) selectivity model. Let us for simplicity take a look at the standard undergraduate textbook type presentation of the model (Borjas 2008).

Suppose that residents of a source country (say Nigeria) are considering migration to a host country (say the US). Earnings in each country depend on a single factor – skills – which is completely transferrable across countries and (for simplicity) the decision to migrate is entirely driven by earnings differentials. Let S denote the skill levels or efficiency units of each labourer. The horizontal axes in Fig. 5.2 (a and b) thus represent skill (or efficiency units) distributions and the diagram maps the payoffs per efficiency unit in each of the two countries. In Fig. 5.2a the payoff line for the host country is steeper than that of the source country, while in Fig. 5.2b, the payoff line for the source country is steeper than that of the source country. In other words, in Fig. 5.2a returns to higher skills in the host country exceed those in the source country, while in Fig. 5.2b returns to lower skills in the host country exceed those in the source country.

It is easy to see how the decision of people in different portions of the skill distribution is made. So long as the payoff for the more skilled (less skilled) workers in the host country exceeds that of the corresponding

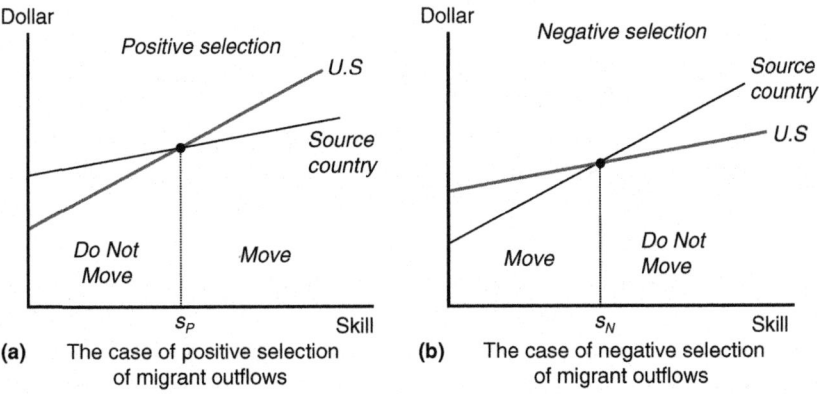

(a)   The case of positive selection of migrant outflows
(b)   The case of negative selection of migrant outflows

Fig. 5.2 Self-selection of the migrant flow. (a) The case of positive selection of migrant outflows. (b) The case of negative selection of migrant outflows. *Source*: Borjas (2008), pp. 343. Permission granted by McGraw-Hill

payoffs in the home country, people with skill levels above (below) threshold S would migrate. In the case of panel A, the payoff for relatively more skilled people in the host country (those exceeding threshold Sp) is higher than that for relatively more skilled people in the home country and the opposite is true for people with skill levels below Sp. Hence, people with skill levels above Sp choose to migrate to the host country and we have a case of the so-called *positive selection*, namely outmigration of relatively more skilled workers. The opposite is true in the case of panel B: returns to skills are higher in the host country than the home country for relatively less-skilled workers, while workers with relatively higher skills receive higher returns in the home country than the host country. Hence, relatively less-skilled people (with skill levels below the Sn threshold) are more motivated to migrate and we have a case of *negative selection*, namely outmigration of workers belonging to the lower skill parts of the distribution.

Given that – on average – developing countries face higher levels of labour market inequalities than developed countries (and hence the relative returns to skills for more skilled workers in these countries exceed those in potential destination countries which are more developed), Roy's model would predict predominantly negative selection from less developed to more economically developed countries. Yet, with the exception of migration flows such as those from Mexico and Puerto Rico to the US, the typical migrant flow from developing to developed countries is characterised by a positive selection (Hanson 2010).

Rosenzweig (2007) explains this controversial finding by arguing that what determines migration choices are cross-country differences in the *level* of wages as opposed to differences in *returns to skills* as predicted by Roy. Following Hanson's (2010) outline of this logic, let us assume that the average annual salary for a Nigerian with primary education is $1000, while that for a US primary education graduate is $20,000. At the same time, let's assume that the average annual salary for a Nigerian with tertiary education is $10,000, while that for a US tertiary education graduate is $60,000. Tertiary education graduates in the US thus get 3 times higher earnings than primary education graduates, while tertiary education graduates in Nigeria get 10 times higher earnings. In Roy's sense, this makes the Nigerian payoff schedule steeper than that of the

US and makes a case for negative selection. At the same time, an average Nigerian university graduate would receive $50,000 more in the US than in Nigeria, while an average primary school graduate would receive only $19000 more in the US than in Nigeria. Thus in terms of *level* of pay (and ignoring all other issues affecting migration), a university graduate would be more motivated to migrate than a primary school graduate.

Whatever the migrant motivations, the overwhelming evidence is one of higher level of skilled than unskilled migration from developing towards developed countries and hence the important development question to ask is what implications skilled migration has for the countries of origin. Early literature on the subject has focused on the negative implications of brain drain. In essence, this traditional framework of analysis focuses on the existence of positive externalities of learning, whereby the social product of human capital exceeds that of private capital. As a consequence, the outmigration of skilled people has negative implications for the migrant exporting developing country (Bhagwati and Hamada 1974; Grubel and Scott 1966; McColloch and Yellen 1977). Furthermore, there are revenue implications of outmigration, given that many educated people are subsidised by the state. Thus, outmigration of educated people deprives the economy of tax revenues to offset the costs of their education (Bhagwati and Rodriguez 1975).

More recently, much of the literature on *brain drain* has focused on *brain gain* implications of the phenomenon (Stark et al. 1997; Stark and Wang 2002; Mountford 1997). The idea is that outmigration of educated people motivates others to acquire education in the hope of migrating. In a world of imperfect information only a fraction of those who acquired education migrates and those who stay back contribute positively to the economy's development. In other words, there are brain gain implications of brain drain.

Following Montford (1997) and Commander et al. (2004) we can assume that the distribution of (innate) ability A is uniform and lies between Amin and Amax and that education yields private returns that increase with ability. We can also assume that the costs of education are constant across the skill distribution. In a world without migration, there will be a point A* where the increasing returns to education will equate the cost of education. Hence, in the case of no possibility of migration, it would be advantageous (dis-advantageous) for people with skill levels exceeding A* to acquire education. If the prospect of migration increases the return to education for all levels of abilities, then individuals with levels of ability lower than A* will have an incentive to acquire education as its return will exceeds its cost. However, not all individuals will actually migrate, therefore the ones who acquired extra education in expectation to migrate, but eventually stayed in their home country, will contribute to the economic development of the source country.

However, the brain gain implication is conditional on the uncertainty of migration. If receiving countries were able to perfectly screen the ability of migrants (i.e. 'cream off only the very best over a certain threshold Am'), and this high degree of selectivity was known to all individuals in the source country, then the motivations for people with abilities below the threshold required by the host country would remain unchanged and the implications of brain drain for the local economy would clearly be negative (Montford 1997; Commander et al. 2004). Given the theoretical controversy in the brain drain-brain gain debate, a large number of empirical studies have tested the hypotheses of brain gain implications of brain drain. Some of the early research looks mainly at the link between outmigration of educated people from developing countries to rich countries and the stock of human capital in the migrant exporting countries and finds positive correlation (Beine Docquier and Rapoport 2001). These results – based on cross-sectional data – are criticised for poor ability of the authors to infer a causal relationship (Hanson 2010). The endogeneity problem is addressed by Beine et al. (2011) in a panel setting, and the positive impact of high-skill migration on human capital formation is confirmed. Given that what is more important for the economic development of the source country is not as much the number of people who decide to invest in education, but the number of educated people who stay back, Beine et al. (2008) move a step forward and compute the net effect of brain drain for each country and region. They show that countries with positive net effects (winners) generally combine low levels of human capital and low high-skill migration rates, while losers are typically characterised by large high-skill migration rates. There appear to be more losers than winners and the losers lose more than the winners gain. While the effect differs across country types – with the main emerging economies, China, India, Indonesia and Brazil experiencing small gains – while small- and medium-sized African and Central American countries experiencing losses, there is an overall gain for the world as a whole. Overall, the results highlight the heterogeneity of brain drain-brain gain implication of outmigration across countries and inspire further research efforts on a case by case basis.

5.4 The Economics of Migrant Remittances

The literature reviewed in the preceding sections highlights heterogeneous implications of migration for migrant exporting developing countries. While growth and poverty alleviation implications in the form of networking, information flow enhancement and brain gain have been acknowledged, there is no consensus on dominance of these effects over negative consequences like brain drain and more general loss of human capital for both individual households and countries. Since a large proportion of migrants from developing countries send remittances to their households and countries of origin, the obvious next question is whether this can compensate for potentially negative net implications of outmigration. This sub-section will first review key issues in the literature on remittance motivations, thus highlighting key characteristics of potential donors and recipients of remittances and establishing why these types of private transfers take place. The section will then explore economic implications of remittances at both the micro- and macrolevel.

The altruistic model of private transfers (as in Stark 1995) is the typical theoretical starting point of analyses of the determinants of private transfers (of which migrant remittances are a substantial part). According to this framework, an individual's utility is a positive function of not only her own welfare (typically measured with consumption), but also of the welfare of others, weighted by the level of the donor's altruism. The key result of the model is that donors/ emigrants with higher earnings are likely to remit more, and these transfers are more likely to benefit lower income households. In the case of the pure altruism hypothesis, an increase by one dollar of the income of the donor, coupled with a one dollar drop in the recipient household's income, should raise the amount transferred by precisely one dollar.

The key null hypothesis in most studies on determinants of migrant remittances is that of the altruistic motive behind transfers. But while the null hypothesis is well defined, it is much more difficult to differentiate across a range of possible alternative hypotheses of absence of altruism, emanating from a range of different theoretical frameworks. Rapoport and Docquier's (2006) review on the economics of migrant remittances provides an excellent unifying framework for the differentiation across different types of non-altruistic behaviour in empirical settings. The authors distinguish between individual motives for remittances and familial arrangements and identify characteristics of donors and recipients of transfers, the empirical results on which show evidence in favour or against behaviours that are inconsistent with the pure form of individual altruism.

Theoretical differences – mainly with respect to assumptions regarding which type of non-altruistic behaviour is dominant – lead to different empirical predictions within the same type of empirical specification. The typical forms of individual non-altruistic behaviour explored are the inheritance-driven, exchange-driven and strategy-driven actions and to establish which one is dominant, authors regress remittances on the income and wealth of both the donor and the recipient of the transfer, as well as other individual and household characteristics of both parties. Within such a unified empirical specification, it is easy to differentiate between altruistic and several different non-altruistic causes for remittances. For example, remittances are expected to be a positive function of the recipients' wealth if inheritance expectations play a role. Moreover, inheritance-inspired behaviour would also postulate an inverse U-shape relationship between the number of siblings and the amount of remittances, while the number of siblings has no clear implications for remittances in any alternative theoretical framework.

By contrast, within a broader strategic behavioural framework, one can witness a set of more complex links between migration and remittances decisions. In the strategic behaviour model of Stark (1995) the skill composition of migrants is heterogeneous and individual productivity is not observed in the host market; thus employers apply statistical discrimination such that migrants are paid the average productivity of the minority group to which they belong. As a result, there is scope for cooperative arrangement between migrants and those left behind, such that migrants 'bribe' their less-skilled remittance recipients to stay back in the country of origin and not dilute the skill pool in the destination country. Empirically, one would therefore expect remittance flows from more educated migrants to less educated recipients. This is not the case for remittance flows that are part of a simpler exchange arrangement, whereby migrants pay their relatives for a simple favour, such as taking care of their family and property in the country of origin. The education of the migrant in such a framework does not have any clear empirical impact on the total value of remittances.

To sum up, unlike in the case of pure altruism, these three types of non-altruistic drives for remittances – inheritance, exchange and strategic motives – justify situations whereby remittances do not allocate towards those in greater need in the community or country of origin. By contrast, while not necessarily driven by pure altruism, familial arrangements may not only improve the welfare of their direct recipients, but also entail positive externalities for the community of origin. For instance, the literature on investment-driven remittances discusses scenarios whereby in the context of missing or imperfect markets, the family sends away its most capable members, in expectations of remittances to be subsequently invested in either human or physical capital accumulation. Even short of such long-term investments, within a familial theoretical framework, migration and remittances can be seen as a form of insurance. While in neither case there is a clear prediction on the link between remittances and either the level of assets or the long-term income of the recipients, remittances are a positive function of the recipient's vulnerability or exposure to shocks.

Identifying the motives behind remittances provides useful information on the pattern of migration and relationship between migrants and those left behind, as well as on the expected consequences of remittances and migration. For instance, it is easy to see that while, irrespective of the motivation of the donor, remittances should improve the welfare of their recipients and have the potential of lifting poor households above the poverty line, the link between remittances and intra-household inequality is much less straightforward. Although the pure altruistic framework predicts allocation of remittances towards those in greatest need, strategic behaviour may lead to a situation whereby remittances are allocated towards less deprived members of the community of origin, thus leading to enhancement rather than reduction of inequality. However, establishing the type of motive that drives remittances is not sufficient for identifying their inequality implications and obtaining unbiased estimates of these implications, given that migrants are not a random sample of the population in the community or country of origin. If – given the fact that migration is not a cost-free process – migrants are part of the better off part of the population, remittances would lead to an increase in inequality in the country of origin even if they are a reflection of altruistic behaviour of donors towards worse off members from their own households.

Prolific empirical literature has explored the theoretical ambiguity related to the inequality implications of remittances. After accounting for migrant selectivity issues, Adams (1989, 1992) finds that while remittances widen inequality in Egypt, they have neutral effect on rural income distribution in Pakistan. Aside from accounting for migrant selectivity, Taylor and Wyatt (1996) consider the implications of remittances for easing the credit constraints of their recipients. Using a small household sample from Mexico, they find that by allowing poorer households' access to credit, remittances lead to income equalisation. McKenzie and Rapoport (2007) confirm the heterogeneity and context-specific implications of remittances on inequality by using two detailed datasets from Mexico: the Mexican Migration Project (MMP), which consists of data from 57 rural communities in areas of high migration and the national demographic dynamics survey (ENADID), which consists of representative sample of rural communities in Mexico. They find that in communities with high level of migration prevalence, such as those occurring in many MMP communities, migration leads to reduction in inequality; however, in communities with more diverse migration experience, such as those surveyed as part of ENADID, migration increases inequality at lower levels of migration stock and then reduce inequality as one approaches the migration levels prevailing in the MMP communities. The result is explained via network effects: as migration networks develop at the family and community level, the likelihood of migration increases, leading to a fall in the costs of migration and an increase in the benefits of migration and remittances. In a related context and a theoretical framework that discusses the role of networking effects, Stark et al. (1986, 1988) find that the effect of remittances depends crucially on how migration facilitating information and contracts are diffused through the village population. If contracts and information are not household-specific, but are diffused across the village population, the effect of remittances is inequality reducing.

While the empirical literature explored in the preceding few paragraphs is preoccupied mainly with identifying the direction and dimension of the impact of remittances on inequality, Dimova and Wolff (2008) focus on identifying the relative strength of the effect of remittances on inequality among a whole range of additional inequality drivers. Using a treatment effects model they first explore the determinants and welfare implications of remittances on recipient households, after accounting for the non-random selection of households into the remittance 'treatment' and find that (i) in keeping with altruistic behaviour, private transfers in Bulgaria allocate to those in greatest need, and (ii) have positive impact on the welfare of their recipients. Using a decomposition method, based on the treatment effects model, the authors then establish that transfers have only a very small positive impact on the expenditure gap between households receiving transfers and households not receiving remittances. Inequality in living standards is mostly driven by unobserved characteristics and to a smaller extent by factors such as education and experience.

While a large part of the microlevel literature on the economic development implications of remittances focuses on aggregate household outcomes such as poverty and inequality, a related literature explores more complex interim impacts such as human capital and physical capital investment, occupational choices and insurance against shocks.

These consequences of remittances are well aligned with the familial arrangements' theoretical framework explored earlier. Once again, one of the most comprehensive theoretical frameworks, explaining the role of migration and remittances on investments in entrepreneurship and human capital is outlined in the review of Docquier and Rapoport (2005). The model that explains the role of migration and remittances on entrepreneurship and thereafter exit from a poverty trap is a formalisation of Roy's (1998, Chapter 7) conceptual framework on the links between credit market and labour market failures. The idea is that in the context of large income inequality – whereby a large proportion of the population fails to provide collateral and is hence excluded from the capital market – combined with poor institutional environment and large level of uncertainty, the capital market breaks down. This spills over into a situation whereby only a handful of entrepreneurs who are able to cover the start-up cost of opening a business co-exist with a large pool of poor workers, thus leading to low level labour market equilibrium at the subsistence wage. Migration and remittances have the capacity of shifting the labour market equilibrium in two different ways: (i) outmigration reduces the excess labour supply in the market, thus pushing up the equilibrium wage; an effect that Docquier and Rapoport consider to be minimal, and (ii) remittances lift the liquidity constraint, thus enhancing the level of entrepreneurship and thereafter labour demand; once again leading to an exit from low level equilibrium.

An analogical effect (along the lines of (i) above, even if the effect of remittances were to be ignored) is explored by Epstein and Kahana (2008) for the case of child labour. The authors extend the classical Basu and Van (1998) model where child labour is a result of excess labour supply to allow for the possibility of migration and demonstrate that by reducing the excess supply of labour and therefore lifting the equilibrium wage, outmigration from a poor country leads to a higher level equilibrium without child labour. Although at the macrolevel, this theoretical model highlights child level alleviating effects of outmigration, at the household level migration is likely to lead to disruptions, especially to labour constrained rural households. Broader negative (rural productivity) implications of migration along those lines are for instance highlighted by Rozelle et al. (1999) in the case of China. These disruptions however can at least to a certain extent be alleviated by remittances sent by the migrants. Dimova et al. (2015) and Bargain and Boutin (2015) show that this is indeed the case in the contexts of Tanzania and Burkina Faso, where the net household level effect of migration and remittances is child labour alleviating.

Given that migration and remittances are shown to reduce child labour and a large portion of the literature on human capital development tends to consider education and child labour as substitutes, it is logical to assume that the net effect of migration and remittances on the human capital development of the next generation should be positive. Rapoport and Docquier (2006) explore explicitly this link within an overlapping generations model and show that when (i) the size of the middle income group in the population is sufficiently large, (ii) members of this group opt for migration and (iii) intergenerational remittances within that group allow future generations' access to education, the economy converges to a long-run, efficient steady state.

A large number of empirical studies have explored the role of migration and remittances on entrepreneurship and human capital investments. Woodruff and Zenteno (2001) research the link between remittances and the creation of microenterprises in urban Mexico. They find that remittances are responsible for 20% of the capital investments in microenterprises overall and to one third of the respective capital investments in the 10 highest migration states in the country. Most of the rest of the literature focuses on the effects of return migration on entrepreneurship; the invariable result being one of positive implications (Ilahi 1999; Massey and Parado 1998; McCormick and Wahba 2001, 2003; Mensard 2004; Dustman and Kirchkamp 2002). Similar conclusions have been reached in the case of human capital investments as a result of migration and remittances (Hanson and Woodruff 2002; Cox et al. 2003).

While the broader set of familial models discussed above focuses predominantly on longer term implications of migration and remittances, related to a large extent to consequences such as investments in physical and human capital, a fast expanding literature explores the use of migration and remittances as insurance. The fast expansion of this type of literature is not surprising, given the amplification of the incidences and consequences of natural disasters in the context of climate change and climate change-induced conflict (IPCC 2014; Maystadt et al. 2014, Maystadt and Eckers 2014). The migration part of this literature invariably finds that households in less developed countries – especially those in more risk-prone rural settings – use migration as both an ex ante and ex post insurance to shocks and describes the heterogeneous (especially with respect to gender) modes of household level adaptation to shocks via migration (Dillion et al. 2011; Halliday 2010; Gray and Mueller 2012; Marchiori et al. 2012). Anecdotal, case study and cross-country macroeconomic evidence all indicate that – contrary to other international financial flows – remittance flows increase or remain stable after large shocks, such as natural disasters, macroeconomic and financial crises, and armed conflicts (Clarke and Wallsten 2004; World Bank 2006; Weiss Fagen and Bump 2005; Yang 2007). Mohaputra et al. (2009) also confirm the positive microlevel implications of remittances in the event of shocks in Bangladesh, Ethiopia, Burkina Faso and Ghana. While a large part of this literature is plagued by the challenge for authors to identify causal relationships, Mitrut and Wolff (2014) disentangle a positive causal effect of the 2004 Indian tsunami on international remittance transfers, using aggregate country data and a synthetic control methodology.

Although the majority of the microeconomic literature on the implications of migration and remittances on occupational choices, long-term investments and adaptation to shocks highlights poverty alleviating and economic development-enhancing implications, an alternative set of studies identifies the tendency of migrant receiving households to consume rather than invest the remittances received, which in turn leads to productivity reduction. A highly cited case in point is Azam and Gubert's (2005) study of the migration and remittance behaviour of the Soninké ethnic group from the border regions of Mali and Senegal, where remittance-enhanced consumption is driven by social norms aimed at status preservation, while remittance receiving households are shown to decrease their productivity upon receipt of the transfers compared to households that do not rely on remittances. This type of dynamics is consistent with Bohning (1975) and Rempel and Lodbell (1978) who argue that remittances reduce investment by promoting greater finance consumption and housing expenditures, but Stark (1991) argues that investments may ultimately increase even if the cash received is not invested immediately.

The microlevel dichotomy related to the use of remittances for either consumption or long-term investments and thereafter productivity or welfare enhancement or deterioration has spillover effects at the macrolevel. Indeed a review of the macrolevel implications of international remittances identifies heterogeneous effects, largely conditional on the type of remittance utilisation. For instance, Durand et al. (1996) find that for every US$2 billion remittances that entered Mexico, there was over a US$6.5 billion production increase in agriculture, manufacturing and services. By contrast, Chamie et al. (2003) find a negative impact of remittances on economic activities in a panel of 113 developing countries.

5.5 Putting It All Together and Moving Forward

5.5.1 Brain Drain, Brain Gain and the Intervening Effect of Remittances

As the literature reviewed in this chapter indicates, the effects of migration and remittances on migrant exporting developing countries are ambiguous. Remittances are generally welfare enhancing. At the same time, they do not necessarily reduce inequality and do not necessarily increase productivity and growth in the long run. Whether brain gain dominates over brain drain is not clear either. Given that skilled outmigration from developing countries dominates unskilled outmigration and there are theoretical predictions on positive implications of skilled migration and remittances by skilled migrants such as brain gain, information exchange and technology inflow, naturally the next question explored in the literature over the past decade has been whether skilled migrants are more likely to remit than unskilled migrants. The starting point of this debate is the proposition that if skilled migrants remit more than unskilled ones, this could offset some of the adverse implications of skilled as opposed to unskilled. With the use of the cross-country data on skilled migration, compiled by Docquier and Marfouk (2004), Faini (2007) tests the hypothesis that skilled migrants are more likely to remit less due to the greater propensity of skilled migrants to stay longer abroad and reunite with their families, and finds evidence in favour of this hypothesis. The negative effect of migrants' education on remittances is confirmed by Niimi et al. (2010), based on data from 82 countries. Moreover, in a different and more generalised context, Dimova and Wolff (2015) confirm the reunification dynamics explored by Faini (2007). While the focus of the majority of the migration-remittance literature is on the intensity and type of migration on remittances, Dimova and Wolff (2015) explore the alternative channel whereby remittances are primarily used to finance and stimulate further migration from the household and community of origin. After accounting for endogeneity, the authors find confirmation of the positive implications of remittances on chain migration in Bosnia and Herzegovina. They also find that migrants generally have superior human capital characteristics than non-migrants.

If this is indeed a dominant pattern of migration from and remittances to developing countries, it could have disastrous economic implications for these countries and respective communities. However, Bollard et al. (2011) argue that the relationship between skilled migration and remittances is much less dramatic and may even, on average, have positive development implications. Using microdata from surveys in 11 major destination countries, the authors find that while the evidence on the link between education of the migrant and his or her probability to remit is mixed, there is a strong positive relation between education and the amount of remittances, conditional on remitting. This line of analysis is still nascent; more research should explore the combined effect of migration and remittances at the microlevel.

5.5.2 The Special Case of Refugees, Displaced People and Remittances

The focus of our preceding discussion was on economic migration and remittances thereof. However, the case of forced migration and the remittances to and from forced migrant requires special attention, given that forced migration due to conflict and natural disasters is at its highest level since World War II and on the rise. According to the latest issue of UNHCR (2015), the number of forcibly displaced people by the end of 2014 had increased to 59.5 million compared to 51.2 million a year earlier and 37.5 million a decade earlier. Nine out of 10 refugees at that time were hosted by developing countries, thus posing substantial developmental pressure on both (relatively low income) countries of origin and (relatively low income) countries of destination (The World Bank 2014). For instance, most of the refugees from Syria have fled to neighbouring countries – Lebanon, Turkey and Jordan. A World Bank (2013) study has estimated a GDP growth reduction in Lebanon of 2.9 percentage points between 2012 and 2014 and an additional fiscal burden of US$2.6 billion on account of the conflict. Many refugees and internally displaced people are affected by protracted periods of displacement; by the end of 2013, two thirds of the world's refugees had been in exile for more than five years and half of them were children.

The fast-growing literature on forced migration has started looking at forced migrants as a special case of economic migrants who have lost their assets and the resettlement and absorption costs of whom are much higher than those of economic migrants, whose inflow is better organised and involves smaller numbers over more extended periods of time (Ibanez and Moya 2009; Fiala 2009). The fledgling literature has identified positive impacts in the form of increase in the demand for goods which stimulates local production and creation of jobs, as well as infrastructural development by donors. It has also highlighted negative implications like environmental degradation and health deterioration, as well as disproportionate negative labour market shocks on certain local population groups, especially low-skilled workers and net buyers of food.

Given the fortuity of available data on refugees from Burindi and Rwanda in the north-western region of Kagera in Tanzania in the mid-1990s, several studies have explored the effect of refugees on the economy of Kagera. Baez (2011) analyses the impact of the refugee inflow on the health of local children and finds several different indications of worsening health conditions 1.5 years after the shock. Within the same context, Alix-Garcia and Saah (2010) find that the refugee inflow led to increase in the prices of agricultural goods (bananas, beans and milk) and a decrease in the price of aid-delivered goods like maize, thus raising important policy questions regarding the appropriate balance of aid and integration of refugees in recipient communities. In a much more extensive study of the multiple impacts of the refugee inflow on the local communities of Kagera, Maystadt and Verwimp (2014) establish that while the aggregate effect of refugees on the local community in terms of real per adult equivalent consumption is positive, there is a non-monotonic relationship whereby negative externalities (environmental degradation, security, disease) could overcome the economic benefits in villages close to the refugees camps. Furthermore, the authors find that the effect on different types of local hosts differs depending on their occupations: while non-agricultural workers gained from the refugee inflow, low-skilled agricultural workers were net losers.

Although in general the effects of large refugee inflows on the host economy have been found to be mixed and necessitating careful evaluation of the balance between humanitarian aid and facilitating the integration of (long-term) refugees in the local economy, countries like Uganda – the third largest refugee hosting country in Africa after Ethiopia and Kenya – have been given as examples of progressive and forward-looking asylum policies (UNHCR 2015). Upon receiving refugee status, refugees in Uganda are given small areas of land in villages integrated within the local host community. This pioneering approach is aimed at enhancing social cohesion and allowing refugees and hosts to live peacefully. Betts et al. (2014) explore the implications of such policymaking and finds that refugees in Uganda are well integrated and tend to make positive contributions to the local economy by creating employment opportunities to Ugandan nationals and creating new technologies. Although rigorous research on the subject is only fledgling, the multiple implications of forced migration appear to be well understood and the typical policy prescriptions are: (i) more and better support for refugees and their hosts, (ii) support for long-term solutions to protracted forced migration situations and (iii) more investments in fragile states and countries prone to natural calamities (Maystadt and Breisinger 2015).

Aside from the study of forced migration itself, a fledgling and fast developing area of research is that of remittances to and from forced migrants. An excellent survey of this literature is provided by Vargas-Silva (2016). As in the case of forced migration, remittances to and from migrants are seen as a special case of the broader category of remittances that are a result of similar motivations, but are also affected by a separate set of factors when sent by the displaced, including the possibility of continuing or new conflicts in the home region or country, the possibility of mass repatriation, the relationship of diaspora groups with the region or country of origin of opposition groups, the higher risk of sudden closure of remittance channels and the complex movement categories of the displaced. For example, the intention of the migrant to stay longer or permanently in the host country has negative impact on remittances (Dustmann and Mestres 2010), while higher income risk in the host country or higher chance of deportation increases remittances as a way to secure place back home (Ahmed 2000; Jacobsen 2005; Delpierre and Verheyden 2014). Once conflict is over, many refugees send money home to assist recovery plans (Rodima-Taylor et al. 2013; Van Hear and Cohen 2015).

Refugees tend to form diaspora communities and remittances are often a result of a social pressure within migrant networks, which is tends to exceed the social pressure among economic migrants (Akuei 2005; Jacobsen 2005; Hammond 2011), often resulting in negative long-term implications, such as failure of the refugees to invest in human capital development (Tharmalingam 2011). The network pressure can go in either direction; for instance, a diaspora network can frustrate the propensity of forced migrant to remit if the regime in the country of origin is part of political opposition vis-à-vis the political ideology of the migrant (Eckstein 2010). While the impact of remittances on the community of the source country is conceptually analogical to that of remittances originating from economic migrants, the few studies on the implications of remittances towards forced migrants show transformative implications. For example, Campbell et al. (2006) and Shandy (2006) show that in the cases of Congolese refugees in Kenya and Sudanees refugees in Ethiopia, remittances gave their recipients the real option to move to a city instead of remaining in the refugee camp.

Betts et al. (2014) even argue that remittances made it possible for Somali refugees to open businesses in Uganda. But although remittances may have transformative implications for both the refugees themselves and for family members in the origin country, who are victims of a crisis, the obvious barriers to such remittances are often difficult to overcome.

5.6   Conclusion

This chapter reviews theories and evidence on the implications of international migration and remittances for the economic development prospects of affected (mostly migrant exporting and remittance receiving) economies. The results of the review indicate that the net effect of migration and remittances in less developed countries is complex and heterogeneous. Although a large outflow of (homogeneous low skill) labour is theoretically shown to reduce the excess labour supply in developing countries, thus raising equilibrium wages and pulling poor economies out of a poverty trap, there is no sufficient empirical evidence that unequivocally supports this proposition. Moreover, the overwhelming evidence is one of skilled migration out of developing countries, the implications of which are neither theoretically nor empirically straightforward. In particular, there is no unambiguous answer as to whether either brain gain or enhanced inflow of capital and technology on account of networking and information sharing by skilled migrants can compensate for the detrimental consequences of loss of human capital in a less developed economy. Furthermore, although large remittance flows towards developing countries tend to dwarf the size and effect of alternative cross-border financial flows and these flows have been found to have positive counter-cyclical influence on crisis-ridden economies, the broader literature on remittances by economic migrants continues to debate on whether the transfers received are used for investment or for consumption and whether they are therefore productive in the long run.

In sum, while the majority of the traditional conceptual questions related to the costs and benefits of migration and remittances for developing countries are answered, there appears to be an emerging consensus that the implications are heterogeneous; hence context-specific validation is required for sound policy advice. This is especially the case in the now buoyant domain of forced migration and remittances from and to refugees and displaced people, where one of the key policy dilemmas is related to the appropriate balance between aid and economic integration, alongside finding innovative ways for easing private transfers.

While researchers and policymakers continue to work on finding optimal solutions to ongoing dilemmas, the conceptual literature on migration and remittances paves its way in new innovative directions. Among the most interesting new areas of research is the transfer of (both financial and non-financial) assets to recipient groups that are not necessarily part of the immediate network of the donor. These include for instance financial transfers to community charity projects, as opposed to private households. A point in case is the paper by Licuanan et al. (2015) who study the motivations behind and the outcomes of donations sent by overseas migrants to community charity projects in the Philippines. An even broader area of ongoing research involves the transfer of cultural norms and political culture. For instance, using Egyptian household data, Bertoli (2015) and Bertoli and Marchetta (2015) explore the transfer of cultural norms by temporary migrants in the Gulf countries and find that these migrants bring back home more conservative norms that involve greater fertility. Similarly, Mahmoud et al. (2013) find that emigration episodes that started in the late 1990s affected strongly the political preferences and electoral outcomes in Moldova, leading to the fall of the last ruling Communist government in Europe. Given the large doze of consensus among development economists that institutions and social norms are the key determinant of long-term development outcomes, this is a truly important research avenue that is worthwhile developing further.

References

Adams, R. (1989). Workers remittances and inequality in rural Egypt. *Economic Development and Cultural Change, 38*(10), 45–71.
Adams, R. (1992). The impact of migration and remittances on inequality in rural Pakistan. *Pakistan Development Review, 31*(4), 1189–1203.

Ahmed, I. (2000). Remittances and their economic impact in postwar Somaliland. *Disasters, 24*(3), 380–389.

Akuei, S. (2005). Remittances as unforeseen burdens: The livelihoods and social obligations of Sudanese refugees. (Global Migration Perspectives Working Paper 18), Global Commission on International Migration.

Alesina, A., & Dollar, D. (2000). Who gives foreign aid to whom and why? *Journal of Economic Growth, 5*(1), 33–63.

Alix-Garcia, J., & Saah, D. (2010). The effect of refugee inflows on host communities: Evidence from Tanzania. *World Bank Economic Review, 24*(10), 148–170.

Aroca, P., & Maloney, W. (2005). Trade and foreign direct investments in Mexico. *The World Bank Economic Review, 19*(3), 449–472.

Azam, J. P., & Gubert, F. (2005). Those in Kayes. The impact of remittances on their recipients in Africa. *Review Economique, 56*, 1331–1356.

Baez, J. (2011). Civil wars beyond borders: The human capital and health consequences of hosting refugees. *Journal of Development Economics, 96*(2), 391–408.

Bandyopadhyay, S., & Wall, H. (2005). Immigration and outsourcing: A general equilibrium analysis. Research division. Federal Reserve Bank of St Louis. (Working Paper Series. 2005–058).

Bargain, O., & Boutin, D. (2015). Remittances and child labour in Africa: Evidence from Burkina Faso. *Journal of Development Studies, 51*(7), 922–938.

Basu, K., & Van, P. H. (1998). The economics of child labor. *American Economic Review, 88*, 412–427.

Beine, M., Docquier, F., & Rapoport, H. (2001). Brain drain and economic growth. Theory and evidence. *Journal of Development Economics, 64*(10), 275–289.

Beine, M., Docquier, F., & Rapoport, H. (2008). Brain drain and human capital formation in developing countries: Winners and losers. *The Economic Journal, 118*, 631–652.

Beine, M., Docquier, F., & Oden-Defoort, C. (2011). A panel data analysis of the brain gain. *World Development, 39*(4), 523–532.

Bertoli, S. (2015) Does return migration influence fertility at home? IZA world of labor: 204

Bertoli, S., & Marchetta, F. (2015). Bringing it all back home: Return migration and fertility choices. *World Development, 65* (2015), 27–40.

Betts, A., Bloom, L., Kaplan, J., & Omata, N. (2014). *Refugee economies: Rethinking popular assumptions.* Report, University of Oxford. http://www.rsc.ox.ac.uk/files/publications/other/refugee-economies-2014.pdf

Bhagwati, J., & Hamada, K. (1974). The brain drain, international integration of markets for professionals, and unemployment. *Journal of Development Economics, 1*(1), 19–42.

Bhagwati, J., & Rodriguez, C. (1975). Welfare theoretic analyses of the brain drain. *Journal of Development Economics, 2*(3), 195–221.

Böhning, W. R. (1975). Some thoughts on emigration from the Mediterranean basin. *International Labour Review, 111*, 251–277.

Bollard, A., McKenzie, D., Morten, M., & Rapoport, H. (2011). Remittances and brain drain revisited: The microdata show that more educated migrants remit more. *The World Bank Economic Review, 25*(1), 132–156.

Borjas, G. (2008). *Labor economics.* New York: McGraw-Hill Companies.

Campbell, E., Kakusu, J., & Musyemi, I. (2006). Congolese refugee livelihoods in Nairobi and the prospects of legal, local integration. *Refugee Survey Quarterly, 25*(2), 93–108.

Chami, R., Fullenkamp, C., & Jahjah, S. (2003). Are immigrant remittances a source of capital for development (IMF Working Paper No 03/89), Washington, DC.

Clarke, G., & Wallsten, S. (2004). *Do remittances protect households in developing countries against shocks? Evidence from a natural disaster in Jamaica.* Washington, DC: Mimeo, The World Bank.

Commander, S., Kangasniemi, M., & Winters, A. (2004). The brain drain: Curse or boon. A survey of the literature. In R. Baldwin & A. Winters (Eds.), *Challenges to globalization. Analysing the Economics.* National Bureau of Economic Research. United States of America: University of Chicago Press.

Cox, D., & Ureta, M. (2003). International migration, remittances and schooling: Evidence from El Salvador. *Journal of Development Economics, 72*(2), 429–461.

Delpierre, M., & Verheyden, B. (2014). Remittances, savings and return migration under uncertainty. IZA (Discussion Paper 1088), Institute for the Study of Labor, Bonn.

Dillion, A., Mueller, V., & Salau, S. (2011). Migratory responses to agricultural risk in Northern Nigeria. *American Journal of Agricultural Economics, 93*(4), 1048–1061.

Dimova, R., & Wolff, F. C. (2008). Are private transfers poverty and inequality reducing? Household level evidence from Bulgaria. *Journal of Comparative Economics, 36*(4), 584–598.

Dimova, R., & Wolff, F. C. (2015). Remittances and chain migration: Longitudinal evidence from Bosnia and Herzegovina. *Journal of Development Studies, 51*(5), 554–568.

Dimova, R., Epstein, G., & Gang, I. (2015). Migration, transfers and child labor. *Review of Development Economics, 19*(3), 735–747.

Docquier, F., & Marfouk, A. (2004). Measuring the international mobility of skilled workers (1990–2000). (Policy Research Working Paper 3381), The World Bank, Washington, DC.

Durand, J., Kandel, W., Parrado, E. A., & Massey, D. S. (1996). International migration and development in Mexican communities. *Demography, 33,* 249–264.

Dustmann, C., & Kirchkamp, O. (2002). The optimal migration duration and activity choice after remigration. *Journal of Development Economics, 67*(2), 351–372.

Dustmann, C., & Mesteres, J. (2010). Remittances and temporary migration. *Journal of Development Economics, 92*(1), 62–70.

Eckenstein, S. (2010). Immigration, remittances and transnational social capital formation: A Cuban case study. *Ethnic and Racial Studies, 33*(9), 1648–1667.

Epstein, G., & Kahana, N. (2008). Child labor and temporary emigration. *Economics Letters, 99,* 545–548.

Faini, R. (2007). Remittances and the brain drain: Do more skilled migrants remit more? *The World Bank Economic Review, 21,* 177–191.

Fiala, N. (2009). The consequences of forced displacement in Northern Uganda. (NiCN Working Paper 65). http://www.hicn.org/wordpress/wp-content/uploads/2012/06/wp65.pdf

Gray, C., & Mueller, V. (2012). Drought and population mobility in rural Ethiopia. *World Development, 40*(1), 134–145.

Grubel, H., & Scott, A. (1966). The international flow of human capital. *American Economic Review, 56,* 268–274.

Halliday, R. (2010). Temperatures and cyclones strongly associated with economic production in the Caribbean and Central America. *Proceedings of the National Academy of Sciences of the United States of America, 107*(35), 15367–15372.

Hammod, L. (2011). Obliged to give: Remittances and the maintenance of transnational networks between Somalis at home and abroad. Bildhaan. *An International Journal of Somali Studies, 10,* 11.

Hanson, G. (2010). International migration and the developing world. In D. Rodrik & M. Rosenzweig (Ed.), *Handbook of development economics* (Vol. 5, pp. 4364–4414). North Holland: Elsevier.

Hanson, G., & Woodruff, C. (2002). *Emigration and educational attainment in Mexico*. San Diego: Mimeo, University of California.

Harrison, A., & Rodriguez-Clare, A. (2010). Trade, foreign direct investments, and industrial policy for developing countries. In D. Rodrik & M. Rosenzweig (Ed.), *Handbook of development economics* (Vol. 5, pp. 4040–4214). North Holland: Elsevier.

Ibañez, A., & Moya, A. (2009). Do conflicts create poverty traps? Asset losses and recovery for displaced households in Colombia. In R. Di Tella. & S. Edwards (Eds.), *The economics of crime: Lessons for and from Latin America* (pp. 137–172). United States of America: University of Chicago Press.

Ilahi, N. (1999). Return migration and occupational change. *Review of Development Economics, 3*(2), 170–186.

IPCC (Intergovernmental Panel on Climate Change). (2014). *Climate change 2014 – Impacts, adaptation and vulnerability*. Geneva: Unpublished.

Jacobsen, K. (2005). *The ecomomic life of refugees*. Bloomfield, CT: Kumarian Press.

Javorcik, B., & Spatareanu, M. (2011). Does it matter where you come from? Vertical spillovers from foreign direct investments and the origin of investors. *Journal of Development Economics, 96*(1), 126–138.

Kose, M. A., Prasad, E., Rogoff, K., & Wei, S. (2010). Financial globalisation and economic policies. In D. Rodrik & M. Rosenzweig (Ed.), *Handbook of development economics* (Vol. 5, pp. 4284–4362). North Holland: Elsevier.

Kugler, M., & Rapoport, H. (2007). International labor and capital flows: Complements or substitutes? *Economics Letters, 94*, 155–162.

Kugler, M., Levintal, O., & Rapoport, H. (2013). Migration and cross-border financial flows (Discussion Paper Series CDP No 17/13), Centre for Research and Analysis of Migration.

Licuanan, V., Mahmoud, T. O., & Steinmayr, A. (2015). The drivers of diaspora donations for development: Evidence from the Philippines. *World Development, 65*, 94–109.

Lucas, R. (1990). Why doesn't capital flow from rich to poor countries? *The American Economic Review, 90*(2), 92–96.

Mahmoud, O., Rapoport, T. H., Steinmayr, A., & Trebesch, C. (2013). The effect of labor migration on the diffusion of democracy: Evidence from a former soviet republic (IZA Discussion Paper No. 7980)

Marchiori, L., Maystadt, J. F., & Schumacher, I. (2012). The impact of climate variations on migration in sub-Saharan Africa. *Journal of Environmental Economics and Management*, *63*(3), 355–374.

Massey, D. S., & Parrado, E. A. (1998). International migration and business formation in Mexico. *Social Science Quarterly*, *79*(1), 1–20.

Maystadt, J. F., & Breisinger, C. (2015). The EU refugee crisis: The tip of a global iceberg. IFPRI Policy Brief 23, November 2015. Washington, DC. http://reliefweb.int/sites/reliefweb.int/files/resources/130022.pdf

Maystadt, J. F., & Eckers, O. (2014). Extreme weather and civil war: Does drought fuel conflict in Somalia through livestock price shocks? *American Journal of Agricultural Economics*, *96*(4), 1157–1182.

Maystadt, J. F., & Verwimp, P. (2014). Winners and losers among a refugee hosting population. *Economic Development and Cultural Change*, *62*(4), 769–809.

Maystadt, J. F., Calderone, M., & You, L. (2014). Local warming and violent conflict in North and South Sudan. *Journal of Economic Geography*, *15*(3), 1–23.

McCormick, B., & Wahba, J. (2001). Overseas work experience, savings and entrepreneurship amongst return migrants to LDCs. *Scottish Journal of Political Economy*, *48*(2), 164–178.

McCormick, B., & Wahba, J. (2003). Return international migration and geographical inequality: The case of Egypt. *Journal of African Economies*, *12*(4), 500–532.

McCulloch, R., & Yellen, J. (1977). Factor mobility, regional development, and the distribution of income. *The Journal of Political Economy*, *85*(1), 79–96.

McKenzie, D., & Rapoport, H. (2007). Network effects and the dynamics of migration and inequality: Theory and evidence from Mexico. *Journal of Development Economics*, *84*(1), 1–24.

Mensard, A. (2004). Temporary migration and capital market imperfections. *Oxford Economic Papers*, *56*, 242–262.

Mitrut, A., & Wolff, F. C. (2014). Remittances after natural disasters: Evidence from the 2004 Indian tsunami. (Working Papers in Economics No 604), University of Gothenburg, Sweden.

Mohaputra, S., Joseph, G., & Ratha, D. (2009). Remittances and natural disasters. Ex-post response and contribution to ex-ante preparedness. Policy Research Working Paper 4972, The World Bank.

Mountford, A. (1997). Can a brain drain be good for growth in the source country? *Journal of Development Economics*, *53*(2), 287–303.

Navaretti, G., De Simone, G., & Sembenelli, A. (2007). Migration and foreign direct investment. A review of the literature. Mimeo, University of Milano, http://www.dagliano.unimi.it/media/Barba_DeSimone_Sembenelli.pdf

Niimi, Y., Ozden, C., & Schiff, M. (2010). Remittances and brain drain: Skilled migrants do remit less. *Annals of Economics and Statistics, 98/99*, 123–141.

Rapoport, H., & Docquier, F. (2006). Chapter 17: The economics of migrants' remittances. In S.-C. Kolm & J. M. Ythier (Eds), *Handbook of the economics of giving, altruism and reciprocity* (Vol. 2, pp. 1135–1198). North Holland: Elsevier.

Razin, A., & Sadka, E. (1997). International migration and international trade. In: M. Rosenzweig and O. Stark. (Ed.) *Handbook of population and family economics* (pp. 852–887). Volume 1B.

Rempel, H., & Lobdell, R. (1978). The role of urban-rural remittances in rural development. *Journal of Development Studies, 14*, 324–341.

Rodima-Taylor, D. et al. (2013). Remittance flows to post-conflict states: Perspectives on human security and development. Pardee Center Task Force Report. Boston University, http://www.bu.edu/pardee/files/2013/10/Pardee-CFLP-Remittances-TF-Report.pdf

Rosenzweig, M. (2007). *Education and migration. A global perspective.* Yale University, Mimeo, http://siteresources.worldbank.org/EXTPREMNET/Resources/489960-1338997241035/Growth_Commission_Workshops_Equity_Rosenzweig_Presentation.pdf.

Roy, A. (1951). Some thoughts on the distribution of earnings. *Oxford Economic Papers, 3*, 135–146.

Roy, D. (1998). *Development economics.* United Kingdom: Oxford University Press.

Rozelle, S., Taylor, J.E., & deBrauw, A. (1999). Migration, Remittances, and Agricultural Productivity in China. *American Economic Review, 9*(2), 287–291.

Shandy, D. (2006). Global transactions: Sudanese refugees sending money home. *Refuge, 23*(2), 28–35.

Stark, O. (1991). *The migration of labor.* Oxford and Cambridge: Basil Blackwell.

Stark, O. (1995). *Altruism and beyond.* Oxford and Cambridge, MA: Basil Blackwell.

Stark, O., & Wang, Y. (2002). Inducing human capital formation: Migration as a substitute for subsidies. *Journal of Public Economics, 86*(1), 29–46.

Stark, O., Taylor, J. E., & Yizhaki, S. (1986). Remittances and inequality. *The Economic Journal, 96*, 722–740.

Stark, O., Taylor, J. E., & Yizhaki, S. (1988). Migration, remittances and inequality: A sensitivity analysis using the extended Gini index. *Journal of Development Economics, 28*, 309–322.

Stark, O., Helmenstein, C., & Prskawetz, A. (1997). A brain gain with a brain drain. *Economics Letters, 55*, 227–234.

Taylor, J. E. & Wyatt, T. J. (1996). The shadow value of migrant remittances, income and inequality in a household-farm economy. *Journal of Development Studies, 32*(6), 899–912.

Tharmalingam, S. (2011). A long distance navigator? Remittance as a transnational practice among Tamils and Somalis in Norway. *Forum for Development Studies, 38*(2), 177–196.

The World Bank. (2006). *Global economic prospects: Economic implications of remittances and migration.* Washington, DC: The World Bank.

The World Bank. (2013). *Lebanon: Economic and social impact assessment of the Syrian conflict.* Washington, DC: The World Bank. http://documents.world bank.org/curated/en/2013/09/18292074/lebanon-economic-social-impact-assessment-syrian-conflict.

The World Bank. (2014). Migration and development brief 23. Special topic: Forced migration. Migration and Remittance Team, Development Prospects Group, http://siteresources.worldbank.org/INTPROSPECTS/Resources/334934-1288990760745/MigrationandDevelopmentBrief23.pdf.

The World Bank. (2015). Migration and development brief 24, migration and remittance team, development prospects group, http://pubdocs.worldbank.org/pubdocs/publicdoc/2015/10/1027614453353157305/MigrationandDevelopmentBrief25.pdf.

UNHRC. (2015). *Global trends, forced displacement in 2014*, Geneva, UNHRC (The UN refugee agency), http://unhcr.org/556725e69.html.

Van Hear, N., & Cohen, R. (2015). Diasporas and conflict. Centre on Migration, Policy and Society, Working Paper 122, Oxford University, https://www.compas.ox.ac.uk/media/WP-2015-122-VanHear_Cohen_Diasporas_Conflict.pdf.

Vargas-Silva, C. (2016). Literature review: Remittances sent to and from refugees and internally displaced people. (KNOMAD Working paper 12), Swiss Agency for Development and Cooperation, http://www.knomad.org/docs/working_papers/KNOMAD%20WP%2012%20Lit%20Review%20Remittances%20tofrom%20Refugees%20and%20IDPs.pdf.

Weiss-Fagen, P., & Micah, B. (2005). Remittances in conflict and crises: How remittances sustain livelihoods in war, crises and transition to peace. *The Security-Development Nexus Program Policy Paper, International Peace Academy*, New York.

Woodruff, C., & Zenteno, R. (2001). *Remittances and micro-enterprises in Mexico*. San Diego: Mimeo, University of California.

Yang, D. (2007). *Coping with disaster: The impact of hurricanes on international financial flows, 1970–2002*. Ann-Harbor: Mimeo, University of Michigan.

Ralitza Dimova is an economist, currently employed by the University of Manchester. Since her graduation from the Catholic University of Leuven with a PhD in Economics, she has worked in a number of countries, including France, Germany and the US. Prior to that she lived and worked for two years in India. As part of a three-year project, sponsored by the British Academy, she has developed an academic network with four countries in Francophone West Africa. Much of her ongoing research focuses on food security, labour markets in developing countries and intergenerational transfers, especially in the context of Cote d'Ivoire and Malawi.

6

Multinational Enterprises and Economic Development in Host Countries: What We Know and What We Don't Know

Rajneesh Narula and André Pineli

6.1   Introduction

Not 40 years ago, multinational enterprises (MNEs) were regarded with considerable suspicion by developing country governments, many of whom regarded MNEs as tools of imperialism and one of the causes of persistent underdevelopment. Unsurprisingly, foreign direct investment (FDI) policies were, in general, overly restrictive.

However, by the early 1990s, the MNE has been rehabilitated. Governments in developing countries removed barriers and began to aggressively woo FDI through a variety of incentives. These included fiscal incentives (tax holidays, lower tax rates), financial incentives

R. Narula (✉)
Henley Business School, University of Reading, Reading, UK
e-mail: r.narula@henley.ac.uk

A. Pineli
Henley Business School, University of Reading, Reading, UK
e-mail: A.G.DeMirandaPinelialves@pgr.reading.ac.uk

© The Author(s) 2017
G. Giorgioni (ed.), *Development Finance*, Palgrave Studies
in Impact Finance, DOI 10.1057/978-1-137-58032-0_6

(grants, subsidised credit, guarantees), donations (land), along with complementary investments in infrastructure and human capital. To some extent, this shift was influenced by the failure of import-substitution policies in promoting industrialisation (Narula 2014). With active support of international agencies, FDI is increasingly perceived as a key component of development policy.[1] Politicians in most countries view inward FDI as a source of employment, and not only those created by the MNE's local affiliate but also those generated along the value chain, and through income multiplier effects, in addition to other impacts on fiscal revenues, exports and so on.

MNEs are also expected to bring new technologies and management practices to the host country. As if those were not enough, FDI is also expected to have a positive impact on gross domestic product (GDP), through an improved allocation of production factors. Unfortunately, a thorough cost/benefit analysis of FDI is seldom performed by governments. Potential negative externalities are often disregarded, while positive externalities are overstated as the costs associated with investments in infrastructure and human capital are rarely taken into account. Indeed, as Narula and Driffield (2012) note, such locational investments are a *sine qua non* for benefits to be internalised by domestic actors. As such, they are not really positive 'externalities' but 'effects', since there is often a price – direct or indirect – to the accrual of benefits (Zanfei 2012).

The development impact of FDI was largely absent of the academic debate until the 1970s.[2] In part, this was due to the lack of specific theories distinguishing direct and portfolio investment and explaining the existence and behaviour of MNEs. Nonetheless, despite significant theoretical developments on these themes in the last few decades, there remains a strongly neoclassical aspect to how governments understand FDI. Perhaps most significantly, most policy makers still do not distinguish between the underlying motives of the MNE investment (Morrissey 2012), nor the

---

[1] The adoption of 'market-friendly' policies, including the withdrawal of impediments to free capital movements, were, in fact, an important component of structural adjustment programmes supported by those multilateral agencies (Narula 2014).

[2] Reuber et al. (1973) and Lall and Streeten (1977) were among the early studies that analysed the theme through a more conventional economics lens.

importance of distinguishing between initial and sequential investments. Fully leveraging the potential of FDI-assisted development requires seeing MNEs as complex organisms that do not have uniformly similar operations in each location, and acknowledging that they are constantly evaluating their options, and consequently the degree of involvement in a given location can decrease as well as increase. Each MNE subsidiary evolves over time, with different effects from initial and sequential investments. Changes in commitment are a response to specific location characteristics of the host, and MNEs make these investments (and disinvestments) in direct response to how these characteristics evolve relative to other alternative locations. In other words, governments often ignore that FDI engagement and its effects are dynamic and ever-evolving. Quantitative studies using country-level data show that the determinants of inward FDI are by and large the same factors usually found to explain GDP level: availability of human capital and infrastructure, good institutions and governance, political stability, sound macroeconomic fundamentals (Narula 1996; Noorbakhsh and Paloni 2001; Globerman and Shapiro 2002; Walsh and Yu 2010). At the firm-level, market characteristics, production costs and availability of resources are the main determinants of the location choice of FDI in developing countries.

The aim of this chapter is to review the literature on the effects of inward FDI in developing and transition economies. The magnitude and importance of FDI to these economies are highlighted by a set of statistics in the next section. Core theories are briefly described in Section 6.3. Section 6.4 assesses the microeconomic effects of FDI on host countries. The macroeconomic effects are dealt with in Section 6.5. The final section presents some concluding remarks.

6.2 The Importance of FDI to Developing Countries

MNEs are certainly the most visible actors of globalisation. Due to data limitations, their engagement in international production is usually measured by FDI flows and stocks, although FDI may no longer constitute their primary form of internationalisation, as MNEs are increasingly using non-equity means of engagement in certain industries (UNCTAD 2011; Collinson et al. 2016).

Data on FDI flows reflect a country's Balance of Payments,[3] on an annual basis. Between 1980 and 2014, global FDI flows increased by a factor of more than twenty (in nominal terms), surpassing the five-fold growth of world GDP and the eight-fold growth in international trade. Considering only developing and transition economies,[4] the growth in inward FDI flows was even bigger, expanding almost a hundred-fold, from US$ 7.4 billion in 1980 to US$ 729 billion in 2014. Developing economies increased their share in world inward FDI flows from less than 14% to almost 60% (UNCTAD 2015).[5] However, FDI flows do not tell very much about the actual contribution of foreign capital to the recipient country's economic activity. Indeed, what really matters in this case is the accumulated FDI, which constitute the country's inward FDI stock.[6] World FDI stocks reached US$ 24.6 trillion in 2014, 10 times the 1990 figures. Developed countries are still the main hosts of FDI, though their share has diminished over time, from 75%, in 2000, to less than two-thirds, in 2014 Table 6.1.

---

[3] When recording Balance of Payments statistics, most countries follow the International Monetary Fund's (IMF) recommendations. The IMF adopts the OECD's definition: 'direct investment is a category of cross-border investment associated with a resident in one country having control or significant degree of influence on the management of an enterprise that is resident in another economy' (IMF 2009, p. 100). According to the IMF's definition, a significant degree of influence occurs when the foreign investor owns from 10% to 50% of the voting rights. The 10% threshold is taken as an indication of a long-lasting relationship between the investor and the invested entity (OECD 2008).

[4] Henceforth referred to as *developing economies*, unless explicitly stated.

[5] UNCTAD continues to classify some high-income economies, such as Hong Kong, Singapore, South Korea and Taiwan, as developing economies, which distorts these figures somewhat.

[6] Ideally, inward FDI stock statistics should show the value of the assets owned by non-residents, which should include reinvested earnings and adjust for intra-company flows. However, few countries collect such data. For countries in which these data are missing, international agencies like UNCTAD estimate FDI stocks taking the accumulation of flows over a certain period as a proxy. This practice is imperfect, as it relies on historical prices instead of market value and disregards reinvested earnings by MNEs on host economies. Nonetheless, the figures tend to be more meaningful than FDI flows when discussing development effects.

Table 6.1 Inward FDI stock, 1990–2014

Region /Country	1990	2000	2010	2014 US$ billion	2014 % World	2014 % Region
		US$ billion		US$ billion	% World	% Region
World	2,197.8	7,203.8	19,607.4	24,626.5	100.0	–
Developed economies	1,686.0	5,476.6	12.789.1	15,591.4	63.3	–
Developing economies	510.1	1,669.8	6,088.7	8,310.1	33.7	–
Transition economies	1.7	57.4	729.6	725.0	2.9	–
Developing and Transition Economies						
Africa	60.7	153.7	586.5	709.2	2.9	–
South Africa	9.2	43.5	179.6	145.4	0.6	20.5
Egypt	11.0	20.0	73.1	87.9	0.4	12.4
Nigeria	8.5	23.8	60.3	86.7	0.4	12.2
Morocco	3.0	8.8	45.1	51.7	0.2	7.3
Tunisia	7.6	11.5	31.4	31.5	0.1	4.4
Latin America and the Caribbean	107.2	461.0	1,594.8	1,893.6	7.7	–
Brazil	37.1	122.3	682.3	754.8	3.1	39.9
Mexico	22.4	121.7	363.8	338.0	1.4	17.8
Chile	16.1	45.8	152.6	207.7	0.8	11.0
Colombia	3.5	11.2	83.0	141.7	0.6	7.5
Argentina	9.1	67.6	88.5	114.1	0.5	6.0
Asia	340.2	1,052.8	3,891.1	5,679.7	23.1	–
Hong Kong	201.7	435.4	1,067.5	1,549.8	6.3	27.3
China	20.7	193.3	587.8	1,085.3	4.4	19.1
Singapore	30.5	110.6	632.8	912.4	3.7	16.1
Indonesia	8.7	25.1	160.7	253.1	1.0	4.5
India	1.7	16.3	205.6	252.3	1.0	4.4
Thailand	8.2	30.9	139.3	199.3	0.8	3.5
South Korea	5.2	43.7	135.5	182.0	0.7	3.2
Transition Economies	1.7	57.4	729.6	725.0	2.9	–
Russia	–	32.2	490.6	378.5	1.5	52.2
Kazakhstan	–	10.1	82.6	129.2	0.5	17.8
Ukraine	–	3.9	58.0	63.8	0.3	8.8
Serbia	–	–	24.9	33.1	0.1	4.6
Turkmenistan	–	0.9	13.4	26.2	0.1	3.6

Source: UNCTAD (2015)

6.3   The Reasons for the Existence of Foreign Direct Investment and Multinational Enterprises

A good understanding of MNEs and why they invest abroad is necessary to underpin the discussion of their effects on host economies. Thus, the main theoretical contributions in the field are summarised in chronological order.

For a long time, theoretical models in economics did not concern themselves with the existence of the MNE. The general equilibrium model developed by Hecksher and Ohlin in the first decades of the twentieth century, to explain the patterns of trade between countries, treated capital as an internationally immobile factor of production.[7] Despite its low predictive power, as highlighted by the Leontief paradox,[8] the model remained the core explanation of international trade for many decades. Moreover, early theoretical models regarded international capital flows as largely interest rate arbitrage, thus largely ignoring differences between portfolio and direct investment. Capital was expected to move from capital-abundant to capital-scarce countries until the full equalisation of the rates of return.[9] This approach prevailed until the late 1950s, when it began to be challenged by some scholars like John Dunning (1958) and Stephen Hymer (1960). Hymer's PhD thesis was a turning point in the study of international production,[10] since it presented convincing arguments, based on

---

[7] Building on the concept of comparative advantage put forth by David Ricardo, the Heckscher-Ohlin (H-O) model replaced Ricardo's idea of comparing relative productivity between countries by a prediction of the patterns of international trade based on factor endowments. The model predicts that a country will specialise in products that use their abundant production factors and import those which require factors which are scarce. The model depends on a set of rather restrictive assumptions, such as the adoption of identical technologies by different countries and constant returns to scale, besides factor immobility between countries.

[8] Leontief (1953) tested the H-O model with US data, arriving at the striking conclusion that imports were more capital-intensive than exports, even though the US was capital rich.

[9] For an overview of that early literature, see Iversen (1935).

[10] Buckley (2011) presents a review of the 'pre-Hymer' literature on international business, recognising its fragmented nature and the lack of a 'packaged form'. For a summary of the key theoretical literature on International Business, see Dunning (2001) and Dunning and Lundan (2008).

observations of the real world, for the differentiation of capital movements. He stressed that the distinctive feature of FDI, as opposed to portfolio investment, was the exercise of control over the firm's foreign assets. Hymer (1960) also sought to identify the conditions under which a firm will establish plants overseas, and proposed that a firm invests abroad through FDI if it is able to earn rents, benefiting either from imperfect competition or from the possession of distinctive assets. Hymer's market power explanation of the existence of the MNE was the dominant explanation until the mid-1970s. Building on the theoretical discussions about the nature of the firm initially advanced by Coase (1937), Buckley and Casson (1976) argued that a firm will undertake cross-border activity as intra-firm activity whenever the net benefits of doing so are larger than through the market. Bounded rationality and market imperfections affect the propensity for firms to internalise the markets for intermediate products and proprietary assets, thereby linking activities located in different countries (Hennart 2001).

In an effort to reconcile Hymer's view with the new internalisation stream, an integrated approach was developed by Dunning (1977, 1981). The 'eclectic paradigm' incorporated various theoretical perspectives to explain 'why', 'where' and 'how' a firm performs activities overseas. According to this approach, international investment requires the fulfilment of three preconditions: (a) the investing firm must own some kind of proprietary assets capable to yield extraordinary rents as a means to overcome the cost disadvantages of being an outsider (ownership advantage); (b) there must be an advantage in producing in the chosen location, otherwise the firm would produce and export from home country (location advantage); (c) there must be a justification for carrying out the activity within the firm, otherwise a market transaction (such as the licensing of the firm's brand or technology to a third party) would be preferred (internalisation advantage).

Building on earlier work by Behrman (1972), Dunning also proposed the consolidation in the literature of four basic motivations driving internationalisation: resource-seeking, market-seeking, efficiency-seeking and strategic asset-seeking (Dunning 1993).[11] Three are asset-exploiting motives – MNEs look for favourable locations where they can exploit their existing ownership advantages; the fourth is an asset-augmenting motive – MNEs seek locations where they can augment their pool of ownership advantages (Narula and Dunning 2000). Though relatively well integrated in the eclectic paradigm, Dunning's motives are, nevertheless, an *ad-hoc* categorisation, picked from real world examples (Cuervo-Cazurra and Narula 2015).[12] Motives for FDI have changed substantially over the years. In the 1950s and 1960s, FDI was overwhelmingly market-seeking, resource-seeking or trade-supportive. Today, the search for specific knowledge assets is much more common, and has been a distinctive feature of acquisitions of firms in developed countries by MNEs from developing countries (Madhok and Keyhani 2012). However, FDI to developing countries is still mostly resource-seeking, particularly among the least developed countries, and market-seeking, with increasing importance of the services sector (Narula 2014).

An offshoot of the eclectic paradigm is the investment development path (IDP) model, put forward by Dunning in 1979 and expanded in a series of works in the following decades (Dunning and Narula 1996; Narula 1996; Narula and Dunning 2000, 2010). Basically it argues that ownership advantages of firms interact with the location advantages of countries, and these interactions help shape development outcomes of both the host and the home economies. The IDP postulates that the evolution of inward and outward direct investment activity in a country varies

---

[11] Dunning (1993) actually proposed a longer list of nine motives, but five were labelled secondary by him and ended up being forgotten by the academic community. Obviously, in real world firms often have more than one motive to invest in a specific location (Cuervo-Cazurra and Narula 2015).

[12] Cuervo-Cazurra et al. (2015) propose a novel classification of internalisation motives, theoretically grounded on behavioural economics and highlighting the roles of firms' ownership advantages (or lack of) and home and host countries' location advantages (or disadvantages). According to the proposed taxonomy, firms expand abroad to: (a) sell more; (b) buy better; (c) upgrade; or (d) escape. The first is close to Dunning's market-seeking motive while the second combines resource-seeking and efficiency-seeking. The third resembles strategic asset-seeking, while the fourth retrieve one of Dunning's (1993) lost motives, and is related to avoiding institutional voids or other poor home country conditions.

systematically according to its relative level of economic development.[13] The IDP is divided into five main stages. In each, the nature and extent of FDI are intrinsically connected to the ownership advantages possessed by domestic and foreign firms as well as the location advantages of countries:

Stage 1 – When a country is very poor, it is not able to attract much FDI due to the narrow availability of location-bound complementary assets, with the exception of FDI aimed at exploiting its natural resources. Likewise, outward FDI tends to be minimal, since the domestic firms do not possess sufficient ownership advantages to venture abroad;

Stage 2 – Inward FDI tends to expand as the host country's location advantages improve, while outward FDI usually remains low. Market-seeking FDI takes place, stimulated by the enlargement of the domestic market due to growing economic activity. The development of some location-bound assets – infrastructure, for example – may encourage the inflow of FDI in export-oriented industries, especially in those capable of taking advantage of low labour costs;

Stage 3 – Inward FDI increases at a lower rate as domestic competitors evolve, while the inverse occurs with outward FDI. Comparative advantages in labour-intensive and resource-intensive industries begin to vanish due to rising wages, and some production capacity is transferred to countries in a lower stage of development. The enlarged domestic market allows for the capture of scale economies and the adoption of more technology-intensive production processes, encouraging efficiency-seeking inward FDI. Domestic firms' success becomes more dependent on their knowledge-intensive ownership advantages, and less on their home country location advantages. The sources of competitive advantages of both domestic and foreign-owned firms begin to shift to intangible assets.

---

[13] The IDP follows the structuralist tradition in which structural change is a central feature of economic development. Economic structure of countries evolve from a dependency on natural assets – land, mineral deposits, unskilled labour – to an increasing dependence on created assets – capital, technology, skilled labour (Narula 1996). Structural change has to do with: Allocation of labour between agriculture, manufacturing and services; capital, skill and knowledge intensity of production techniques; consumption patterns (subsistence, standardised, differentiated goods); and sources of comparative advantages (natural assets, created assets), among others (Lall 1996). Hence, transition to higher stages of the IDP depends on the development of the infrastructure, human capital and institutions demanded at each level of economic development.

Stage 4 – This stage is reached when the country's outward FDI stock exceeds inward FDI stock. The majority of domestic firms are able to compete with foreign MNEs in both the domestic and foreign markets. Inward FDI is deeply embedded in the local economy and is increasingly motivated by strategic asset seeking. Outward FDI is still on the rise, motivated by the loss of competitiveness at home and the accumulation of ownership advantages by domestic firms.

Stage 5 – Some trends of the previous stage are deepened. Domestic MNEs improve their capacity of allocating functions according to the comparative advantages of each invested country. The increasing geographical dispersion of assets makes the domestic MNEs' interests less convergent with their home governments'. In this stage, there is no prediction of the net investment position of the country.[14]

Though it is possible to link IDP stages to GDP per capita ranges, as several empirical studies have done (e.g., Narula 1996; Dunning and Narula 1996; Duran and Ubeda 2001; Boudier-Bensebaa 2008),[15] the IDP is idiosyncratic. Every country follows its own path, with unique stage thresholds levels. Thus, even when countries present a similar GDP per capita, their economic structures may be very different, due to different natural resource endowments, institutions, government policies and accidents of history, resulting in different location advantages as well as different ownership advantages of domestic firms (Lall 1996; Narula 1996). It can be said that even within a single country, different industries/sectors may be at different stages of the IDP. Indeed, dualism is still a common pattern among developing economies, in which a 'traditional' sector persists alongside a 'modern' sector (Singer 1970). Furthermore, economic development is path dependent – earlier strategies continue to influence outcomes even after being abandoned. In other words, history matters[16]!

---

[14] For a more detailed description of the IDP stages, see Dunning and Narula (1996).

[15] Duran and Ubeda (2001) confirmed that structural variables has a strong explanatory power on inward FDI for developing countries, but not for developed countries. Narula (1996) showed that created assets are important determinants of both inward and outward FDI among developed countries, but not among developing countries.

[16] Nevertheless, Narula and Dunning (2010) acknowledge that the oversimplification of the role of policies and their influence on the interaction between location advantages of countries and ownership advantages of firms constitute a weakness of the IDP.

The IDP is a dynamic model, in which not only firms' ownership advantages and countries' location advantages are evolving but also the interactions between them are changing in nature. In this sense, it is reasonable to expect that the way inward FDI affects the recipient economy depends on those advantages and their interactions, which in turn are related to the level of economic development of country.

6.4   The Effects of MNEs on Host Economies – A Microeconomic View

Foreign MNEs tend to be different from domestic firms in several aspects. They not only differ in size, but MNEs are in a better position to exploit cross-border efficiencies, particularly in sectors where scale economies matter. The technologies employed by MNEs, particularly those from developed countries, are usually more capital-intensive than those in use in the host economy and they tend to concentrate in more dynamic sectors. MNEs also have a higher propensity to import and export than local firms. Therefore, the presence of MNEs is expected to affect the host economy in a number of ways, from the employment level to the fiscal revenues. Most important, MNEs may employ production factors more efficiently than local firms, so their presence would be expected to enhance the overall productivity of the economy. Contrary to what is assumed in neoclassical economic models, state-of-art technologies are often inaccessible through the market, so their introduction by the MNEs may enhance the average productivity and accelerate structural transformation in host countries. These are regarded as the direct effects of FDI.

Nevertheless, the presence of MNEs also produce effects on other economic agents, notably on domestic firms. These are the external effects induced by FDI, and it is important to know the channels through which they occur. Indeed, aside from the direct and more visible impacts on employment and income generation, government officials frequently justify the bundle of subsidies they offer to attract FDI on the basis of the potential indirect benefits, such as the transfer of managerial know-how and production techniques to indigenous firms. In the literature, externalities and spillovers are widely employed as synonyms, although some scholars do differentiate between them. For Narula and Driffield (2012), for example, spillovers imply a process of learning by the recipient firm. Therefore, all spillovers are externalities, but not all externalities are spillovers.

MNE externalities can be classified as pecuniary or non-pecuniary externalities. The first come from the violation of the assumption of independence of economic agents – meaning that the behaviour of one agent affects other agents – and are transmitted through prices in the market. Benefiting from pecuniary externalities is relatively easy since they are internalised by simply paying lower prices on intermediate goods produced by more productive MNEs, for example (Castellani 2012). Non-pecuniary externalities are not transmitted through the market, and arise mainly from the public good nature of knowledge – whence they are also known as knowledge or technological externalities. Once introduced in the host economy by an MNE, knowledge can be used by other firms without compensation to its creator. However, that does not mean that it can be internalised without costs. On the contrary, the capture of FDI knowledge spillovers requires costly efforts by the host country and its firms (Zanfei 2012). Though this differentiation between pecuniary and knowledge externalities is important, in practice it is very difficult to distinguish between them (Castellani 2012). There have been a large number of empirical studies on externalities, much of which deals with productivity externalities from FDI, with a focus on the performance of domestic firms, while a less-developed literature deals with the linkages fostered by MNEs. However, the evidence from this body of work is, unfortunately, far from conclusive.

6.4.1 Intra-Sectoral Effects of MNE Presence

MNE effects on their domestic competitors are called horizontal spillovers, while the effects on the firms situated in a preceding or a successive stage of the value chain are known as backward and forward vertical spillovers, respectively. Horizontal spillovers occur through three main channels:

(a) The competition effect: The arrival of a new (foreign) competitor affects equilibrium prices, not only in the related product markets but also in input and factor markets. These are the typical pecuniary externalities. By reducing the monopoly power of domestic firms in some sectors, the entry of MNEs may contribute to enhance allocative efficiency (Caves 1974). Although it may encourage domestic firms to be more efficient,[17] more competition means fewer opportunities to exploit scale economies, with possible (negative) effects on sectoral productivity (Aitken and Harrison 1999).[18] The composite effect on competing domestic firms tends to be negative. They may be crowded-out by foreign competitors. However, it is reasonable to suppose that a considerable part of domestic firms in developing countries does not compete directly with MNEs since the former target lower-end markets while the MNE usually target higher-end markets.

(b) The demonstration/imitation effect: Production techniques and managerial practices used by the MNE may be more efficient than those used by domestic firms (indeed, this is a necessary condition for the occurrence of FDI). Their use by the MNE 'demonstrates' their superior attributes, and local competitors are able to observe and imitate them through, for example, reverse-engineering.

(b) The labour turnover effect: MNEs train their local employees, who accumulate managerial and technical know-how. This acquired knowledge leaks from the MNE when workers move to a collocated competitor or start their own firm. However, MNEs seek to minimise such spillovers often by paying above-market salaries to retain such employees (Fosfuri et al. 2001).[19]

---

[17] Zanfei (2012) criticises the use of the term 'externality' for this type of competition effect since the increase in the domestic firm's efficiency is determined by its own strategy and resource commitment and not by the behaviour of other firms.

[18] In the long run this effect should disappear as the least productive firms exit the market.

[19] Several empirical studies have confirmed that MNEs pay higher salaries. See Aitken et al. (1996), for Mexico and Venezuela, Lipsey and Sjoholm (2004), for Indonesia, and Chen et al. (2011), for China.

In both demonstration/imitation and labour turnover effects, the extent of potential spillovers depends upon the nature of the assets of the MNEs' affiliates – more specifically, their degree of imitability. Thus, the level of intellectual property rights' protection in the host country would play a role, but the true effect is uncertain. Strong protection encourages the transfer of more valuable assets by the MNE's headquarters to its affiliate, but at the same time reduces the chances of imitation. Therefore, there must be an 'optimum' level of intellectual property rights that maximises the spillover potential.

6.4.2 Inter-Sectoral Effects of MNE's Presence

In 1958, Albert Hirschman made a seminal contribution to the infant field of economic development studies. Assuming that 'the lack of interdependence and linkage is of course one of the most typical characteristics of underdeveloped economies', Hirschman (1958) became an advocate of an unbalanced growth strategy, where a handful of particular investments was able – through pecuniary externalities – to stimulate further investments in sectors that could supply inputs or buy their intermediate products. In such a strategy, FDI could play a vital role, as a trigger of the whole process.

Lall (1978, 1980) slightly modified Hirschman's concept of linkages, defining them as the 'direct relationships established by firms in complementary activities which are external to 'pure' market transactions' (Lall 1980, p. 204). According to Lall, because most markets for manufacturing intermediate goods exhibit certain imperfections, this justifies the adoption of one of three possible solutions: (a) vertical integration; (b) extra-market linkages; or (c) government intervention. Therefore, linkage creation is an outcome of a 'make or buy' choice, an intermediate solution between arms-length transaction and complete internalisation. Through the linkages, the MNEs can provide technical, managerial and financial assistance to their suppliers, for example. As the MNE expects a benefit from this type of relationship, it has incentives to create and deepen backward linkages. Therefore, it is more appropriate to refer to these as 'knowledge transfer' or 'technological transfer' instead of spillovers, since it derives from an intentional action by the MNE.

However, MNEs may also affect local suppliers and buyers through other channels. On the one hand, the increased demand enable domestic suppliers to benefit from scale and specialisation economies, while the MNEs' production itself increases supply for downstream sectors, possibly bringing prices down. On the other hand, when the MNEs introduce requirements for product quality or on-time delivery for their supplies – even where linkages do not exist – they induce an effect analogous to demonstration effect[20] – a non-pecuniary effect. Unfortunately, empirical studies generally do not distinguish between knowledge transfer and knowledge spillovers. Although such a distinction may seem of little importance for a host economy eager to receive FDI, in terms of policy design it is rather relevant, since transfer means an intended decision by the MNE while spillovers is an unintended consequence of its presence. Knowledge transfer is admittedly Pareto-improving, since it is expected to increase profits of both sides of the relationship.

Besides the aforementioned effects, backward linkages may also produce pecuniary effects on downstream sectors, including the MNE's own sector. In the theoretical models presented in Rodriguez-Clare (1996) and Markusen and Venables (1999), the entry of an MNE increase demand for inputs in the upstream sector. Due to higher specialisation and increasing returns to scale, domestic firms that use the same inputs also benefit. Therefore, backward linkages entail positive horizontal productivity externalities. In Rodriguez-Clare's (1996) model, positive effects are more likely when the goods produced by the MNEs are more complex, the communication costs with parent company are higher and when the level of economic development in home and host countries are not too different.

6.4.3 The Empirical Evidence on FDI Spillovers

In empirical studies, the occurrence of spillovers is assessed only indirectly. In the case of horizontal spillovers, researchers usually estimate an equation in which the productivity of the domestic firms of a certain

---

[20] Nevertheless, it must be noticed that, in this case, the effect is not likely to squeeze the MNE's rents, differently to what might occur when the leakage benefits its direct competitors (Kugler 2000).

sector depends on the foreign presence in the same sector, controlling for other observable determinants. Foreign presence in supplier (or buyer) sectors is the variable of interest if the focus is on backward (or forward) spillovers. Foreign presence is commonly measured by the foreign-owned firms' share in sectoral total sales or output, although a few studies use employment or equity instead.

The estimation of vertical spillovers requires the knowledge of the economy's input-output relationships, but due to data limitations, it is common to employ a single-year input-output matrix for the whole period analysed. Hence, it does not capture the dynamic effects of the investment on the input-output structure. Moreover, input-output relations of domestic firms and MNEs (in a same sector) are taken as identical, what implicitly means that they employ the same technology. This clearly leads to an overestimation of local sales and purchases of MNEs, as MNEs are known to import and export relatively more than domestic firms. Even more relevant is the fact that it contradicts the essence of the idea of spillovers, which depends on the leakage of the MNE's superior technology and knowledge to local firms (Barrios et al. 2011).

A key requirement of such analyses is the estimation of the productivity of the firms. Some studies use the labour productivity, usually calculated dividing physical output or sales by the number of employees. However, most recent studies increasingly use total factor productivity instead. This procedure requires sound information about the capital employed by the firms, but these are difficult to find because of poor accounting records (Driffield and Jindra 2012). It is also necessary to choose a functional form for the production function – Cobb-Douglas is usually chosen. Conversion of longitudinal data to constant prices is an additional problem, since the use of the same price index to deflate fixed capital of all the firms of a same sector contradicts the very logic of allocative efficiency.

It is easy to see that such an empirical approach does not allow for differentiation of pecuniary and non-pecuniary externalities on productivity. Also, in the usual econometric specification the channels through which spillovers occur is ignored, that is, they are treated as a 'black box'.

So far, the empirical evidence about FDI spillovers has been inconclusive. Gorg and Strobl (2001), in their meta-analysis of early spillovers studies, concluded that the lack of uniformity in samples, variable definitions and estimation procedures could be the root of the mixed results.[21] However, the increasing convergence of methods over the last years, especially the more frequent practice of estimating horizontal and vertical spillovers simultaneously, seems to have clarified the situation somewhat. An awkward aspect of these studies is that economic importance of the findings is rarely discussed. Nevertheless, the extensive meta-analyses conducted by Havranek and Irsova (2011, 2012) and Irsova and Havranek (2013) found that estimated horizontal spillovers are typically economically irrelevant; the effects of MNEs on their local customers are likewise negligible; and only backward spillovers are economically meaningful. According to their estimations, a 10 percentage-point increase in foreign presence in a sector is associated with an increase of 9% in the productivity of local suppliers, on average (Havranek and Irsova 2011).[22] Empirical evidence on the competition effect is also inconclusive. Kosova (2010) found evidence that the entry of a foreign MNE initially displaces domestic firms in Czech Republic. However, after two years, the increased demand and technology spillovers offset that initial effect, and FDI becomes benign to domestic firms. Nevertheless, it seems that the claim 'the more FDI, the better' does not hold in respect to spillovers. In fact, Wang and Yu (2008) found that a moderate foreign

---

[21] The first studies used cross-sectional data aggregated at sectoral level, finding mostly positive and statistically significant spillovers. Haddad and Harrison (1993) is the first known published study that employed firm-level panel-data – which became the norm in the 2000s – but failed to find significant spillovers. According to some meta-analyses (Gorg and Strobl 2001; Meyer and Sinani 2009), cross-sectional studies tended to overestimate the real horizontal spillovers, since they do not control for possible reverse causality, that is, FDI flowing to more productive industries, and for unobservable heterogeneity among firms.

[22] There is some evidence of publication bias (Gorg and Strobl 2001; Havranek and Irsova 2011, 2012), a problem that occur when studies providing the 'right' results are more likely to be selected for publication. The selection mechanism is usually guided by the preference of editors and referees for statistically significant results validating hypothesis or theories. According to Havranek and Irsova (2012), findings seems to obey a research-cycle: pioneer studies tend to report large and significant estimates because only strong results convince the journal editors about the relevance of the theme; as time passes, sceptical results become preferred, as they are considered more interesting.

presence is beneficial to Chinese domestic firms, but a crowding-out effect is observed in labour-intensive sectors when the MNEs' share approaches two-thirds of the industry. A similar result was found by Buckley et al. (2007), who also noticed that this effect is stronger when FDI comes from Taiwan, Honk Kong or Macau, in comparison to other sources. They suggest that this may be due to the kind of ownership advantages of the ethnic-Chinese foreign firms, which tend to be more similar to domestic firms' advantages – they are typically smaller than MNEs from other countries – so the competition effect is more likely to overcome the limited demonstration and labour turnover effects.

One serious problem with this empirical literature on spillovers is that most studies implicitly assume that the elasticity of the productivity of domestic firms to foreign presence is constant, that is, an increase of the MNEs' share from 0% to 10% produce the same effect as an increase from 90% to 100%. However, it is hard to believe that the competition effect is equal in both cases. In fact, Altomonte and Pennings (2009) found, in the case of Romania, that the first foreign investment in a specific industry and region boosts total factor productivity of domestic firms by nearly 3.5%. However, the effect weakens as new foreign competitors enter, eventually becoming negative (after the arrival of the 12th MNE).

There are very few studies which have tried to measure the labour turnover effects. Among these, Gorg and Strobl (2005) found that the productivity of domestic manufacturing firms in Ghana seems to be positively influenced by their owners' previous experience in multinationals of the same sector, while Poole (2013) found that workers of Brazilian domestic firms earn higher salaries when the number of former MNE employees working in the firm increases, what the author interpret as an evidence of spillover through the labour turnover effect.

Girma et al. (2015) is the first study that simultaneously investigates the direct and indirect (via spillovers) effects of the presence of MNEs on the productivity of the firms (both domestic and foreign-owned). Their results show that in China the direct effect is positive and increases as the MNEs' share in a region-sector cluster rise (except in the 0%-10% range, where it falls), while the indirect effect on domestic firms is negative, reaching the strongest impact when the foreign share is around 40% in the cluster. The overall effect on productivity is positive, but not monotonically related with foreign presence: it declines between 0% and 20% of foreign share, when the marginal indirect effect outweighs the marginal direct effect, then it begin to increase.

Conceptually, it is uncontroversial that the potential for spillovers only materialise under certain conditions, the most important being the capability of domestic firms of 'internalising' the externalities. In this respect, two aspects have received considerable attention. The first is the degree of backwardness of domestic firms in relation to the technological frontier represented by the MNEs investing in the country. Earlier theoretical models (Findlay 1978) concluded that a larger technological gap augments the potential for benefiting from the MNE presence. Demonstration effects would be particularly strong in earlier development stages as local firms would have a lot to learn, while at higher stages imitation would become increasingly hard and costly as the MNEs would have incentives to protect their distinctive proprietary assets (Meyer and Sinani 2009).[23]

More recent conceptual models have questioned the technological gap model, emphasising a second aspect: that domestic firms must have a minimum level of absorptive capacity in order to exploit external knowledge (Cohen and Levinthal 1989). Absorptive capacity can be defined as the 'ability to internalise knowledge created by others and modifying it to fit their own specific applications, processes and routines' (Narula and Marin 2003, p. 23). It is not difficult to perceive that both aspects are interrelated and run in opposite directions, that is, it is reasonable to expect that the higher the technological gap, the lower the absorptive

---

[23] Meyer and Sinani (2009) developed some hypotheses linking the occurrence of horizontal spillovers to the level of economic development of the countries. According to their reasoning, in low-income countries technological gap is wide, so domestic firms benefit from FDI since the MNEs would not have incentives to prevent the diffusion of standardised knowledge to firms that does not target the same market (upper-end domestic or export) as them. Moreover, the marginal cost of adopting some processes is low, while the benefits may be large. In middle-income countries, crowding-out is more likely, since the scope for imitation is narrower and concentrated in proprietary assets, and direct competition between MNEs and domestic firms is more probable as their ownership advantages are less different than in the former case, although a gap remains. Finally, in high-income countries, the competition effect is benign, since it forces domestic firms to react to foreign presence by means of improving their capabilities.

capacity of the firm. There is plenty of empirical evidence that investments in research and development (R&D) enhance the firm's absorptive capacity (Cohen and Levinthal 1990), but they have diminishing returns and tend to be less effective as the firm approaches the technological frontier (Criscuolo and Narula 2008). Furthermore, domestic absorptive capacity and external knowledge must match for actually realising the potential benefits accruing from FDI (Lorentzen 2005).

It must be underlined, however, that a firm's absorptive capacity does not depend exclusively on its own efforts. Its success or failure occur in orchestration with an entire 'system', as learning and innovation involves interactions not only with its competitors, customers and suppliers but also with the macro environment, which refers to factors such as culture, institutions, infrastructure and so on, that mould the mechanisms of knowledge creation and distribution within a country (Lorentzen 2005; Barnes and Lorentzen 2006; Criscuolo and Narula 2008). If the 'right' institutions are absent in this environment, it is much harder for domestic firms to absorb and efficiently employ external knowledge (Lorentzen 2005).

In empirical studies, the technological gap is commonly proxied by some measure of the difference between the productivity of the domestic firm and that of the most productive firms in the sector. Absorptive capacity is usually proxied by a measure of human capital or R&D expenditure, although technological learning in developing countries tends to rely less on R&D than in developed countries (Lorentzen 2005). Unfortunately, most studies that have investigated empirically both factors focused on developed economies. Flores et al. (2007), for instance, identified a technological gap interval – domestic firm's productivity between 50% and 80% of the MNEs' productivity in a sector – in which the FDI horizontal spillovers are biggest in the case of Portugal. In one of the few studies focusing on a developing economy, Blalock and Simon (2009) confirmed that human capital and absorptive capacity, measured by R&D expenditure, moderate the effect of MNEs' presence on the productivity of competing domestic firms in Indonesia. They also found that the larger the technological gap, the larger the productivity increase due to spillovers. In the case of Argentina, Narula and Marin (2003) found positive knowledge spillovers from FDI among a subset of domestic firms with high absorptive capacity – defined as firms that have invested more in new equipment oriented to product or process innovation or in training activities – but failed to find a significant result in the whole sample of domestic firms. Laborda Castillo et al. (2014) is another example of the moderating role of absorptive capacity, in this case for Chilean enterprises.

If domestic firms' heterogeneity matters, so should the heterogeneity of MNEs. Indeed, MNEs are not all equal. The potential for linkages creation and spillovers depends on the nature of the investing MNE, although empirical studies often ignore this. On the one hand, the ownership advantages of the investing MNE reflect its sectoral characteristics and its home country location advantages – in the case of developed countries' MNEs, they derive mainly from created assets (Narula 1996, 2014). On the other hand, the functions the MNE's headquarters delegate to its affiliate depend not only on its overall strategy but also on the location advantages the MNE sees in the host country.

Motives for FDI may also vary according to the country of origin of the MNE, as natural resources endowment and market size are largely recognised as important determinants of FDI. Different motives provide different potential for linkages and spillovers (UNCTAD 2001; Narula 2014). Nevertheless, the literature linking FDI motives to effects on host economies is intriguingly scarce, as underlined by Driffield and Love (2007).

Most studies implicitly assume that MNE's affiliates possess the same set of ownership advantages as their parent companies. This means an almost automatic transfer of assets from parent to subsidiary, thus ignoring the fact that this process is costly, so the parent may choose to transfer only a subset of the assets considered relevant to that location. Bell and Marin (2004) criticise the conventional approach, calling for opening the 'black box' that lies between the investment decision of the MNE's parent company and the observed domestic firms' productivity growth – or the whole process of knowledge transfer, firstly, from parent to subsidiary and, secondly, its leakage and absorption by domestic firms. A modified version of their conceptual model, which highlights the 'black box' domain in the case of horizontal spillovers, is given in Fig. 6.1.

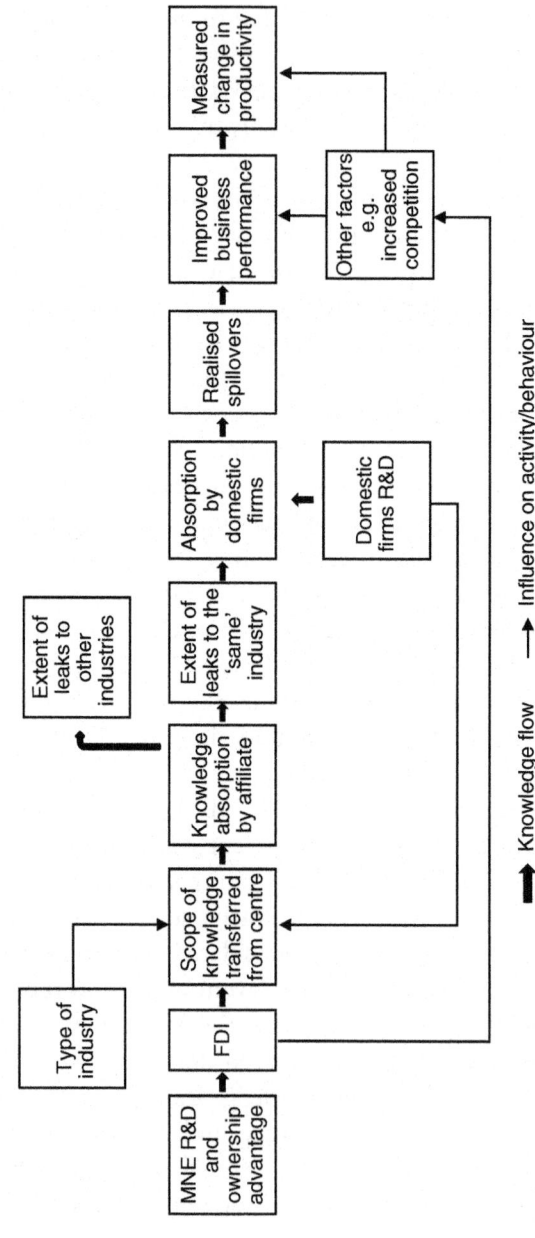

Fig. 6.1 Opening the 'black box' of FDI horizontal effects. *Source:* Authors, modified from Bell and Marin (2004)

Assuming homogeneity among subsidiaries also imply a complete disregard of asset-augmenting activities performed by them (Dunning and Narula 1995). In fact, recent literature has been emphasising the differences between 'competence-exploiting' and 'competence-creating' MNEs' subsidiaries, the former concentrating in exploiting existing assets of the whole company in the host country, while the later receive or gain mandates to perform asset augmenting activities, such as development of new products or new technologies, which can be later incorporated to the whole company's assets (Cantwell and Mudambi 2005). Over the years, the affiliate will possibly develop its own unique set of ownership advantages (Birkinshaw and Hood 1998), which will depend on the subsidiary's autonomy and initiative and on the host country's location-bound advantages. Domestic capacity, expressed in terms of both domestic firms' capabilities and environmental attributes, is a fundamental determinant of high competence foreign affiliates (Barnes and Lorentzen 2006).

'Competence-creating' subsidiaries are more embedded in host economies' innovation system, so it seems reasonable to assume that their knowledge assets are more likely to leak to domestic firms than in the case of 'competence exploiting' subsidiaries. Some studies indeed seem to corroborate this hypothesis. Marin and Sasidharan (2010) found that, in India, the occurrence of horizontal spillovers depends upon the technological activity carried out by MNEs' subsidiaries. Only 'competence-creating' subsidiaries – identified by high R&D expenditure and export intensity – generate positive spillovers, while 'competence exploiting' subsidiaries generate no spillovers. Likewise, Todo and Miyamoto (2006) found that only MNE subsidiaries that perform R&D locally generates significant positive horizontal spillovers in Thailand. Marin and Bell (2006) provide some evidence that only 'technologically active' subsidiaries – defined according to a set of variables related to R&D, training and investment in technological goods – generate positive horizontal spillovers to domestic firms in Argentina. In another paper, they found some evidence of interdependence of technological activities performed locally by MNEs' subsidiaries and domestic firms (Bell and Marin 2004).

However, using a different econometric approach, Chudnovsky et al. (2008) were not able to confirm those findings as their results show negligible spillovers from foreign presence in Argentina and the incapacity of higher degrees of innovative activities by MNE's affiliates to enhance the possibilities of spillovers.

The degree of control of the MNE's parent over its affiliate is expected to influence the extent of cross-border knowledge transfer, and, hence, the potential of knowledge leakages to domestic firms. When in a partnership, the MNE tends to transfer less sophisticated knowledge to its affiliate, but this tends to be the more easily absorbable by the domestic firms in the same sector (Javorcik and Spatareanu 2008). Abraham et al. (2010) found that international joint ventures in China are more likely to impact positively the productivity of domestic firms than wholly foreign-owned firms. In the case of Indonesia, according to Blomstrom and Sjoholm (1999), there is no difference between minority and majority foreign participation regarding its capacity of generating spillovers. For Romania, Javorcik and Spatareanu (2008) found that negative horizontal spillovers from FDI, due to competition effect, were lower when the foreign investment was made through a joint venture.

6.4.4 The Empirical Evidence on MNE Linkages in Host Economies

The connection between MNE linkages and host countries' economic development is not straightforward. MNEs' subsidiaries created to operate in enclaves develop few linkages with the domestic economy, so tend to exert a lesser development impact. However, higher domestic purchases by MNEs do not necessarily lead to higher economic development. Indeed, import-substituting industrialisation (ISI), followed by a number of developing countries from the 1950s to the 1970s, was relatively successful in inducing local procurement, through import restrictions and local content policies, among others. However, most of these linkages were inefficient, due to small scale and technological backwardness, only surviving due to autarky.[24] In turn, an export-oriented development strategy, followed by some Asian countries[25] from the late 1960s, was less prone to create domestic linkages, for its own internal logic of specialisation. Nevertheless, it favoured efficiency by means of larger scale and exposure to international competition.

So far, studies on FDI linkages have attracted much less attention than FDI spillovers, due, in part, to unavailability of data, particularly in developing countries. Existing literature is comprised mainly of case studies (Lall 1980; Altenburg 2000; Giroud 2003, 2007; Hansen and Schaumburg-Muller 2006). However, case studies may overestimate the benefits brought by MNEs if they overlook the linkage-breaking effect caused by the displacement of domestic firms by the foreign competitors. Due to differences in sources of ownership advantages, linkages built by MNEs tend to be qualitatively different from those forged by domestic firms. In Lin and Saggi's (2005) theoretical model, when the MNE has only a moderate technological advantage over local competing firms, the net linkage effect is positive, but when the advantage is large, linkages shrink. Therefore, it is the net effect that must be evaluated (Rodriguez-Clare 1996).

Quantitative empirical studies usually follow Hirschman (1958) and ignore forward linkages. MNEs' backward linkages are empirically assessed by some measure of their purchases in the domestic market, usually the share of total inputs bought from domestic suppliers. However, Alfaro and Rodriguez-Clare (2004) consider this proxy inadequate, and propose an alternative measure, the ratio of the value of inputs bought domestically to the number of workers hired by the firm.

---

[24] One of the most widespread criticisms against FDI-assisted development was the inadequacy of the technologies brought in by the MNEs, which were regarded as being excessively capital-intensive for countries where the abundant production factor was unskilled labour (Ahmad 1978; Lall 1978). However, this criticism implicitly supposes that capital-intensive technologies can be adapted relatively easily depending on factor prices conditions, what is rarely true. Furthermore, by doing this, the MNE would be giving up one of its most important ownership advantages, say, superior technology.

[25] Countries like South Korea and Taiwan cannot be seen as followers of a purely export-oriented strategy from the 1960s to the 1980s since they maintained a large set of policies very similar to those adopted by Latin American countries at that time (Amsden 1989; Wade 1990).

The potential for linkage creation by MNE investments depends, to a large extent, on the same factors already cited in the case of spillovers: the nature of the MNE and its affiliate, investment motives, mode of entry, among others. Domestic-oriented affiliates tend to create more linkages than export-oriented affiliates, since they are less dependent on low cost inputs (in international terms) to be competitive. An MNE which enters through the acquisition of a domestic firm will have a higher number of local connections, since it tends to maintain at least some of the existing suppliers and buyers (UNCTAD – United Nations Conference on Trade and Development 2001). However, a newcomer through greenfield investment creates new linkages, instead of simply building upon the existing ones, and this should also be considered when evaluating linkages.

Based on the Rodriguez-Clare's (1996) theoretical model, Alfaro and Rodriguez-Clare (2004) searched for linkages derived from MNE presence in four Latin American countries – Brazil, Chile, Mexico and Venezuela. Although in all the countries investigated the share of inputs sourced domestically by MNEs is lower than that by domestic firms, their estimated linkage coefficient – measured by ratio of the value of inputs bought domestically to the number of workers hired by the firm – is higher for MNEs in all the cases except Mexico. Pooling data of MNEs present in four European transition economies, Jindra et al. (2009) found that subsidiary's autonomy, initiative and technological capability is positively related to the extent of backward linkages (measured by the share of inputs bought from domestic suppliers). They also found evidence that greenfield investments provide fewer backward linkages. Ha and Giroud (2015) found that innovation performance of South Korean domestic firms (measured by patent counts) is positively affected by the presence of 'competence-creating' subsidiaries of MNEs,[26] and negatively by 'competence-exploiting', in buyer sectors.

---

[26] The classification of subsidiaries was done through the application of factor analysis to a questionnaire answered by the firms about the importance they attribute to innovation initiatives. Competence-creating subsidiaries were associated mainly to product diversification, market power expansion and introduction of new products. Competence-exploiting subsidiaries were associated to labour and product cost reduction and flexible production.

The opposite effect was found for supplier sectors. In sum, albeit promising results, more empirical studies are needed to draw a clearer picture of the determinants of the linkage's extent and depth, expanding the focus of the analysis to domestic suppliers' characteristics.

6.5   The Effects of MNEs on Host Economies – A Macroeconomic View[27]

It is widely accepted that the output level of an economy depends on its stock of capital. Therefore, economic growth depends on the additions to that capital stock. In Solow-type neoclassical growth models, there is no distinction between domestic and foreign investment: both give the same contribution to capital accumulation and, therefore, to economic growth. Endogenous growth models, however, differentiate these sources of investment on a technological basis. It is usually assumed that foreign investors bring in more efficient technologies. Therefore its impact on economic growth would be higher than that coming from domestic investment.

Nonetheless, FDI does not necessarily mean capital formation. The financial resources brought by foreign investors can be used to create new assets, but can also be used to acquire existing ones. In this case, there is no investment in the national accounts sense.[28] However, even

---

[27] The focus of this section is the effects of FDI on economic growth. However, FDI flows also affect the external equilibrium of the host economy. FDI is considered a more stable means of financing current account deficits than foreign portfolio investment flows (Lipsey et al. 1999), as well as a less risky alternative to foreign debt, since the related income payments tend to be procyclical. Krugman (2000) makes a point of the negative association between portfolio investment (out)flows and FDI (in)flows during the Asian financial crisis of the late 1990s.

[28] The term 'investment' has different meanings in the System of National Accounts (SNA) and in the Balance of Payments (BP). In the SNA, investment is a synonym of gross fixed capital formation and means the *additions* (in a given period) to the stock of fixed assets that can be used to produce more goods in the future (UN 2003). Therefore, this concept of investment includes machinery, buildings, roads etc., but excludes non-produced fixed assets such as land. In the BP, investment is a financial flow. The funds may be used to acquire existing assets or to build new ones. Inflows of investment increase the financial liabilities of the country, outflows of investment increases the financial assets of the country. The sum of the assets and liabilities indicates the net investment position of the country.

when the foreign investor effectively makes a contribution to host country's capital stock, there is no guarantee that the net effect on aggregate investment will be positive. In any economy, at any time, there are a limited number of profitable investment opportunities. It is quite possible that FDI simply crowds-out domestic investment, totally or partially. Should this happen, the net effect would be smaller than the original investment. However, it is also possible that the investment done by the foreign firm engender new profitable opportunities in the economy, which would be taken by domestic firms. In this case, FDI would crowd-in domestic investment. Therefore, the direction and magnitude of this effect is an empirical matter.

So far, few studies have investigated empirically the effect of FDI on domestic investment. Using a sample of 69 developing countries in the period 1970–1989, Borensztein et al. (1998) have found a positive, albeit not statistically robust, impact of FDI on domestic investment. For the period 1971–2000, Agosin and Machado (2005) have found a crowding-out effect among Latin American countries and a neutral effect among Asian and African countries. Clearly, more studies are needed, preferably adding some variables only available at the aggregate level, in order to understand under which conditions FDI crowds in or, alternatively, crowds out, domestic investment.

When it comes to the relationship between inward FDI and economic growth, the majority of empirical works seems to find a positive correlation, at least for developing countries. One of the few exceptions is Mencinger (2003), which found a negative relationship between FDI and GDP growth for a sample of transition economies in the period 1994–2001.[29] However, positive effects of FDI on economic growth are not automatic. According to Balasubramanyam et al. (1996), FDI is positively correlated with GDP growth, but their results are statistically significant only for developing countries pursuing export promotion policies, instead of import substitution policies. However, the criteria

---

[29] According to the author, this result may had been driven by the prevalence of acquisitions, many of them through privatisation, and the use of the proceeds of the sales in consumption instead of domestic investment, since he had failed to find a positive relationship between FDI and total capital investment (Mencinger 2003).

used to classify the countries in their sample are quite controversial since it is based on actual exports rather than a direct policy measure. Borensztein et al. (1998) also found a positive correlation between FDI and GDP growth within a sample of developing countries, but the size of this effect depends on the availability of human capital in the host economy. They attribute this result to the need of adequate absorptive capacity for a country benefit from the inflow of advanced technology brought along by foreign investors. Their findings were confirmed by Wang and Wong (2009a), who found a direct effect of FDI on aggregate total factor productivity in a sample of developing countries, but only when a threshold level of human capital is reached.

Using data from the period 1975–1995, Alfaro et al. (2004) found that the positive effect of FDI on GDP growth depended on the level of development of host country's financial market. Wang and Wong (2009b) found a positive correlation between greenfield FDI and GDP growth, but a negative relationship between mergers and acquisitions (M&A) and economic growth. However, these conclusions should be taken carefully. Indeed, Blonigen and Wang (2005) provide convincing econometric evidence that pooling advanced and developing economies in empirical FDI studies, as those studies have done, can induce misleading conclusions. When replicating the study of Borensztein et al. (1998) with an augmented sample incorporating a set of developed economies, they failed to find the same effect of FDI on GDP growth.

As highlighted in the introduction of this chapter, the set of determinants of inward FDI usually found in econometric studies is very close to the set of determinants of GDP growth. Therefore, it is expected that both variables move in the same direction, what had been confirmed by the empirical studies cited above, although not without some mediating factors. However, as correlation does not mean causality, it is important to examine separately the findings of studies concerned with the latter question. Carkovic and Levine (2005) are very critical about previous studies on the basis of inadequate control of simultaneity bias and country-specific effects, among others problems. After controlling these factors, they failed to find a strong independent impact of FDI on growth, for a panel of 72 countries for 1960–1995. Their results also indicate that the lack of an impact of FDI on GDP growth does not depend on the stock of human capital, the level of per capita income, or the level of financial development of the country. However, their sample pools developed and developing countries, and therefore is subject to the criticism mentioned above.

Li and Liu (2005) found evidence of a mutual causality between FDI and GDP growth in a sample of developing countries in the period 1970–1999. The positive effect of FDI on growth is larger the higher the level of human capital and the lower the technological gap (measured as the difference of per capita income of the country and the US's). Allowing for heterogeneous effects among countries, Nair-Reichert and Weinhold (2001) found a causal relationship between FDI and GDP growth, in a panel comprised of 24 developing countries in the period 1971–1995, with some evidence that this relationship is higher in more open economies. Employing an unusual test for causality, Chowdhury and Mavrotas (2006) found that GDP causes FDI in Chile, while there is a feedback between these variables in Malaysia and Thailand, in the 1969–2000 period. Alguacil et al. (2011) found that the effect of FDI on growth is much more robust in a sample of 13 low and lower-middle income (5 Latin American and 8 Asian) than in a sample of 13 upper-middle income countries (all but one from Latin America), in the period 1976–2005. They suggest that this may be an indication that FDI is less likely to crowd out domestic investment in less-developed countries. Herzer et al. (2008) examined the relationship between FDI and growth using co-integration techniques on a country-by-country basis. They analysed 28 developing countries, but found a long-run relationship only in 4 (Sri Lanka, Nigeria, Tunisia and Egypt), and in all these cases, there was a reinforcing relationship between FDI and growth.

In sum, the evidence to date seems to validate the hypothesis of the existence of a relationship between FDI and GDP growth, possibly flowing in the both directions. Nevertheless, the relationship only seems to hold for a subset of developing countries with some specific attributes, although there is no consensus about what these attributes are. At the very least, we can say that there are doubts whether the estimation of macroeconomic models is an adequate way to assess the effects of FDI in host economies. One problem of cross-country studies is that they assume an identical production function across countries. To what extent are the empirical results driven by this kind of underlying assumption?

6.6 Concluding Remarks

The aim of this chapter was to present an overview of the current scholarly knowledge about the development effects of MNEs on host developing countries. The mechanisms linking FDI and development are relatively well-understood, but there are considerable practical challenges in achieving FDI-assisted development.

MNEs can have a decisive influence on the development path of countries. Attracting MNEs is not, of course, the only development strategy available to developing countries, but it can be more efficient than the alternative strategy that restricts the mobilisation of resources to domestic sources. FDI, as well as other forms of MNE local engagement, may function as a shortcut to structural change and help to break the vicious circle of poverty and underdevelopment (Narula and Dunning 2000).

In the formulation of their economic development strategies, governments have to decide if they will be passive or pro-active and whether such policies will be comprehensive or selective. Passive policies tend to reinforce static location advantages of the country, while a pro-active approach tends to be more concerned with complementary policies needed to upgrading, such as skills development. Selective policies are more subject to political capture, corruption and inefficient allocation of the country's scarce resources, but a comprehensive approach can lead to excessive spread of resources and tend to give a lower weight to the strengthening of domestic enterprises. The most successful catching-up cases in the post-World War II era – Japan, Taiwan and South Korea – followed restrictive FDI policies, prioritising technology transfer agreements, licensing and reverse engineering as vehicles to internalise foreign knowledge (Narula and Dunning 2010). It must be said that the world have changed substantially over the last three decades, what means that pursuing similar strategies today will not necessarily produce the same outcomes. The key to understanding these successful catching-up stories is that it was not FDI *per se* that determined their growth, but the associated knowledge transfer and linkages, and the capacity of domestic firms to absorb, internalise and upgrade their knowledge assets by taking advantage of the spillovers.

Waiving restrictions on FDI is not the same thing as having a congruent set of policies towards FDI. Developing countries must create an environment conductive to fully exploit the potential benefits resulting from the presence of foreign MNEs. Moreover, a sound FDI policy must not be exclusively concerned with attracting capital investment, but must give the same importance to enhance the local embeddedness of the MNEs. It is important to underline that FDI projects are not all equal. The quality of FDI a country receives is at least as important as the quantity. Quality has to do with the MNE's investment motivations, the affiliates' mandate and autonomy, and these will have a direct impact over the potential for linkages and spillovers.

It is important that FDI policy be linked to industrial policy and trade policy. Indeed, in the twenty-first century industrial policy is crucial to achieving internationally competitive industries. 'Modern' industrial policies should focus on deepening and widening the country's location advantages, to encourage the expansion of MNEs' activities, and the strengthening of domestic firms' capacity to absorb the knowledge spillovers and connecting to the value chains set up by MNEs. This may be done through a variety of interventions, from investment in human capital and technological capabilities to the promotion of industrial clusters to facilitate knowledge flows.

The dependence on incentives and subsidies as a means to attract MNEs is fraught with difficulty, and is necessarily a short-term solution. From an economic viewpoint, FDI incentives can only be justified if they are not larger than the overall expected benefits from the foreign investment.[30] The evidence would suggest that such incentives are less important for long-term achievements than developing and upgrading

---

[30] See Blomstrom and Kokko (2003) for a number of convincing arguments against FDI incentives.

the quality and extent of a country's absorptive capacity through improvements in its knowledge infrastructure.

It is also worth noting that the usual means of measuring linkages and spillovers are increasingly outdated, and do not allow us to capture the structure of modern cross-border value chains. Countries increasingly specialise in tasks, instead of products, and their economic structures and international trade reflect these changes. MNE affiliates also reflect these new realities, with growing specialisation and strong competition between subsidiaries of the same MNE. The dependency upon registered equity investments to construct the measures of foreign presence overlooks the increasing separation between control and ownership by MNEs. MNEs can no longer be viewed as a synonym to FDI (Narula and Dunning 2010; UNCTAD – United Nations Conference on Trade and Development 2011; Collinson et al. 2016), that is, MNEs are increasingly able to control the value chain in the absence of ownership. The truncated miniature replica that constituted the dominant pattern of the typical MNE affiliate is now a relic of the past (Pearce 2001). MNEs currently use a multitude of arrangements to access the desired location advantages of other countries, ranging from traditional FDI to outsourcing, with a myriad of partial internalisation schemes in the middle. It is hard to be specific on the extent to which non-equity modes of internationalisation are replacing FDI (or whether they are in addition to) because reliable data do not as yet exist. However, if traditional FDI measurements suffer from data inconsistency and problems of classification, these 'new' modes of governance are even harder to quantify.

References

Abraham, F., Konings, J., & Slootmaekers, V. (2010). FDI spillovers in the Chinese manufacturing sector. *Economics of Transition, 18*(1), 143–182.

Agosin, M., & Machado, R. (2005). Foreign investment in developing countries: Does it crowd in domestic investment? *Oxford Development Studies, 33*(2), 149–162.

Ahmad, J. (1978). Import substitution: A survey of policy issues. *The Developing Economies, 16*(4), 355–372.

Aitken, B., & Harrison, A. (1999). Do domestic firms benefit from foreign direct investment? Evidence from Venezuela. *American Economic Review, 89*(3), 605–618.

Aitken, B., Harrison, A., & Lipsey, R. (1996). Wages and foreign ownership: A comparative study of Mexico, Venezuela and the United States. *Journal of International Economics, 40*(3–4), 345–371.

Alfaro, L., & Rodriguez-Clare, A. (2004). Multinationals and linkages: An empirical investigation. *Economia, 4*(2), 113–169.

Alfaro, L., Chanda, A., Kalemli-Ozcan, S., & Sayek, S. (2004). FDI and economic growth: The role of local financial markets. *Journal of International Economics, 64*(1), 89–112.

Alguacil, M., Cuadros, A., & Orts, V. (2011). Inward FDI and growth: The role of macroeconomic and institutional environment. *Journal of Policy Modeling, 33*(3), 481–496.

Altenburg, T. (2000). Linkages and spillovers between transnational corporations and small and medium-sized enterprises in developing countries: Opportunities and best policies. In UNCTAD (Ed.), *TNC-SME linkages for development: Issues – experiences – best practices*. New York and Geneva: United Nations.

Altomonte, C., & Pennings, E. (2009). Domestic plant productivity and incremental spillovers from foreign direct investment. *Journal of International Business Studies, 40*, 1131–1148.

Amsden, A. (1989). *Asia's next giant: South Korea and late industrialization*. Oxford and New York: Oxford University Press.

Balasubramanyam, V. N., Salisu, M., & Sapsford, D. (1996). Foreign direct investment and growth in EP and IS countries. *The Economic Journal, 106* (434), 92–105.

Barnes, J., & Lorentzen, J. (2006). Learning, upgrading, and innovation in the South African automotive industry. In R. Narula & S. Lall (Eds.), *Understanding FDI-assisted development*. London: Routledge.

Barrios, S., Görg, H., & Strobl, E. (2011). Spillovers through backward linkages from multinationals: Measurement matters! *European Economic Review, 55*(6), 862–875.

Behrman, J. (1972). *The role of international companies in Latin America: Autos and petrochemicals*. Lexington, MA: Lexington Books.

Bell, M., & Marin, A. (2004). Where do foreign direct investment-related technology spillovers come from in emerging economies? An exploration in

Argentina in the 1990s. *The European Journal of Development Research*, *16*(3), 653–686.

Birkinshaw, J., & Hood, N. (1998). Multinational subsidiary development: Capability evolution and charter change in foreign-owned subsidiary companies. *Academy of Management Review*, *23*, 773–795.

Blalock, G., & Simon, D. (2009). Do all firms benefit equally from downstream FDI? The moderating effect of local suppliers' capabilities on productivity gains. *Journal of International Business Studies*, *40*, 1095–1112.

Blomstrom, M., & Kokko, A. (2003). The economics of foreign direct investment incentives. In H. Herrmann & R. Lipsey (Eds.), *Foreign direct investment in the real and financial sector of industrial countries*. Heidelberg and New York: Springer.

Blomstrom, M., & Sjoholm, F. (1999). Technology transfer and spillovers: Does local participation with multinationals matter? *European Economic Review*, *43*, 915–923.

Blonigen, B., & Wang, M. (2005). Inappropriate pooling of wealthy and poor countries in empirical FDI studies. In T. H. Moran, E. M. Graham, & M. Blomström (2005) (Eds.), *Does foreign direct investment promote development?* Washington, DC: Institute for International Economics.

Borensztein, E., De Gregorio, J., & Lee, J. W. (1998). How does foreign direct investment affect economic growth? *Journal of International Economics*, *45*(1), 115–135.

Boudier-Bensebaa, F. (2008). FDI-assisted development in the light of the investment development path paradigm: Evidence from central and eastern European countries. *Transnational Corporations*, *17*(1), 37–68.

Buckley, P. (2011). The theory of international business pre-Hymer. *Journal of World Business*, *46*, 61–73.

Buckley, P., & Casson, M. (1976). *The future of the multinational enterprise*. London: Macmillan.

Buckley, P. J., Clegg, J., & Wang, C. (2007). Is the relationship between inward FDI and spillover effects linear? An empirical examination of the case of China. *Journal of International Business Studies*, *38*(3), 447–459.

Cantwell, J., & Mudambi, R. (2005). MNE competence-creating subsidiary mandates. *Strategic Management Journal*, *26*, 1109–1128.

Carkovic, M., & Levine, R. (2005). Does foreign direct investment accelerate economic growth? In T. Moran et al. (Eds.), (2005). *Does Foreign direct investment promote development?* Washington, DC: Institute for International Economics.

Castellani, D. (2012). In praise of pecuniary externalities. *The European Journal of Development Research, 24*(1), 15–19.

Caves, R. (1974). Multinational firms, competition, and productivity in host-country markets. *Economica, 41*(162), 176–193.

Chen, Z., Ge, Y., & Lai, H. (2011). Foreign direct investment and wage inequality: Evidence from China. *World Development, 39*(8), 1322–1332.

Chowdhury, A., & Mavrotas, G. (2006). FDI and growth: What causes what? *The World Economy, 29*(1), 9–19.

Chudnovsky, D., López, A., & Rossi, G. (2008). Foreign direct investment spillovers and the absorptive capabilities of domestic firms in the Argentine manufacturing sector (1992–2001). *The Journal of Development Studies, 44*(5), 645–677.

Coase, R. (1937). The nature of the firm. *Economica, 4*, 386–405.

Cohen, W., & Levinthal, D. (1989). Innovation and learning: The two faces of R&D. *The Economic Journal, 99*, 569–596.

Cohen, W., & Levinthal, D. (1990). Absorptive capacity: A new perspective on learning and innovation. *Administrative Science Quarterly, 35*(1), 128–152.

Collinson, S., Narula, R., & Rugman, A. (2016). *International business.* London: Pearson.

Criscuolo, P., & Narula, R. (2008). A novel approach to national technological accumulation and absorptive capacity: Aggregating Cohen and Levinthal. *The European Journal of Development Research, 20*(1), 56–73.

Cuervo-Cazurra, A., & Narula, R. (2015). A set of motives to unite them all? Revisiting the principles and typology of internationalization motives. *The Multinational Business Review, 23*(1), 2–14.

Cuervo-Cazurra, A., Narula, R., & Un, C. A. (2015). Internationalization motives: Sell more, buy better, upgrade and escape. *Multinational Business Review, 23*(1), 25–35.

Driffield, N., & Jindra, B. (2012). Challenging the production function approach to assess the development effects of FDI. *The European Journal of Development Research, 24*(1), 32–37.

Driffield, N., & Love, J. (2007). Linking FDI motivation and host economy productivity effects: Conceptual and empirical analysis. *Journal of International Business Studies, 38*, 460–473.

Dunning, J. (1958). *American investment in British manufacturing industry.* London: Allen & Unwin.

Dunning, J. (1977). Trade, location of economic activity, and the multinational enterprise: A search for an eclectic approach. In P. O. Hesselborn,

B. Ohlin, & P. M. Wijkman (Eds.), *The international allocation of economic activity*. London: MacMillan.

Dunning, J. (1981). *International production and the multinational enterprise*. London: Allen & Unwin.

Dunning, J. (1993). *Multinational enterprises and the global economy*. Cheltenham: Edward Elgar.

Dunning, J. (2001). The key literature on IB activities: 1960–2000. In A. Rugman & T. Brewer (Eds.), *The Oxford handbook of international business*. Oxford: Oxford University Press.

Dunning, J., & Lundan, S. (2008). *Multinational enterprises and the global economy*. Cheltenham: Edward Elgar.

Dunning, J., & Narula, R. (1995). The R&D activities of foreign firms in the United States. *International Studies of Management & Organization, 25*(1–2), 39–74.

Dunning, J., & Narula, R. (1996). The investment development path revisited: Some emerging issues. In J. Dunning & R. Narula (Eds.), *Foreign direct investment and governments: Catalysts for economic restructuring*. Basingstoke: Edward Elgar.

Duran, J., & Ubeda, F. (2001). The investment development path: A new empirical approach and some theoretical issues. *Transnational Corporations, 10*(2), 1–34.

Findlay, R. (1978). Relative backwardness, direct foreign investment, and the transfer of technology: A simple dynamic model. *Quarterly Journal of Economics, 92*(1), 1–16.

Flôres Jr, R. G., Fontoura, M. P., & Guerra Santos, R. (2007). Foreign direct investment spillovers in Portugal: Additional lessons from a country study. *The European Journal of Development Research, 19*(3), 372–390.

Fosfuri, A., Motta, M., & Rønde, T. (2001). Foreign direct investment and spillovers through workers' mobility. *Journal of International Economics, 53*(1), 205–222.

Girma, S., Gong, Y., Görg, H., & Lancheros, S. (2015). Estimating direct and indirect effects of foreign direct investment on firm productivity in the presence of interactions between firms. *Journal of International Economics, 95*(1), 157–169.

Giroud, A. (2003). *Transnational corporations, technology and economic development: Backward linkages and knowledge transfer in South East Asia*. Cheltenham: Edward Elgar.

Giroud, A. (2007). MNE vertical linkages: The experience of Vietnam after Malaysia. *International Business Review, 16*, 159–176.

Globerman, S., & Shapiro, D. (2002). Global foreign direct investment flows: The role of governance infrastructure. *World Development, 30*(11), 1899–1919.

Gorg, H., & Strobl, E. (2001). Multinational companies and productivity spillovers: A meta-analysis. *The Economic Journal, 111*, 723–739.

Gorg, H., & Strobl, E. (2005). Spillovers from foreign firms through worker mobility: An empirical investigation. *Scandinavian Journal of Economics, 107*(4), 693–709.

Ha, Y., & Giroud, A. (2015). Competence-creating subsidiaries and FDI technology spillovers. *International Business Review, 24*, 605–614.

Haddad, M., & Harrison, A. (1993). Are there productivity spillovers from direct foreign investment? Evidence from panel data from Morocco. *Journal of Development Economics, 42*, 51–74.

Hansen, M., & Schaumburg-Muller, H. (Eds.) (2006). *Transnational corporations and local firms in developing countries: Linkages and upgrading.* Copenhagen: Copenhagen Business School.

Havranek, T., & Irsova, Z. (2011). Estimating vertical spillovers from FDI: Why results vary and what the true effect is. *Journal of International Economics, 85*(2), 234–244.

Havranek, T., & Irsova, Z. (2012). Publication bias in the literature on foreign direct investment spillovers. *Journal of Development Studies, 48*(10), 1375–1396.

Hennart, J. (2001). Theories of the multinational enterprise. In A. Rugman & T. Brewer (Eds.), *The Oxford handbook of international business.* Oxford: Oxford University Press.

Herzer, D., & Klasen, S. (2008). In search of FDI-led growth in developing countries: The way forward. *Economic Modelling 25*(5), 793–810.

Hirschman, A. (1958). *The strategy of economic development.* New Haven: Yale University Press.

Hymer, S. (1960). *The international operations of national firms: A study of direct foreign investment.* Cambridge, MA and London: MIT Press (published in 1976).

IMF – International Monetary Fund. (2009). *Balance of payments and international investment position manual: Sixth edition.* Washington, DC: IMF.

Irsova, Z., & Havranek, T. (2013). Determinants of horizontal spillovers from FDI: Evidence from a large meta-analysis. *World Development, 42*, 1–15.

Iversen, C. (1935). *Aspects of the theory of international capital movements.* Copenhagen: Levin & Munksgaard.

Javorcik, B., & Spatareanu, M. (2008). To share or not to share: Does local participation matter for spillovers from foreign direct investment? *Journal of Development Economics, 85,* 194–217.

Jindra, B., Giroud, A., & Scott-Kennel, J. (2009). Subsidiary roles, vertical linkages and economic development: Lessons from transition economies. *Journal of World Business, 44*(2), 167–179.

Kosova, R. (2010). Do foreign firms crowd out domestic firms? Evidence from the Czech republic. *The Review of Economics and Statistics, 92*(4), 861–881.

Krugman, P. (2000). Fire-sale FDI. In S. Edwards (Ed.), *Capital flows and the emerging economies: Theory, evidence, and controversies.* Chicago: University of Chicago Press.

Kugler, M. (2000). *The diffusion of externalities from foreign direct investment: Theory ahead of measurement.* Southampton: University of Southampton, Discussion Papers in Economics and Econometrics.

Laborda Castillo, L., Sotelsek Salem, D., & Moreno, J. D. J. (2014). Foreign direct investment and productivity spillovers: Firm-level evidence from Chilean industrial sector. *Latin American Business Review, 15*(2), 93–122.

Lall, S. (1978). Transnationals, domestic enterprises, and industrial structure in host LDCs: A survey. *Oxford Economic Papers, 30*(2), 217–248.

Lall, S. (1980). Vertical inter-firm linkages in LDCs: An empirical study. *Oxford Bulletin of Economics and Statistics, 42*(3), 203–226.

Lall, S. (1996). The investment development path: Some conclusions. In J. Dunning & R. Narula (Eds.), *Foreign direct investment and governments: Catalysts for economic restructuring.* London and New York: Routledge.

Lall, S., & Streeten, P. (1977). *Foreign investment, transnationals and developing countries.* London: Macmillan.

Leontief, W. (1953). Domestic production and foreign trade: The American capital position re-examined. *Proceedings of the American Philosophical Society, 97*(4), 332–349.

Li, X., & Liu, X. (2005). Foreign direct investment and economic growth: An increasingly endogenous relationship. *World Development, 33*(3), 393–407.

Lin, P., & Saggi, K. (2005). Multinational firms and backward linkages: A critical survey and a simple model. In T. H. Moran, E. M. Graham, & M. Blomström (Eds.), *Does foreign direct investment promote development?* Washington: DC: Institute for International Economics.

Lipsey, R., & Sjoholm, F. (2004). Foreign direct investment, education and wages in Indonesian manufacturing. *Journal of Development Economics, 73,* 415–422.

Lipsey, R. E., Feenstra, R. C., Hahn, C. H., & Hatsopoulos, G. N. (1999). The role of foreign direct investment in international capital flows. In M. Feldstein (Ed.), *International capital flows.* Chicago: University of Chicago Press.

Lorentzen, J. (2005). The absorptive capacities of South African automotive component suppliers. *World Development, 33*(7), 1153–1182.

Madhok, A., & Keyhani, M. (2012). Acquisitions as entrepreneurship: Asymmetries, opportunities, and the internationalization of multinationals from emerging economies. *Global Strategy Journal, 2*(1), 26–40.

Marin, A., & Bell, M. (2006). Technology spillovers from foreign direct investment (FDI): The active role of MNC subsidiaries in Argentina in the 1990s. *Journal of Development Studies, 42*(4), 678–697.

Marin, A., & Sasidharan, S. (2010). Heterogeneous MNC subsidiaries and technological spillovers: Explaining positive and negative effects in India. *Research Policy, 39,* 1227–1241.

Markusen, J., & Venables, A. (1999). Foreign direct investment as a catalyst for industrial development. *European Economic Review, 43,* 335–356.

Mencinger, J. (2003). Does foreign direct investment always enhance economic growth? *Kyklos, 56*(4), 491–508.

Meyer, K., & Sinani, E. (2009). When and where does foreign direct investment generate positive spillovers? A meta-analysis. *Journal of International Business Studies, 40,* 1075–1094.

Morrissey, O. (2012). FDI in sub-Saharan Africa: Few linkages, fewer spillovers. *European Journal of Development Research, 24*(1), 26–31.

Nair-Reichert, U., & Weinhold, D. (2001). Causality tests for cross-country panels: A new look at FDI and economic growth in developing countries. *Oxford Bulletin of Economics and Statistics, 63*(2), 153–171.

Narula, R. (1996). *Multinational investment and economic structure: Globalisation and competitiveness.* London and New York: Routledge.

Narula, R. (2014). Foreign direct investment as a driver of industrial development: Why is there so little evidence? In R. Van Tulder, A. Verbeke, & R. Strange (Eds.), *International business and sustainable development.* Bingley: Emerald.

Narula, R., & Driffield, N. (2012). Does FDI cause development? The ambiguity of the evidence and why it matters. *The European Journal of Development Research, 24*(1), 1–7.

Narula, R., & Dunning, J. (2000). Industrial development, globalization and multinational enterprises: New realities for developing countries. *Oxford Development Studies, 28*(2), 141–167.

Narula, R., & Dunning, J. (2010). Multinational enterprises, development and globalization: Some clarifications and a research agenda. *Oxford Development Studies, 38*(3), 263–287.

Narula, R., & Marin, A. (2003) *Foreign direct investment spillovers, absorptive capacities and human capital development: Evidence from Argentina.* Geneva: International Labour Office Working Paper no. 96.

Noorbakhsh, F., & Paloni, A. (2001). Human capital and FDI inflows to developing countries: New empirical evidence. *World Development, 29*(9), 1593–1610.

OECD – Organization for Economic Cooperation and Development (2008) *OECD benchmark definition of foreign direct investment:* (fourth edition). Paris: OECD Publishing.

Pearce, R. (2001). Multinationals and industrialisation: The bases of 'inward investment' policy. *International Journal of the Economics of Business, 8*(1), 51–73.

Poole, J. (2013). Knowledge transfers from multinational to domestic firms: Evidence from worker mobility. *The Review of Economics and Statistics, 95*(2), 393–406.

Reuber, G. (1973). *Private foreign investment in development.* Oxford: Clarendon Press.

Rodriguez-Clare, A. (1996). Multinationals, linkages, and economic development. *American Economic Review, 86*(4), 852–873.

Singer, H. (1970). Dualism revisited: A new approach to problems of the dual society in developing countries. *Journal of Development Studies, 7*(1), 60–75.

Todo, Y., & Miyamoto, K. (2006). Knowledge spillovers from foreign direct investment and the role of local R&D activities: Evidence from Indonesia. *Economic Development and Cultural Change, 55*(1), 173–200.

UN – United Nations. (2003). *National accounts: A practical introduction.* New York: United Nations.

UNCTAD – United Nations Conference on Trade and Development. (2001). *World investment report 2001: Promoting linkages.* United Nations: New York and Geneva.

UNCTAD – United Nations Conference on Trade and Development. (2011). *World investment report 2011: Non-equity modes of international production and development.* United Nations: New York and Geneva.

UNCTAD – United Nations Conference on Trade and Development. (2015). *World investment report 2015: Reforming international investment governance.* United Nations: New York and Geneva.

Wade, R. (1990). *Governing the market: Economic theory and the role of government in East Asian industrialization.* Princeton: Princeton University Press.

Walsh, J., & Yu, J. (2010) *Determinants of Foreign direct investment: A sectoral and institutional approach.* Washington, DC: IMF (Working Paper 10/187).

Wang, C., & Yu, L. (2008). Do spillover benefits grow with rising foreign direct investment? An empirical examination of the case of China. *Applied Economics, 39*(3), 397–405.

Wang, M., & Wong, S. (2009a). Foreign direct investment and economic growth: The growth accounting perspective. *Economic Enquiry, 47*(4), 701–710.

Wang, M., & Wong, S. (2009b). What drives economic growth? The case of cross-border M&A and greenfield FDI activities. *Kyklos, 62*(2), 316–330.

Zanfei, A. (2012). Effects, not externalities. *The European Journal of Development Research, 24*(1), 8–14.

Rajneesh Narula is the John H. Dunning Chair of International Business Regulation at the Henley Business School, University of Reading, UK. His research and consulting have focused on the role of multinational firms in development, innovation and industrial policy, R&D alliances and outsourcing.

André Pineli is researcher on international economics and political economy at the Institute for Applied Economic Research (IPEA), Brazil. He is currently PhD student in International Business and Strategy at the Henley Business School, University of Reading. His research focuses on foreign direct investment, multinational enterprises and their development effects on home and host countries.

7

The Impact of Microfinance on Poverty Alleviation: Making Sense of the Evidence

Supriya Garikipati

7.1 Introduction

Microfinance is the provision of small-scale financial services and products to poor individuals and households. The focus is to provide financial services to low-income households with the aim to improve their income and standard of living (Armendáriz and Morduch 2007). Low-income households typically have limited access to conventional services provided by mainstream banks and other financial institutions. The professed promise of microfinance is to bridge this gap by reaching out to low-income households and help in the fight against poverty and vulnerability (Yunus 2008). Reducing poverty mainly entails increasing productivity and incomes and reducing vulnerability entails improving gender equality and welfare outcomes for all members of low-income households, but especially for women and children

S. Garikipati (✉)
University of Liverpool Management School, Liverpool, UK
e-mail: s.garikipati@liverpool.ac.uk

© The Author(s) 2017   **189**
G. Giorgioni (ed.), *Development Finance*, Palgrave Studies
in Impact Finance, DOI 10.1057/978-1-137-58032-0_7

(Torre and Vento 2006). At the forefront of achieving this promise is the provision of small loans to the poor also known as microcredit. Microcredit is often the main and sometimes the only service provided by Microfinance Institutions (MFIs) – however microcredit is really just one component of microfinance services. However, because of its prominent place among the products offered by MFIs, the terms 'microfinance' and 'microcredit' are at times used interchangeably (Harper 2003).[1] In this chapter we will restrict discussion to the provision of microcredit only.

The main credit disbursal model used by MFIs has been the provision of small loans to poor women via neighbourhood group. Groups take over client selection and monitoring thus mitigate the difficulties arising due to asymmetric information between lenders and borrowers, making it viable for MFIs to lend without the need for physical collateral (Gatak and Guinnane 1999). Targeting women also helps MFIs meet the double bottom line of financial and social objective (Garikipati et al. 2017). Women are more compliant with repayments and inclined to share incomes generated from credit with their children. The incentive for women to participate comes from the expected benefits to their agency and empowerment via an increased role in the household economy. These claims and features have made microfinance programs – mainly group lending to poor women – an attractive addition to poverty alleviation strategies all over the developing world. Over the last three decades, the industry has experienced rapid growth. At the turn of 2012, its global business touched a total loan portfolio of around USD 40 billion and a client base of around 205 million, of whom over 84% were women (Microcredit Summit Report 2015).

While the microfinance industry became part of the development policy orthodoxy in low-income countries, the debate around its

---

[1] The microfinance industry has a much broader focus than microcredit alone – the services provided by most MFIs across the world now include micro-savings, micro-insurance, capacity building for entrepreneurship. MFIs may also provide intermediation services to their clients, some of which include money transfer services, financial literacy and group building sessions (Roodman 2012). The main focus of these products and services is to promote poor livelihoods.

social efficacy has also gained in intensity (Daley-Harris 2009). The promise of microfinance to alleviate poverty and empower women meant that MFIs became the beneficiaries of significant subsidies and support from various donors, making it possible for them to focus on reaching the target group and serving poor clients more efficiently. A large number of MFIs rely heavily on subsidies and donor funds – prominent among them are BRAC and Grameen in Bangladesh; the Self-Help-Group-Bank-Linkage Programme in India (Hudon 2016). In terms of both the number of people targeted and the financial input that it receives, microfinance has become the biggest development programmes globally (Van Rooyen et al. 2012). This donor dependency has clearly heightened the expectations for microfinance to live up to its promises and demonstrate its impact in a manner that is both scientifically rigorous and also accessible to donors and development practitioners (Helms 2006). Microfinance has thus become the centre of intense debate and public discourse.

Top among these discussions is the social efficacy of microfinance – mainly its promise to alleviate poverty and empower women. The vast literature that has emerged over the last three decades is intensely polarised with discussants holding diametrically opposite views – some maintaining that microfinance is effective in meeting its social promises while others providing evidence to the contrary. Overtime the waters have become very murky and it is not clear that we have a meaningful and usable verdict. This is despite having more systematic reviews than any other area of development policy - a total of five so far and still counting (see Duvendack et al. 2011; van Rooyen et al. (2012); Vaessen et al. (2013); Awaworyi (2014); Brody et al. (2016). As it stands, there is no clear conclusion on the social effectiveness of microfinance. This grey space is heavily in need of clarity and the laying down of some clear established empirical facts that are meaningful for policy and practice. This chapter attempts to provide such a synthesis of the existing evidence with the intent to arrive at some meaningful conclusions on the social effectiveness of microfinance.

Measuring the impact of microfinance interventions is arguably a challenging task because of various potential biases mainly arising from self-selection and program placement. Several approaches have been put forward to help deal with these biases.[2] Studies that synthesise any 'evidence-based' policy literature typically rank quantitative studies according to methodological rigour, and include only those which have addressed problems of endogeneity and selection bias – with randomised control trials representing the 'gold standard'. It is important to state that this chapter is not intended as such a systematic review. Most empirical studies that examine the social impact of microfinance fall short of these exacting standards – and a systematic review would mean that the overwhelming majority of studies relevant to this chapter would be excluded which would 'effectively (wipe) clean the memory banks of past knowledge' (Bedecarrats et al. 2015, p. 16 as quoted in Kabeer 2017). Instead we review the broad assessment literature, but focus on specific questions of social efficacy of microfinance, especially with respect to its ability to alleviate poverty and improve incomes of the poor. We do this to arrive at answers for material questions of interest from a broader evidence-base.

7.2   Does Microfinance Alleviate Poverty?

The microfinance industry has sustained growth and interest around the world mainly with the promise to help alleviate poverty. Its ability to alleviate poverty is however intensely debated. Many remain sceptical about the positive impact of microfinance and it is in the interest of all stakeholders (governments, donors, practitioners and clients) to understand what its true impact on poverty is – in other words what works and what does not work in microfinance with respect to pulling people out of the vicious cycles of low incomes and low productivity.

The theory of 'positive change' in microfinance assumes that a borrower is constrained in taking up income-generating activity either by a

---

[2] While the common trend among empirical assessments is to adopt a framework that considers microcredit as an exogenous 'treatment' on individuals or households, studies have also used quasi-experimental techniques (see, e.g., Pitt and Khandker 1998; Garikipati 2008) and randomised control trials (see, e.g., Karlan and Zinman 2007; Banerjee et al. 2009; Karlan et al. 2009; Feigenberg et al. 2010). For detailed discussion on impact assessment methods used in the literature on microfinance and their validity, see Morduch (1999), Duvendack et al. (2011); Berhane and Gardebroek (2011) and Roodman and Morduch (2013).

high marginal credit cost or by lack of capital. Access to regulated capital, which eases the constraints, should hence allow for the increase of profits, income and hence welfare (Duvendack et al. 2011). The theory of positive change is indeed supported by evidence suggesting that microfinance is effective and benefits clients (see, e.g., Sebstad and Chen, 1996; Morduch 1999; Khandker 2005; Rosenberg 2010; Imai and Azam 2012). The 'negative impact' theory discusses entirely different linkages – for instance, families building microenterprises may have an incentive to use the labour of their children and not school them (Wydick 1999). The negative linkages are also supported by a variety of studies (see, e.g., Hulme and Mosley 1996; Copestake 2002; Hoque 2005; Nghiem et al. 2012). Hence, as it stands, the evidence on the impact of microfinance on poverty across the world remains mixed.

The situation is somewhat abetted by recent systematic reviews by Duvendack et al. (2011), van Rooyen et al. (2012), Vaessen et al. (2013) and Awaworyi (2014) that synthesise existing literature on the impact of microfinance on poverty. The inferences drawn from these studies mainly suggest that there is no visible impact of microfinance on profits and incomes and hence on poverty. For instance, van Rooyen et al. (2012) conclude that while microcredit positively influences the level of economic activities undertaken by the poor, there is evidence of lower income associated with being a microfinance borrower for relatively longer periods. This may suggest that high interest rates charged in the sector are a disproportionate drain on poor incomes. Similarly, in an empirical synthesis of the literature, Awaworyi (2014) finds a significant and positive impact of microcredit on assets, but the effect is weak and thus of little practical economic relevance. Worryingly, his evidence also indicates a negative impact on income growth – suggesting once again the negative impact of high interest rates levied by MFIs. These syntheses have also been useful in explaining some of the heterogeneity in reported findings on the impact of microfinance interventions. For instance, in their synthesise Duvendack et al. (2011) suggests that the differential effects on socio-economic outcomes can often be explained by the characteristics associated with microfinance programmes. Methodological variations in impact assessment are also responsible for some of the heterogeneity in findings (see also Kabeer 2005a).

Instead of reinventing the wheel by way of resynthesising the evidence-based assessment literature, in the interest of paucity and clearer conclusions, in this chapter the focus is on examining the evidence around the impact of microfinance on poverty. We consider a variety of measures of poverty: income, consumption, expenditure, profits and assets. We consider both amount borrowed (loan size) and access to credit (programme membership or receipt of loan) as relevant measures of microfinance. Non-quantitative studies that rely only on descriptive measures of assessment (client experiences or researcher observations) are beyond the remit of this study. We also exclude studies that examine impacts on poverty indices constructed out of multiple measures of poverty (like Imai et al. 2010, 2012),[3] and those that consider micro-savings as a measure of microfinance (e.g., Ashraf et al. 2010; Dupas and Robinson 2013). We believe these sacrifices are worth making in the interest of getting discerned and distinct conclusions. We discuss the results that emerge from a review of the studies roughly in order of how long they have existed for and how well they are established within in the literature.

Before we do this however, there is a need for a word of caution. The attempt here is to synthesise the literature in a way that is accessible to a variety of audience. While we want to arrive at clear and meaningful ideas that can help interpret the inestimably large literature on microfinance impact assessment that has accumulated by now – we fully recognise the danger of arriving at simple generalisations. Indeed if anything is clear from this literature it is that the vast global initiative of microfinance can hardly be expected to have one single, consistent impact story over the long assortment of product variations and geographical differences. Hunting for generalisations is futile and the focus of debate must move on to understanding the variety of experiences. That must indeed be the real quest (see also Copestake et al. 2016). It is essential that the conclusions presented below are understood to have the severely limited objective of reviewing the literature by way of presenting an overview of impact outcomes that have been consistently observed across studies.

---

[3] Evidence presented in both studies supports the poverty-reducing effect of microfinance.

The first and long-standing conclusion that emerges from the literature is the positive impact microfinance has on the non-poor borrowers. Microcredit schemes typically target the poor; however, at times beneficiaries may be from households that are somewhat above the poverty line – the better-off amongst the poor. Studies find that these borrowers benefit from microcredit – early work by Hulme and Mosley (1996) demonstrates this for a range of countries. This fits with the theoretical expectation that microfinance will have a positive impact if borrowers have viable investments and the necessary business skills. The better-off amongst the poor are more likely to have these conditions compared to the very poor – who may also be denied highly productive activities because of start-up costs or other constraints (Wood and Sharif 1997). Where MFIs serve non-poor clients, the impacts of the interventions are usually positive. Evidence emerging from rural China and rural India also support this hypothesis (Li et al. 2011; Garikipati 2012). Other studies also support this idea indirectly – for instance, Stewart et al. (2012) proposes that any risk from microcredit can be mitigated by targeting at clients with a level of financial security – suggesting that there is risk involved in targeting the poorest of the poor. Zeller et al. (2001) indicate that access to credit can reduce risk through livelihood diversification, which has the potential to raise incomes – which once again suggests that the better-off among the poor are more likely to reap the benefits of credit. Studies however suggest that with the right type of support and training even the poorest of borrowers can succeed (see, e.g., Hulme and Moore (2007) on BRAC's ultra-poor programme called Income Generation for Vulnerable Group Development).

The second result that can be gleaned from the literature is the positive impact of microfinance on consumption and expenditure – especially in the short run. This is entirely unsurprising given that an injection of credit whether used for production or consumption will result in expenditure, at least in the short run. Several studies examine the impact of microfinance on at least one proxy for consumption. Khandker (2005), Cuong (2008), Gertler et al. (2009), Attanasio et al. (2011); Berhane and Gardebroek (2011), Imai and Azam (2012) and Kaboski and Townsend (2012) present evidence supporting the positive effect of microfinance on consumption, especially in the short run. Pitt and Khandker (1998) also find this but mainly for female borrowers. Evidence presented by Hoque (2004),

Banerjee et al. (2009), Augsburg et al. (2012) and Nghiem et al. (2012) indicate that the effects of microfinance on consumption is insignificant mainly due to the small value of microloans issued. The available evidence however overwhelmingly favours increased consumption in the short run. Impact on consumption in the long run is of course related to profits and income growth overtime (Crépon et al. 2014). We deal with these next.

The third result that we can comment on with some certainty is the positive impact that credit has on business profits. The emerging consensus is that microloans that are put into productive use impact positively on the productivity of microenterprises, especially when borrowers have the essential business skills. Tedeschi (2008), Copestake et al. (2001) and McKernan (2002), Crépon et al. (2014) provide evidence to support the positive effects of microfinance on microenterprise profits. Furthermore, two factors seem to support higher profit – longevity of membership and flexible repayment terms. Copestake et al. (2001) find that clients who remain in microcredit programmes rather than leave after their first loans also tend to have more profitable businesses. In contrast those clients who left after receiving their first loan were worse off. Rigid nature of loan repayment schedule at a Peruvian MFI meant negative impact on business profits as it did not give borrowers, who had mostly invested in their farms, the opportunity to start receiving returns on their investment before repayments were due (Copestake et al. 2005). So it seems that as long as clients don't rush out of the door and MFIs are prepared to flex repayment schedules around the needs of their clients, microfinance should help improve the profitability of microenterprises. Banerjee et al. (2009) and Attanasio et al. (2011) are two studies that do not support the result on positive impact on profits – in fact the latter finds a significant negative impact – it is important to note that these two studies were randomised evaluations where intention to treat rather than actual intervention was used to measure access to microfinance.

In common parlance, an increase in profit should also mean an increase in income – but this linear relationship does not seem to be borne out in the case of microfinance – not only because credit may be diverted into consumption expenditure but even when credit is used for productive purposes. For instance, in a randomised evaluation, Crépon et al. (2014) find that although business profits of microfinance clients increase, their incomes do not because of the off-setting effect of lost wages from casual work. So what about the effect on incomes of the relatively poor borrowers who are less able to diversify incomes? The suggestion emerging from the studies discussed above is that the poor are less likely to have access to productive opportunities and necessary skills so the impact of microfinance on their incomes is likely to be less positive. In fact the next conclusion that we can draw from the literature is that the impact on income is uncertain. A great many studies find no significant impact on income like Abou-Ali et al. (2009), Cotler and Woodruff (2008), Takahashi et al. (2010), Imai and Azam (2012), Kaboski and Townsend (2012) Nghiem et al. (2012) and Crépon et al. (2014). Some studies even find a negative association (Attanasio et al. 2011), whereas some do find a significant positive impact – like, Copestake et al. (2005), Cuong (2008) and Kouassi (2008). However, even these studies tend to find associated conditions with the positive results – for instance, Copestake et al. (2001) find that clients who leave the programme after their first loan tend to be worse off and it is only those who persevere benefit in terms of higher household incomes. Overall, the lesson that emerges is that impact on income cannot be taken for granted and there may be associated conditions that need attention.

The final result is on the impact of microfinance on asset accumulation – most of the literature suggests a positive association, although an empirical synthesis of the literature shows that the impact is modest at best and hence may have little economic significance. One of the issues with using assets as a proxy for poverty is the need for longitudinal data that goes back a sufficient period. There is likely to be some trade-off in the short-run between consumption expenditure and asset expenditures – which are likely to only settle overtime – so to generate a sufficiently robust picture we would need data that covers a sufficiently long period. The results emerging from the literature suggest a positive impact of microfinance on long-term asset accumulation with an important caveat – the association is modest to the extent where it is unlikely to be economically meaningful. Of the studies that examine this relationship, Pitt and Khandker (1998), Cotler and Woodruff (2008), Garikipati (2008), Gertler et al. (2009) and Islam (2011) suggest a positive but most suggest a modest impact of microfinance on asset accumulation while Takahashi et al. (2010), Attanasio et al. (2011) and

Kaboski and Townsend (2012) suggest a negative impact. In a systematic empirical review that includes most of these studies, Awaworyi (2014) concludes that although the effect of microcredit on assets is positive, the effect-size represents no meaningful economic significance.

Overall we can conclude that while the better-off amongst the poor are in a good position to benefit from microfinance initiatives, the benefits for poor clients are not assured nor is their direction of change clear. While microfinance is likely to have a positive impact on consumption and expenditure, especially in the short run – the long-run benefits on income growth and asset creation are uncertain. Moreover, even when these benefits are experienced, they are likely to be modest which really brings into question the poverty alleviation capacity of microfinance. Where clients use their loans for productive purposes, loans do seem to help with improving profitability, but clients require staying capacity and leaving the programme prematurely can leave clients worse-off. Certainly it seems that with respect to poverty alleviation the gains from microfinance are measurably small – relying on market-based credit alone to alleviate poverty is wish-full thinking. Recent systematic reviews such as Duvendack et al. (2011), Awaworyi (2014) among others report along similar lines – very modest effect of microfinance and certainly of little significance in terms of their economic importance. There is certainly no strong evidence to support the claim that microfinance has a positive effect on the economic well-being of the poor. Some of the emerging literature in fact suggest that microfinance creates a debt burden for the poor which because of its institutional backing could have ever more of a real and perceived negative impact on the borrowers (see Guérin 2013). Of course the lack of sufficiently lengthy longitudinal data impedes us from making conclusions on the long-term impact of microfinance. Credit may increase income eventually, however given that borrowers incur debts that must be repaid, sometimes starting immediately, the expected positive impacts of microcredit on some economic outcomes may not be immediate or significant (Stewart et al. 2012). Relying on the market to fight poverty is unlikely to work unless significant and long-term adjustments are made to microfinance products. For instance, repayments could be linked to business profit – this is broadly the model used for repayments of graduate loans in several parts of the developed world; what works for graduates in developed countries may also work for the very poor in the developing world.

7.3 Some Concluding Comments

It must be noted of course that this work focused on the credit element of microfinance only. It is clear that the financial needs of the poor extend beyond credit to that of savings, insurance and financial capacity building (see Collins et al. 2009; Duvendack et al. 2011). These needs have remained largely unmet but by a handful of MFIs and therein lies a critic of the industry which has cheery picked credit over other financial needs of the poor – mainly because of its potential to earn a profit. While it is important to explore sustainable approaches to lift people out of poverty, it is equally important to ensure that the poor are not exposed to exploitation in the name of market based solutions. The recent microfinance crisis in Andhra Pradesh, India, has really brought home the point that perhaps working with the poor is not the right space for institutions that are driven solely by profit (see Haldar and Stiglitz 2013). There does seem an inherent limit in extending the microfinance model to for-profit only institutions.

It is worth reflecting on the heterogeneity in reported estimates across the studies. One clear lesson to carry away from this is that it may be futile to find one universal truth with respect to the impact of microfinance on poverty. Not only are results different because of study-level methodological drivers, but the main difference comes from the programme-specific attributes and client characteristic. A general result that emerges is that credit-only programmes do worse than credit-plus programmes. Several studies and systematic reviews by now agree that MFIs that offer credit-plus programmes, which combine credit with other services, especially services that enhance capacity for business and financial training, are likely to have better results (Armendáriz and Morduch 2007; Banerjee 2009; Duvendack et al. 2011). Some programmes may combine other products from the range available to microfinance institutions like micro-insurance or micro-savings (for e.g., see Dupas and Robinson 2013). Consistently results suggest that programmes like Grameen and BRAC show positive results because of the focus on group building activities build into the schemes. For the same reason relatively smaller programmes run by committed NGOs may have better results when compared to large state-run programme. The potential for positive changes to occur via microfinance are dependent upon 'context, commitment and capacity' (Kabeer 2005b).

Finally, a word must be put in for the need for long-term studies – given that the short-term impact is uncertain or even detrimental – mainly because of rigid repayment rules – the questions that is begging an answer is the long-run impact of microfinance. Are things likely to improve overtime as clients settle into a rhythm of progressive loans and rigid repayment disciplines? The hope of a positive answer is undeniably what keeps the juggernaut of microfinance chugging – indeed there are studies that suggest such an answer (see, e.g., Copestake et al. 2001; Stewart et al. 2012). Given that investments into microenterprises are likely to take time to yield returns, it may take time for investment to translate into increased consumption expenditure. It is unlikely that cross-sectional studies will capture these transitions effectively. The need for longitudinal studies hence cannot be overemphasised.

While its ability to alleviate poverty is uncertain at best, it is undeniable that its 'market friendly' flexible lending mechanisms will ensure microfinance's popularity for the foreseeable future (Copestake 2002). Hence a clear policy directive seems to be in order. Without being too prescriptive, the accumulated literature allows us to put forward some distinct policy relevant statements – using credit as a standalone policy is unlikely to help alleviate poverty and indeed may increase indebtedness and suffering in the short run. This is especially true if the target clients are ultra-poor. If a credit-driven intervention is to be used, then combining it with other microfinance services must be considered (like savings and insurance). The inherent limits on expansion of the sector to for-profit institutions must also be heeded and unhindered scaling up using purely market-driven models of credit disbursement must be avoided. In short, credit as a tool for alleviation of poverty must be used with caution and perhaps with great hesitation.

References

Abou-Ali, H., El-Azony, H., El-Laithy, H., Haughton, J., & Khandker, S. R. (2009). Evaluating the impact of Egyptian social fund for development programs. The World Bank, Policy Research Working Paper Series 4993.

Armendáriz, B., & Morduch, J. (2007). *The economics of microfinance the economics of microfinance.* Cambridge: The MIT Press.

Ashraf, N., Karlan, D., & Yin, W. (2010). Female empowerment: Impact of a commitment savings product in the Philippines. *World Development, 38*(3), 333–344.

Attanasio, O., Augsburg, B., Haas, R., Fitzsimons, E., & Harmgart, H. (2011). *Group lending or individual lending? Evidence from a randomised field experiment in Mongolia.* Institute for Fiscal Studies, IFS Working Papers: W11/20.

Augsburg, B., De Haas, R., Harmgart, H., & Meghir, C. (2012). Microfinance at the Margin: Experimental Evidence from Bosnia and Herzegovina. Rocheste.

Awaworyi, S. (2014). The impact of microfinance interventions: A meta-analysis. Monash University Department of Economics Working Paper Series, 03–14.

Banerjee, A., Duflo, E., Glennerster, R., & Kinnan, C. (2009). The miracle of microfinance? Evidence from a randomized evaluation. Department of Economics Massachusetts Institute of Technology MIT Working Paper, 1–40.

Bedecarrats, F., Guérin, I., and Roubaud, F. (2015). *The gold standard for randomised evaluations: from discussion of method to political economy* (Working Paper WP/2015-01). Paris: University of Paris.

Berhane, G., & Gardebroek, C. (2011). Does microfinance reduce rural poverty? Evidence based on household panel data from Northern Ethiopia. *American Journal of Agricultural Economics, 93*(1), 43–55.

Brody, C., De Hoop, T., Vojtkova, M., Warnock, R., Dunbar, M., Murthy, P., & Dworkin, S. L. (2016). *Economic self-help group programs for improving women's empowerment: A systematic review.* London: International Initiative for Impact Evaluation.

Collins, D., Morduch, J., Rutherford, S., & Ruthven, O. (2009). *Portfolios of the poor: How the world's poor live on $2 a day AQ20.* Princeton, NJ: Princeton University Press.

Copestake, J. (2002). Inequality and the polarizing impact of microcredit: Evidence from Zambia's copperbelt. *Journal of International Development, 14*(6), 743–755.

Copestake, J., Bhalotra, S., & Johnson, S. (2001). Assessing the impact of microcredit: A Zambian case study. *The Journal of Development Studies, 37*(4), 81–100.

Copestake, J., Dawson, P., Fanning, J. P., McKay, A., & Wright-Revolledo, K. (2005). Monitoring the diversity of the poverty outreach and impact of microfinance: A comparison of methods using data from Peru. *Development Policy Review, 23*(6), 703–723.

Copestake, J., Cabello, M., Goodwin-Groen, R., Gravesteijn, R., Humberstone, J., Johnson, S., Nino-Zarazua, M., Titus, M. (2016). Towards a plural history of microfinance. *Canadian Journal of Development Studies, 37*(3), 279–297.

Cotler, P., & Woodruff, C. (2008). The impact of short-term credit on microenterprises: Evidence from the Fincomun-Bimbo program in Mexico. *Economic Development & Cultural Change, 56*(4), 829–849.

Crépon, B., Devoto, F., Duflo, E., & Pariente, W. (2014), Estimating the impact of microcredit on those who take it up: Evidence from a randomized experiment in Morocco, Working Paper, MIT.

Cuong, N. V. (2008). Is a governmental micro-credit program for the poor really pro-poor? Evidence from Vietnam. *The Developing Economies, 46*(2), 151–187.

Daley-Harris, S. (2009). *State of the microcredit summit campaign report 2009.* Washington, DC: Microcredit Summit.

Dupas, P., & Robinson, J. (2013). Savings constraints and microenterprise development: Evidence from a field experiment in Kenya. *American Economic Journal: Applied Economics, 5*(1), 163–192.

Duvendack, M., Palmer-Jones, R., Copestake, J., Hooper, L., Loke, Y., & Rao, N. (2011). *What is the evidence of the impact of microfinance on the well-being of poor people?* London: EPPICentre.

Feigenberg, B., Field, E. M., & Pande, R. (2010). *Building Social Capital Through Microfinance.* HKS Faculty Research Working Paper Series, RWP10-019, John F. Kennedy School of Government, Harvard University.

Garikipati, S. (2008). The impact of lending to women on household vulnerability and women's empowerment: Evidence from India. *World Development, 36*(12), 2620–2642.

Garikipati, S. (2012). Microcredit and women's empowerment. *Through the Lens of Time Use Data from Rural India. Development and Change, 43*(3), 719–750. doi: 10.1111/dech.2012.43.issue-3

Garikipati, S., Johnson, S., Guérin, I., & Szafarz, A. (2017). Microfinance and gender: Issues, challenges and the road ahead. *The Journal of Development Studies, 53*(5), 641–648.

Gatak, M., & Guinnane, T, W. (1999). The economics of lending with joint liability: Theory and practice. *Journal of Development Economics, 60*(1999), 195–228.

Gertler, P., Levine, D. I., & Moretti, E. (2009). Do microfinance programs help families insure consumption against illness? *Health Economics, 18*(3), 257–273.

Guérin, I., Kumar, S., & Agier, I. (2013). Women's empowerment: Power to act or power over other women? Lessons from Indian microfinance. *Oxford Development Studies, 41*(sup1), S76–94. doi: 10.1080/13600818.2013.781147.

Haldar, A., & Stiglitz, J. (2013). The Indian microfinance crisis: The role of social capital, the shift to for-profit lending and implications for microfinance theory and practice, Working Paper in Global Thought Series, University of Columbia.

Harper, M. (2003). *Microfinance: Evolution, achievements and challenges.* London: ITDG Publishing.

Helms, B. (2006). *Access for all: Building inclusive financial systems.* Washington, DC: World Bank.

Hoque, S. (2004). Micro-credit and the reduction of poverty in Bangladesh. *Journal of Contemporary Asia, 34*(1), 21–32.

Hoque, S. (2005). Micro-credit and empowerment of women: Evidence from Bangladesh. *Asian Economic Review, 47*(3), 411–420.

Hudon, M. (2016) Use of donor funds in financing MFIs. Working Paper: WP-CEB 07-020, CERMi, Brussels.

Hulme, D., & Moore, K. (2007). *Assisting the poorest in Bangladesh: Learning from BRAC's 'targeting the ultra poor' programme,* Brooks World Poverty Institute Working Paper No. 1, University of Manchester.

Hulme, D., & Mosley, P. (1996). *Finance against poverty.* London: Routledge.

Imai, K. S., & Azam, M. D. S. (2012). Does microfinance reduce poverty in Bangladesh? New evidence from household panel data. *Journal of Development Studies, 48*(5), 633–653.

Imai, K. S., Arun, T., & Annim, S. K. (2010). Microfinance and household poverty reduction: New evidence from India. *World Development, 38*(12), 1760–1774.

Imai, K. S., Gaiha, R., Thapa, G., & Annim, S. K. (2012). Microfinance and poverty – A Macro perspective. *World Development, 40*(8), 1675–1689.

Islam, A. (2011). Medium-and Long-Term Participation in Microcredit: An Evaluation Using a New Panel Dataset from Bangladesh. *American Journal of Agricultural Economics, 93*(3), 847–866.

Kabeer, N. (2005a). Direct social impacts for the Millennium development goals. In J. Copestake, M. Greeley, S. Johnson, N. Kabeer, A. Simanowitz, & K. Knotts (Eds.), *Money with a mission, volume 1: Microfinance and poverty reduction.* London: ITDG.

Kabeer, N. (2005b). Is microfinance a 'magic bullet' for women's empowerment? Analysis of findings from South Asia. AQ26 Economic and Political Weekly, 4709–4718.

Kabeer, N. (2017). Economic pathways to women's empowerment and active citizenship: What does the evidence from Bangladesh tell us? *The Journal of Development Studies, 53*(5), 649–663.

Kaboski, J. P., & Townsend, R. M. (2012). The impact of credit on village economies. *American Economic Journal. Applied Economics, 4*(2), 98–133.

Karlan, D., Goldberg, N., & Copestake, J. (2009). Randomized control trials are the best way to measure impact of microfinance programmes and improve microfinance product designs. *Enterprise Development and Microfinance, 20*(3), 167–176.

Karlan, D. S., & Zinman, J. (2007). *Expanding credit access: Using randomized supply decisions to estimate the impacts.* CEPR Discussion Papers: 6180.

Khandker, S. R. (2005). Microfinance and poverty: Evidence using panel data from Bangladesh. *World Bank Economic Review, 19*(2), 263–286.

Kouassi, M. J. (2008). *Microfinance and health: A study of selected countries.* Ph.D. Washington, DC: Howard University.

Li, X., Gan, C., & Hu, B. (2011). The welfare impact of microcredit on rural households in China. *Journal of Socio-Economics, 40*(4), 404–411.

McKernan, S.-M. (2002). The impact of microcredit programs on self-employment profits: Do noncredit program aspects matter? *Review of Economics and Statistics, 84*(1), 93–115.

Morduch, J. (1999). The microfinance promise. *Journal of Economic Literature, 37*(4), 1569–1614.

Nghiem, S., Coelli, T., & Rao, P. (2012). Assessing the welfare effects of microfinance in Vietnam: Empirical results from a quasi-experimental survey. *Journal of Development Studies, 48*(5), 619–632.

Pitt, M. M., & Khandker, S. R. (1998). The impact of group-based credit programs on poor households in Bangladesh: Does the gender of participants matter?. *The Journal of Political Economy, 106*(5), 958–996.

Roodman, D. (2012). Due diligence: An impertinent inquiry into microfinance. CGD Books.

Roodman, D., & Morduch, J. (2013). The impact of microcredit on the poor in Bangladesh: Revisiting the evidence. NYU Wagner Research Paper No. 2231535, 1–49.

Rosenberg, R. (2010). Does microcredit really help poor people? *CGAP Focus Note, Number 59*.

Sebstad, J., & Chen, G. (1996). *Overview of studies on the impact of microenterprise credit*. Washington, DC: Management Systems International.

State of the Microcredit Summit Campaign Report. (2015). Mapping pathways out of poverty. The Microcredit Summit Campaign.

Stewart, R., Van Rooyen, C., Korth, M., Chereni, A., Rebelo Da Silva, N., & De Wet, T. (2012). Do micro-credit, micro-savings and micro-leasing serve as effective financial inclusion interventions enabling poor people, and especially women, to engage in meaningful economic opportunities in low – and middle-income countries? A systematic review of the evidence. EPPI-Centre, Social Science Research Unit, Institute of Education, University of London.

Takahashi, K., Higashikata, T., & Tsukada, K. (2010). The short-term poverty impact of small-scale, collateral-free microcredit in Indonesia: A matching estimator approach. *Developing Economies, 48*(1), 128–155.

Tedeschi, G. A. (2008). Overcoming selection bias in microcredit impact assessments: A case study in Peru. *Journal of Development Studies, 44*(4), 504–518.

Torre, M. L., & Vento, G. (2006). *Microfinance*. New York: Palgrave Macmillan.

Vaessen, J., Leeuw, F., Bonilla, S., Rivas, A., Lukach, R., & Bastiaensen, J., Hombrados, J, G., & Waddington, H. (2013). *The effect of microcredit on women's control over household spending in developing countries*. London: International Initiative for Impact Evaluation.

van Rooyen, C., Stewart, R., & De Wet, T. (2012). The impact of microfinance in sub-Saharan Africa: A systematic review of the evidence. *World Development, 40*(11), 2249–2262.

Wood, G., & Sharif, I. (1997). *Who needs credit?: Poverty and finance in Bangladesh*. London: Zed Books.

Wydick, B. (1999). The effect of microenterprise lending on child schooling in Guatemala. *Economic Development and Cultural Change, 47*(4), 853–869.

Yunus, M. (2008). Turning beggars into entrepreneurs. *NPQ: New Perspectives Quarterly, 25*(2), 88–89. Doi: 10.1111/j.1540-5842.2008.00990.x.

Zeller, M., Sharma, M., Ahmed, A. U., & Rashid, S. (2001). *Group-based financial institutions for the rural poor in Bangladesh: An institutional – and household-level analysis research report 120.* Washington, DC: International Food Policy Research Institute.

Supriya Garikipati completed her doctoral studies in development economics from the University of Cambridge in 2001, soon after which she joined the Department of Applied Economics at Cambridge as a Research Associate. She moved to Liverpool in 2003, where she is a Reader in International Development at the University of Liverpool Management School. She is also the Director of Research Impact for the School and convenor of the – Development Research Initiative (DRIve) – which facilitates networking among academics and practitioners working in international development.Within the discipline of development, her research mainly examines the impact of public policy interventions with a focus on gender and poverty. Her work includes the impact assessment of India's microfinance program, an assessment of its pro-poor approach to economic liberalisation and the impact of feminisation of agricultural labour in India. More recently, she has started to explore the driving factors behind fundamental human behaviour like trust and discrimination and their impact on development policy. One of her current projects examines the interplay of colour, caste and class in modern India, especially the implications for its employment and marital markets. She is also interested in women's reproductive health and has two active projects in this area – one exploring holistic menstrual care services for slum women and another to enhance reproductive health curriculums for adolescent school girls to improve their reproductive knowledge outcomes. While the geographical focus of her research is mainly India, Dr Garikipati also has research interests in the development experiences of Africa and the UK.

Dr Garikipati's work has been published in several high-ranking development journals like *Development and Change; European Journal of Development Research; Journal of Development Studies; Journal of International Development; Journal of Peasant Studies; World Development; World Economy* and many more. She has also co-edited several special issues in journals and contributed to significant reference books in this area. She has led on several international projects sponsored, among others, by DFID, British Academy, Newton Trust and ESRC.

8

The Stock Market Development and Economic Growth Puzzle: Empirical Evidence from Africa

Gideon Boako and Paul Alagidede

8.1 Introduction

Like the chicken and egg puzzle, the debate among economists on whether financial market development leads economic growth or whether the former is a consequence of increased economic activity still lingers on. Inspired by the pioneering work of Irving Fisher in 1907 on the nexus between asset markets and real economic growth, several approaches have been adopted in different dimensions to examine the dynamic interactions between financial development and economic growth. Historically, Schumpeter (1911) highlights the role played by the banking system and technological innovations in driving economic growth, arguing that the push in innovation and future growth is as a result of the banking sector's ability to advance credits to businesses or productive investments (see also Hicks 1969). Levine (2005) advances claims to support Schumpeter's view by outlining several channels by

G. Boako (✉) · P. Alagidede
University of the Witwatersrand Business School, Johannesburg, South Africa
e-mail: gboako@gmail.com; Paul.Alagidede@wits.ac.za

which financial institutions and markets could spur economic growth: (i) through the mobilization and pooling of savings from investors, (i) provision of efficient payment services to facilitate the exchange of goods and services, (iii) undertaking proper corporate governance strategies (iv) proper allocation of savings into productive uses and (v) increasing liquidity, diversifying, and reducing intertemporal risk. In contrast to the above, Gurley and Shaw (1955, 1960) and Goldsmith (1969) suggest that a developing economy fosters an inter-mediated bank debt finance and later the emergence of equity markets as an additional instrument for raising external funds. Robinson (1952) believes that banks react positively to economic growth. Additionally, Demirguc-Kunt and Levine (1996, p. 225) argue that a country's 'financial structure – the mix of financial intermediaries and markets – changes as the country develops'.

From the above, it thus appears that the contention on the lead-lag relationship between finance and growth in the extant literature and theory appears far from settled. This chapter makes a contribution by exploring the current literature on the subject and examine a specific aspect of financial development on growth in Africa – the stock market channel. The focus on Africa arises from the sparse nature of related studies on the continent (see Ngare et al. 2014). Given the recent volatile growth trajectory and efforts at enhancing balanced and sustainable economic performance, an understanding of the relationship between stock market development and economic growth could well inform economic policy. Further, Africa has witnessed tremendous upsurge in the number of stock markets since the late 1980s. Evidence of their role in indigenisation and the entire economic development process is essential in enabling the markets function efficiently.

8.2   Overview of Stock Markets Development in Africa

During the past three decades, tremendous efforts have been pursued to ensure the growth and development of Africa's nascent equity markets. Part of the drive are efforts aimed at integrating African stock markets at the regional and global levels. This has led to the adoption of various strategies including the formation of regional blocks and associations to monitor and coordinate the transformation agenda. Inspired by such initiatives as the Abuja Treaty establishing the African Economic Community (AEC) on 12 May 1994; the Common Markets for Eastern and Southern Africa (COMESA); the Southern African Development Community (SADC); the West African Monetary Union (WAMU), the Bourse Régionale des Valeurs Mobilières in West Africa; and many others, significant strides have been made to formally integrate and harmonize African stock markets regionally and globally. Perhaps, on the wings of these are the improvements in the overall equity market performances across the continent, though at a modest pace and levels below other emerging markets. As can be seen from Table 8.1, with about 27 properly functioning exchanges (ASEA 2014), total number of listed companies in Sub-Saharan African (SSA) equity markets increased from 911 in 2005 to 932 in 2011, though highly incomparable to corresponding figures from South Asia, East Asia, and Pacific. With the exception of South Africa, liquidity levels of African stock exchanges are very low, exerting significant setbacks on the growth of markets. Between 2005 and 2011, total market capitalization of SSA stocks increased from US$605,113 to US$951,930, with South Africa alone accounting for 93.4% (2005) and 90.0% (2011). Growth in turn-over ratios (values of traded shares as a percentage of market capitalization) in SSA appears stalled between 2005 and 2011, decreasing marginally from 37.3% to 37.2%.

Based on the development indicators shown in Table 8.1, stock markets in Africa can be categorized into four, similar to the classifications by Smith et al. (2002):

i. South Africa – the largest and the oldest stock market in SSA.
ii. A group of medium-sized markets, consisting of Egypt, Kenya, Nigeria, Morocco, Tunisia, and Zimbabwe.
iii. A group of small, but rapidly growing markets, consisting of Botswana, Cote d'Ivoire, Ghana, Namibia, and Mauritius.
iv. A group of very small markets consisting of Libya, Malawi, Mozambique, Sudan, Swaziland, Tanzania, Uganda, and Zambia which are struggling to take off.

Table 8.1 Indicators of capital market development in SSA and the rest of the world

	Market Capitalization				Market Liquidity		Turnover Ratio		Listed Companies	
	US$ million		% of GDP		Value of shares traded (%of GDP)					
	2005	2011	2005	2010	2005	2010	2005	2011	2005	2011
Sub-Saharan Africa	605,113	951,930	128.6	149.5	43.3	46.6	37.3	37.2	911	932
South Africa	565,408	856,711	228.9	278.4	81.2	93.5	39.3	39.8	388	355
Nigeria	19,356	39,270	17.2	26.3	1.7	2.7	11.5	9.2	214	196
Kenya	6,384	10,203	34.1	46.0	2.7	3.5	9.8	7.1	47	58
Botswana	2,437	4,107	23.8	27.4	0.4	0.9	1.8	3.6	18	23
Cote D'ivoire	2,327	6,288	14.2	31.2	0.2	0.6	1.4	1.8	39	33
Ghana	1,661	3,097	15.5	11.3	0.6	0.3	3.2	4.1	30	36
Zambia	989	4,009	13.8	17.4	0.2	1.6	2.0	-	15	20
Tanzania	588	1,539	4.2	5.5	0.1	0.1	2.3	2.5	6	17
East Asia & Pacific	1,212,704	4,638,422	40.1	79.9	25.6	113.3	68.4	154.3	3,931	5,181
Europe & Central Asia	789,576	1,116,849	48.7	51.8	22.7	42.7	61.6	121.1	6,564	4,368
Latin Amercia & Carribean	1,028,157	2,274,1911	40.5	57.6	9.9	22.9	28.4	46.4	1,504	1,446
Middle East & North Africa	135,018	265,561	36.8	34.6	7.2	7.5	39.3	19.4	1,531	1,012
South Asia	609,110	1,095,645	58.8	81.9	55.7	52.6	111.6	55.4	6,050	6,400
Euro Area	6,357,326	5,482,967	62.7	51.7	73.1	47.1	120.5	110.4	6,737	6,250

Source: World development indicators (2012).

In Table 8.2, we analyse the development characteristics of 21 African equity markets as at end of 2014. It is observed that the primary activities on most African stock markets are the issuance of bonds and equities with predominantly online and intraday trading mechanisms. The exceptional market is the South African Johannesburg Stock Exchange (JSE) that issues bonds, equities, and derivatives with online, margin, and intraday trading mechanisms.[1] Despite the continent's tremendous efforts towards global commodity production, the markets for commodities in national stock exchanges are virtually non-existing. From Table 8.2, it is noticed that most African stock markets have electronic trading systems, trade for averagely 5 hours, and have a three-day settlement period. These developments are, however, new and may not be seen to have impacted the performances of individual markets (UNDP 2003; Moin 2007). As Ntim et al. (2011) observe, as at 2005, only the markets in Egypt, Nigeria, and South Africa had electronic trading systems. Despite the major setbacks, one interesting development in the continent's stock markets is the openness to foreign participation, though individual countries have some restrictions to non-resident foreign investors' holdings on local bourses.

It does appear that the struggle to move African stock markets from manual and automation trading systems is yielding significant results. That notwithstanding, structural developments in stock markets in Africa still lag behind their global and other merging market counterparts. Currently, African stock markets are organized as mutual entities (Senbet and Otchere 2008) whilst demutualization is the order of the day. Demutualization breaks the jinx of monopoly, enhances gains from competition, and improves corporate governance. Additionally demutualization transforms an exchange from a non-profit entity into a profit entity through a change in the legal status and governance structure in the exchange (Senbet and Otchere 2008). Though data on the status of demutualization on African stock exchanges is not known with exactitude,

---

[1] *It is worth noting that the Egyptian Stock Market also has intraday, online, and margin trading mechanism.*

Table 8.2 Institutional, operational, and infrastructural development characteristics of African stock markets as at end of 2014

Market	Trading mechanism			Trading hours	Trading system	ASEA status	Foreign investment	Commodities exchange	Clearing and settlement	Demutualization	Primary market activity
	Margin	Intraday	Online								
Botswana	No	Yes	Yes	10^{30}–13^{30}	Automated	Yes	Yes	No	T + 3	No	Bond & equity
Cote D'Ivoire	No	Yes	No	8^{30}–10^{30}	Electronic	Yes	Yes	No	T + 3	No	Bond & equity
Tunisia	No	No	Yes	9^{00}–14^{10}	Electronic		Yes	No	T + 3	–	Bond, cash & equity
Casablanca	No	Yes	Yes	9^{00}–15^{40}	Electronic		Yes	No	T + 3	–	Bond & equity
Tanzania	No	No	Yes	10^{00}–14^{00}	Automated		Yes	No	T + 3	–	Bond & equity
Cameroon		Yes		9^{00}–11^{00}	Electronic		Yes	No	T + 3	–	Bond & equity
Egypt	Yes	Yes	Yes	9^{45}–14^{30}	Electronic		Yes	No	T + 3	–	Bond, cash & equity
Ghana	Yes	No	Yes	9^{30}–15^{30}	Automated		Yes	No	T + 3	–	Bond & equity
South Africa	Yes	Yes	Yes	9^{00}–17^{00}	Electronic		Yes	Yes	T + 5	–	Derivatives, interest rate & equity
Rwanda	No	Yes	No	9^{00}–12^{00}	Electronic		Yes	No	T + 2	Yes	Bond & equity
Zambia	Yes	Yes	Yes	11^{00}–14^{00}	Automated		Yes	Yes	T + 3		Bond & equity
Malawi	Yes	Yes	Yes	10^{30}–13^{30}	Manual		Yes	No	T + 5	No	Equity
Mauritius	No	Yes	Yes	9^{00}–13^{30}	Electronic		Yes	No	T + 3	–	Bond & equity
Mozambique	No	Yes	Yes	8^{00}–16^{00}	Electronic		Yes	No	T + 3	–	Bond & equity
Kenya	No	Yes	No	9^{00}–15^{00}	Electronic		Yes		T + 3	–	Bond & equity
Namibia	Yes	Yes	No	9^{00}–17^{10}	Electronic		Yes	No	T + 5	–	Bond & equity
Nigeria	Yes	Yes	Yes	9^{30}–14^{30}	Electronic		Yes	No	T + 3	–	Bond & equity
Uganda	No	No	No	10^{00}–12^{00}	Manual		No	No	T + 5	–	Bond, cash & equity
Zimbabwe	No	Yes	No	10^{00}–11^{00}	Manual		Yes	No	T + 7	–	Equity
Sudan	No	Yes	No	10^{00}–11^{00}	Electronic		Yes	No	T + 5	–	Equity
Cape Verde	No	Yes	Yes	8^{30}–15^{00}	Automated		No	No	T + 0	–	Bond & equity

Source: African Securities Exchanges Association (ASEA), World Federation of Exchanges (WFE), and websites of all exchanges.

some countries have initiated the process and it is expected that within the next decade some successes will be chalked.[2]

In Table 8.3, results of statistical properties of some individual African stock markets and four regional markets are shown. The evidence from Table 8.3 (Panels A, B, and C) shows that daily mean returns and standard deviations (SDs) of all markets were higher during the 2007–2009 global financial crisis (GFC) period than the two non-crisis periods. The higher mean returns and SDs (our crude measure of risk) in Panel B may be attributed to the effects of the GFC. All the series exhibit positive skewness and depict excess kurtosis across samples. Thus, the probability distributions are skewed to the right and have leptokurtic behaviour with fat tails than a corresponding normal distribution. These signs fail to accept the assumptions of normality of the series, which is corroborated by the high significance of the JB test for normality. A robustness examination of the descriptive features for the full sample period using both returns and log series (though not shown for brevity of exposition) confirms the above results, except that individual African markets display both positive and negative skewness with the log index series. Bekaert and Harvey (2014) explain that individual emerging markets are generally positively skewed; however, growth experiences appear country-specific, whereas some of the downside moves are common across countries, causing negative skewness at the index level. The results give some indication that, though smaller and relatively illiquid, individual and regional stock market indices in Africa exhibit certain characteristics that quite mimic the behaviour of highly developed and emerging markets in other economies.

8.2.1 Stock Market and Economic Growth: Survey of the Theoretical Literature

Both the theoretical and empirical strands on the financial development and economic growth literature have been extensively explored. From the Schumpeterian 1911 argument stressing the role of technological

---

[2] For example, the Ghana Stock Exchange (GSE) initiated the process of market demutualization in 2015 though implementation has stalled.

Table 8.3 Descriptive statistics of African stock markets

	Mean (%)	Std. (%)	Skew.	Kurt.	JB @ 1%	Min.	Max.
Panel A: Pre-crisis period – 3 January 2003 to 14 September 2008							
Botswana	0.286	1.317	6.460	53.938	117830.6	0.000	0.160
Egypt	1.166	1.431	2.033	8.397	1948.1	0.000	0.093
Ghana	0.208	1.114	7.127	59.503	144883.9	0.000	0.128
Kenya	0.756	0.913	4.026	30.091	34080.7	0.000	0.111
Morocco	0.774	0.779	2.711	15.836	8284.7	0.000	0.081
Nigeria	0.867	0.901	3.351	27.645	27830.7	0.000	0.104
South Africa	1.143	1.014	1.795	7.398	1375.0	0.000	0.069
Tunisia	0.454	0.382	1.561	6.586	964.6	0.000	0.028
East Africa	0.088	0.121	3.787	24.872	22858.7	0.000	0.012
North Africa	0.060	0.065	2.578	11.991	4582.6	5.59E-07	0.005
Southern Africa	1.134	1.008	1.791	7.376	1364.2	0.000	0.068
West Africa	0.759	0.771	2.695	17.898	10709.6	0.000	0.079
Panel B: Crisis period – 15 September 2008 to 31 May 2009							
Botswana	1.040	0.906	1.386	5.480	87.0	0.000	0.049
Egypt	0.729	0.708	1.182	4.171	43.8	0.000	0.033
Ghana	0.635	1.144	3.761	19.492	2067.3	0.000	0.071
Kenya	1.365	1.393	2.208	9.507	389.1	0.000	0.083
Morocco	1.522	1.382	1.672	6.547	149.5	0.000	0.074
Nigeria	1.627	1.538	1.566	6.896	157.2	0.000	0.089
South Africa	3.164	2.636	1.472	5.431	91.7	0.000	0.129
Tunisia	0.849	0.894	2.502	12.550	731.4	7.05E-05	0.064
East Africa	0.236	0.256	1.987	7.292	215.3	0.000	0.014
North Africa	0.147	1.343	1.643	6.272	135.3	2.61E-05	0.007
Southern Africa	3.158	2.630	1.482	5.473	93.8	0.000	0.129
West Africa	1.519	1.280	1.680	7.831	217.7	0.000	0.079
Panel C: Post-crisis period – 1 June 2009 to 29 December 2014							
Botswana	0.551	0.530	2.594	15.737	11200.2	0.000	0.054
Egypt	1.089	1.393	2.322	10.464	4575.4	0.000	0.109
Ghana	0.651	0.787	2.562	11.849	6190.0	0.000	0.059
Kenya	0.548	0.538	2.607	14.589	9560.7	0.000	0.052
Morocco	0.973	0.981	2.354	11.637	5729.3	0.000	0.087
Nigeria	0.916	0.896	1.996	8.882	2992.6	0.000	0.073

Table 8.3 (continued)

	Mean (%)	Std. (%)	Skew.	Kurt.	JB @ 1%	Min.	Max.
South Africa	1.169	1.010	1.843	8.254	2438.4	0.000	0.076
Tunisia	0.511	0.492	2.597	13.856	8574.5	3.89E-06	0.038
East Africa	0.092	0.093	2.167	10.011	4022.5	0.000	0.007
North Africa	0.078	0.088	2.933	16.023	12080.1	2.30E-07	0.008
Southern Africa	1.148	1.016	1.913	8.600	2723,3	0.000	0.076
West Africa	0.883	0.757	1.951	8.825	2910.4	0.000	0.063

Notes: Std.: standard deviation; Skew: skewness; kurt: kurtosis; JB.: Jarque-Bera; Min.: Minimum; Max.: Maximum.

innovation as the driving force of long-run economic growth suggesting that innovation influences the financial sector's capacity to advance credit to 'growth agents'; several others have given varied views on exactly the channels of theoretical linkages existing between financial sector development and economic growth (see for example, Hicks 1969; Goldsmith 1969; Shaw 1973; McKinnon 1973; Robinson 1952; Castaneda 2006; etc.). Whilst the theoretical explorations have variedly considered economic growth linkages with stock markets fundamental measures of development such as market capitalizations, earnings ratio, liquidity levels, and so on, others consider the nexus with economic growth from the point of financial intermediaries such as banks (example, Bagehot 1873; Schumpeter 1911). For example, the early 1990s studies on the nexus between financial development and growth stemmed from the insights and techniques of endogenous growth models, mainly linking growth rates to preferences, technology, income distribution, and institutional arrangements (Pagano 1993). It is important to stress that both early and recent literature do not practically converge on strictly common theoretical linkages between financial sector development and economic growth.

Pagano (1993) applied a simple endogenous growth model and captured four potential effects of financial development on economic growth: the proportion of saving funnelled to investment, improvement in the allocation of capital, the social marginal productivity of capital, and the effects on savings rates (see Pagano 1993 for detailed explanations). In a related fashion, Levine (2005) proposes that financial institutions can affect economic growth through the following channels: (i) easing the exchange of goods and services through the provision of payment services, (ii) mobilization and pooling of savings from investors, (iii) acquiring and processing information about enterprises and possible investments projects, (iv) investment monitoring and corporate governance, (v) reducing intertemporal risk, diversifying, and liquidity enhancement.

Central to the discussions on finance-growth nexus are four main theoretical strands: financial deepening promotes economic growth (Schumpeter 1911; McKinnon 1973; Shaw 1973), economic growth enhances financial development, financial development and economic growth are 'mutually causal' (Demetriades and Hussain 1996; Greenwood and Smith 1997), and the hypothesis that no causal relationship exist between finance and economic growth (Lucas 1988; Graff 1999). This leads principally to two main hypotheses: 'supply leading' and 'demand-following' hypotheses (see Menyah et al. 2014). The 'supply leading' hypothesis underscores the influential role of financial development in spurring economic growth through increases in savings growth rates which lead to higher capital formation, to in turn affect economic growth (Menyah et al. 2014; King and Levine 1993). The study by Schumpeter (1911) shows the importance of the banking system in economic growth and outlines circumstances under which banks can spur innovation and future growth through the funding of investments projects. Conversely, the 'demand-following' hypothesis suggests that finance can only be seen as a by-product of economic growth, and not the reverse (Robinson 1952). Menyah et al. (2014) expounds on this hypothesis with the view that a booming economy enhances the springing up and growth of financial institutions, financial products and services in the market leading to increased demand for financial assets. Earlier, Gurley and Shaw (1955, 1960) and Goldsmith, Raymond (1969) suggest that as economies develop, self-financed capital investment gives way to bank-intermediated debt finance and later to the emergence of equity markets as an additional factor instrument for raising external funds. In fact, Lucas (1988) believed that economist 'badly over-stress' the role of the financial system in growth. These two hypotheses aside, some schools of thought suggest that both financial sector development and economic growth are potentially *sine qua non* to the enhancement and sustainability of each other – hence, the emphasis on the 'mutually causal' relationship between the two (see for example, Blackburn et al. 2005; Greenwood and Smith 1997).

Drawing on the functional approach of Levine (1997), financial markets facilitates the efficient functioning of private and public investment projects. Through ownership representation of large-caped/valued assets, financial markets ensure markets liquidity and promote the efficient allocation of capital (Nieuwerburgh et al. 2006). By giving investors a wide range of assets to invest in, financial institutions allow for diversification and risk-mitigation, as well as improving the quality and quantity of international funds. Narrowly on stock markets development and economic growth, the theoretical literature has largely dwelled on three main channels: liquidity, integration, and diversification (see also Castenada 2006). On liquidity – *the implied cost of trading shares* – it is argued that liquidity reduces the disincentives to investing long-duration projects since investors can easily sell their stake for savings before the maturity of projects (Bencivenga et al. 1995). Florackis et al. (2014) contend that markets liquidity can act as signalling mechanism, showing the information set of investors. Thus, during periods of negative economic outlook or uncertainties, investors in liquid markets move their capital away from high-risk investments and invest in safe short-term securities, preferably government debts. The account by Devereux and Smith (1994), supported by Obstfeld (1994), suggests that highly integrated markets facilitate international risk sharing, which induces portfolio shift from safe, low-return investments, thereby resulting in enhanced growth. In contrast, Levine and Zervos (1998) contend that both liquidity and higher risk-sharing and international capital market integration may induce saving rates to fall to levels that can easily slow overall economic growth. The study by Saint-Paul (1992) emphasizes the role of portfolio diversification through growth. The model by the author suggests that efficient risk-sharing through stock markets encourage producers to specialize, and thus enhance productivity, which effectively translates into higher steady-state growth rate in the presence of externalities a la Romer.

Despite their positive effects, some studies also show that the effects of liquidity, integration, and diversification of stock markets on economic growth can be negative. For example, Levine (1997) contends that higher capital markets liquidity can lead to negative economic growth. In the opinion of Demirgui-Kunt and Levine (1996) this can happen through three channels: reduction in savings, impact on uncertainty, and increases in euphoria and myopia associated with stock market liquidity. On diversification, Devereux and Smith (1994) suggest that depending on what characterizes risk-aversion of investors, the potential of risk mitigation by diversifying might reduce precautionary savings.

8.2.2 Stock Market and Economic Growth: Survey of the Empirical Literature

Although the empirical literature on financial systems and economic growth is vast, those focusing mainly on stock markets development variables and economic growth appear scanty, and with much attention to developed than developing or emerging markets. Empirically, the seminal contributions of McKinnon (1973), Shaw (1973), and Levine and Zervos (1998) support the idea that financial development exerts positive impacts on growth. However, Gurley and Shaw (1955) and Jung (1986) argue that development of the financial sector does not necessarily lead to economic growth. Recently, whilst Chaiechi (2012), Zhang et al. (2012), Bittencourt (2012) contend that financial sector development positively influences economic growth, Carp (2012) believes otherwise, with Blackburn et al. (2005) and Odhiambo (2007) implying mutually causal effects between the two.

Despite the conventionality of extant studies on the financial development and economic growth literature, not much focus on stock markets. Among the few are: Levine and Zervos (1998), Mayer (1988), Beck and Levine (2002), Caporale et al. (2004). The empirical findings on stock market-economic growth nexus literature mainly support one of the four theoretical hypothesis outlined above (i.e. supply-following, demand-leading, mutual causality, or no causality). Empirical studies supporting the supply-leading hypothesis produce mixed results. Chaiechi (2012) establish that stock market capitalization and domestic credit availability are strongly responsible for stimulating investment, saving and productivity growth in Hong Kong. Moreover, the studies of Harris (1997), Levine and Zervos (1998), Caporale et al. (2004), Tang (2006), Saci et al. (2009), among others, establish that stock markets development positively promote economic growth. On the other hand, some other studies contend that by promoting asymmetric information on companies, the effect of stock markets on growth becomes detrimental to savings growth, and hence economic development (see for example, Devereux and Smith 1994; Morck et al. 1990; Stiglitz 1985). Another argument is that liquid stock markets may lead to lower savings rates due to externalities in capital accumulation (Enisan and Olufisayo 2009). Example of studies supporting the demand-following hypothesis are Odhiambo (2010), Liang and Teng (2006), Zang and Kim (2007). Whilst Rousseau and Vuthipadadorn (2005) and Apergis et al. (2007) support the mutually causal hypothesis, authors like Lucas (1998) find no such relationship, and Tiwari et al. (2015) find uni-directional causation from stock markets to economic growth. In fact, Levine and Zervos (1998) in one breadth suggest that stock market size, volatility, and international integration are not robustly linked with growth – see also De Gregorio and Guidotti (1995).

Methodological approach for estimating the relationship between stock market development and economic growth vary from one study to the other. The studies of Atje and Jovanovic (1993) and Harris (1997) using cross-sectional data estimation techniques conclude that stock markets development enhance economic growth – see also studies using panel and cross-sectional data such as King and Levine (1993), Fernadez and Galetovic (1994), Saci et al. (2009), Zhang et al. (2012), Bittencourt (2012). The common critique of the cross-sectional approach is that it fails to capture individual country market conditions such as financial institutions, policy regimes, and governance effectiveness (Arestis and Demetriades 1997). In fact, Arestis et al. (2001) suggest that the contribution of stock markets on economic growth may tend to be exaggerated by studies that utilize cross-country growth regressions. Bayraktar (2014) advises that because country's characteristics are different, measures that take into account country-specific characteristics can provide useful information on the development level of stock markets across countries, and consequently provide a more accurate categorization based on different problems such as unsustainable expansions or shallow financial markets.

Unlike other developed economies that have some considerable attention in the literature, African countries have not enjoyed the same attention from authors on the finance-growth nexus theme. Enisan and Olufisayo (2009) examine the long-run and causal relationship between stock market development and economic growth of seven sub-Saharan African countries. Applying the autoregressive distributed lag (ARDL) model and Granger causality test; the authors find evidence of positive co-integration and causality of stock market development and economic growth for Egypt and South Africa, with the causality running from stock markets to growth. The causality, however, was found to be bi-directional for Cote D'Ivoire, Kenya, Morocco, and Zimbabwe. Ahmed and Mmolainyane (2014) study the impact of financial integration on growth in Botswana from 1974 to 2009 and find a direct and robust significant association between financial integration and economic growth. The conclusion by the authors is that, the government of Botswana could strengthen and develop the capital market to internationally acceptable standards as a means to attract both local and foreign investors and encourage foreign direct investments in non-mining sectors – see also, Akinboade (1998) and Eita and Jordaan (2010). However, Meshach (2007) report that financial integration has no strong positive impact on GDP per capita growth in Botswana. By examining the relationship between private capital flows and economic growth in Africa during 1990 and 2007, Agbloyor et al. (2014) suggests that strong financial markets are needed for private capital flows to impact economic growth positively.

Studies on Africa examining the link between financial development and economic growth report varying results. Agbetsiafia (2004) and Ndako (2010) report of a uni-directional causality running from financial development to economic growth. However, Atindehou et al. (2005) find evidence of weak causal relationship for 12 African countries studied. Whilst Quartey and Prah (2008) for Ghana and Odhiambo (2007) for Kenya and South Africa find evidence in support of the demand-following hypothesis, the finding by Odhiambo (2007) in the case of Tanzania supported the supply-leading hypothesis.

8.3 What Determines Stock Market Development?

Although finance literature is replete with studies on the nexus between stock market development and economic growth, the question of what exactly is the definition of stock market development and the determining factors of stock markets development appear far from settled. The theoretical literature also appears silent on the issues raised above. That notwithstanding, some extant studies highlight the multifaceted nature on the issue of determinants of stock market development (Demirgui-Kunt and Levine 1996). Common among the determinants identified in the literature are market size, market liquidity, and integration with global capital markets. Some studies also corroborate the above but present some interesting dimensions. Some recent studies also highlight the effects of factors such as institutions, legal frameworks, corporate governance, macroeconomic variables and so on, as drivers of stock market development (Billmeier and Masa 2009). For example, Pagano (1993) argues that the existence of transparency and regulations increases investor confidence and exerts significant impact on financial markets development. The conclusion of Billmeier and Masa (2009) is that both institutions and remittances have significant positive impact on stock market capitalization, a metric identified in the literature as synonymous to stock markets development.

Bayraktar (2014) observes that the first natural step to understand and compare stock markets is to identify some performance benchmarks and measurements. The summary of the papers by Demirgui-Kunt and

Levine (1996), Levine and Zervos (1998), and Nieuwerburgh et al. (2006) identify the following fundamental factors as the determinants of stock market development[3]:

- Size – capitalization: the value of listed domestic shares on domestic exchanges per gross domestic product (GDP).
- Liquidity indicators: measured by two metrics: (a) turn-over ratio, which is the value of trades of domestic shares on domestic exchanges per value of listed domestic shares; and (b) value traded which equals the value of trades of domestic shares per GDP.
- Concentration as a measure of financial depth
- International integration measures
- The cumulative number of initial public offerings (IPO)
- Volatility: measured as a 12-month rolling standard deviation estimate based on market returns
- Institutional development.

Of the above indicators, market size appears to be the dominant determinant of stock market development agreed upon in the literature (see also Bayraktar 2014). Beck et al. (2000) outlines common indicators of stock market capitalization in percent of GDP as: indicators of activity (as the ratio of stock market total value traded in percent of GDP), and indicators of efficiency (as the stock market turnover ratio) – see also studies such as Arestis et al. (2001), Beck and Dimirguc-Kunt (2009), Cihak et al. (2012), and Barajas et al. (2013). The common practice among most of these studies is the comparison of the size of market capitalization in percent of GDP across countries as one indicator of financial deepening and identifies countries with high shares as those with strong financial deepening (Bayraktar 2014). However, Bayraktar (2014) criticizes this approach arguing that since countries have different stock market characteristics, the share measure does not consider any hints about the capacity of countries and their effort in the stock market development process. Instead, the author argues in favour of a more

---

[3] See the cited references for details.

comprehensive measure that takes into account individual country characteristics to give accurate picture of the state of financial systems. In line with this, Bayraktar (2014) uses regression estimates to construct benchmarks to compare capacity and efforts for market capitalization for different countries. Here market capitalization capacity is defined as the predicted value of stock market capitalization estimated through panel regressions, considering a country's specific macroeconomic, financial, and institutional characteristics. Similarly, a market capitalization effort is defined as an index of the ratio of actual market capitalization to a country's capacity for market capitalization.

8.3.1 Evolution of Stock Market Development and Economic Growth in Africa

Figures 8.1(a) and (b) depict trends of stock markets and economic developments in Africa. The figures show how average percentage turn-over ratios of domestic shares and market capitalizations (%) of African stocks are related to average continental GDP growth (%), FDI-net inflows (% of GDP), gross savings (% of GDP), and gross capital formation (% of GDP).

A-priori to the trend analysis, stock markets have been noted to play significant roles in the development of the economy. This has been identified in the risk-sharing enhancing opportunities (diversification) of stock markets, ability to promote investments productivity and efficiency, stimulate the acquisition of information about firms and potential investors, and assisting in the raising of liquidity (Greenwood and Smith 1997; Levine and Zervos 1998). Figure 8.1(a) presents the following observations about the average continental market capitalizations of listed firms and four measures of economic development – FDI-net inflows (% GDP), percentage GDP growth, gross capital formation (% GDP), and gross savings (% GDP):

(a) Excluding the period before 1996 where percentage GDP growth and market capitalization appear to move in sync, a negative relationship is observed for the two variables from 1997 to 2014. GDP growth is observed to increase (bend upwards) whilst market

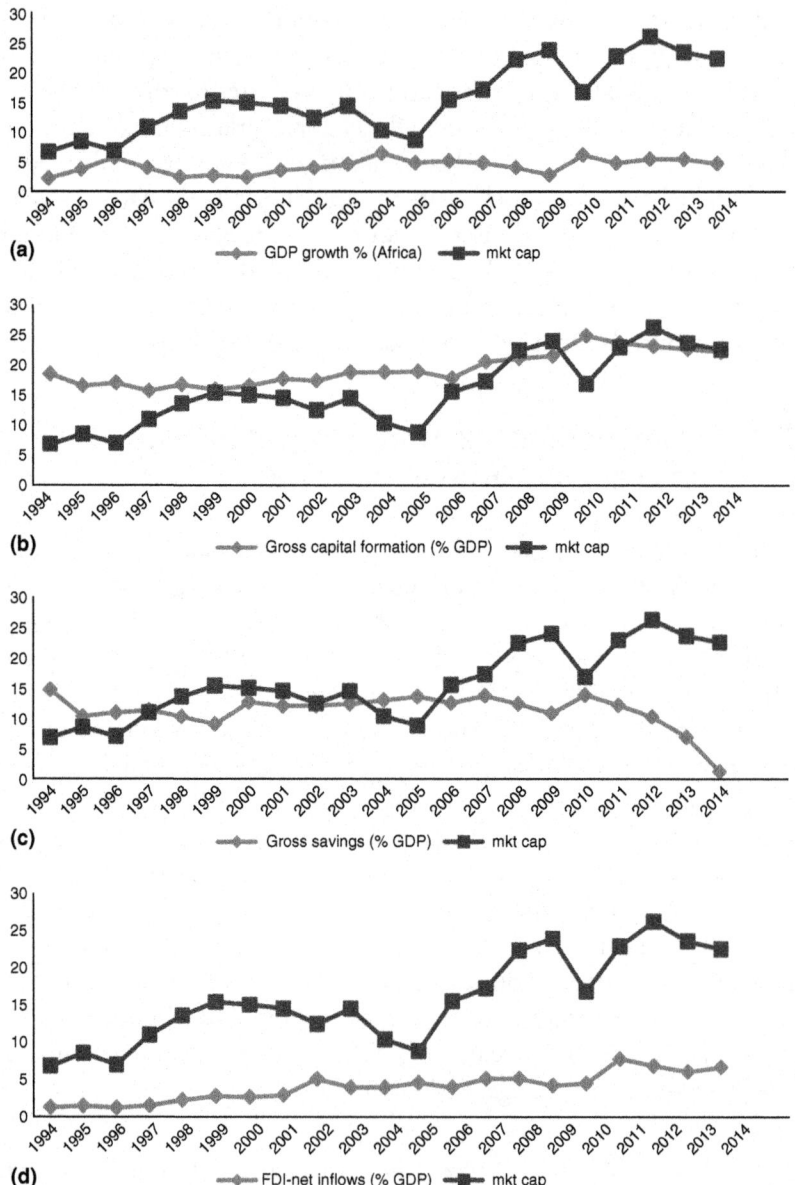

Fig. 8.1 Graphs of economic development indicators and a measure of stock market performance (proxied by market capitalization). All variables are continental averages

capitalization decreases (bend downwards). However, the growth pattern of the two variables is not uniform as some cyclical sharp declines (rises) are observed for GDP growth (market capitalizations) for the periods 2004–2005 and 2010 respectively.

(b) In 1999 gross capital formation (% GDP) and market capitalization nearly converged at 15%; however, the preceding period of 1996–1998 saw the latter rising whilst the former declined. Despite this, growth in gross capital formation was higher throughout the period until 2008–2009 and 2012–2013 where the average market capitalization of listed firms in the continent outgrew the continental average gross capital formation (% GDP).

(c) Between 1998–2003 and 2006–2014 average market capitalization was higher than average gross savings (% GDP). In 1995, 1997, and 2002, both variables assumed growths very closer to each other.

(d) Similar to GDP growth, trends in FDI-net inflows in Africa have been very anaemic to growth trends of listed domestic firms market capitalization. The highest percentage growth in FDI-net inflows of 6.7 recorded in 2014 is even lower than the smallest percentage market capitalization of 6.9 recorded in 1994.

From Fig. 8.1(b), it is observed that both FDI-net inflows (% GDP) and GDP growth (%) have positive asymptotic co-movement with average stocks traded of listed firms from 1994 to 2014. However, although similar positive co-movement is observed in the cases of gross savings and gross capital formation, they individually appear to close-up with stocks traded along the paths. Despite the positive relationships, stocks traded has always dominated all the measures of economic development.

In view of the above observations, it is plausible to posit that, while Africa's economic growth may be stimulated by a number of factors, developments in the capital markets (stocks) could also have its own influence to exert either positively or negatively.

It is instructive to note that relative to other regions, evidence of stock market development in Africa is very harrowing. In Sub-Saharan African (SSA) total market capitalization of equity markets increased from US $605,113 million in 2005 to US$732,438 million in 2012. Of this, South Africa alone accounted for US$565,408 million and US$612,308 million in 2005 and 2012 respectively. The total number of listed companies on all exchanges in SSA moved marginally from 911 (2005) to 923 (2012) compared to other emerging economies such as East Asia Pacific with 3,931 (5,311) and South Asia: 6,050 (6,496) in years 2005 (2012) respectively. In a similar fashion, by 2012, turn-over ratios (values of traded shares as a percentage of market capitalization) in SSA markets increased slightly from 37.3% in 2005 to 47.2% in 2012, anaemic to that of East Asia Pacific of 68.4% (2005) and 127.7% (2012).[4] The above statistics suggests that, except South Africa, African stock markets are generally small in size, immature, and have low levels of liquidity (Figs 8.1 and 8.2).

8.4 Empirical Analysis: Stock Markets- Economic Growth Nexus in Africa

8.4.1 Summary Statistics and Correlations

We start the empirical assessments of the relationship between stock market development and economic growth in Africa with descriptive statistics and correlation matrix. We use annual averages of two measures of stock market performance (*stocks traded and market capitalization*), and four measures of economic development (*FDI-net inflows, Gross capital formation, Gross savings, and GDP growth*). The summary statistics are presented in Table 8.4. The results depict substantial variance among the variables. For example, average annual continental growth in gross capital formation, gross savings, and market capitalization were very high at respectively 19.4%, 11.3%, and 15.7% from 1994 to 2014. The net inflow of FDIs into Africa for the same period was very low (at a growth of 4.0%) similar to the GDP growth rate of 4.4%. It follows from the mean values that, though listed firms recorded higher market capitalizations, trading activities slowed, perhaps on account of the low

---

[4] Unless stated otherwise, figures are gleaned largely from World Development Indicators Database (2015) – http://wdi.worldbank.org/table/5.4

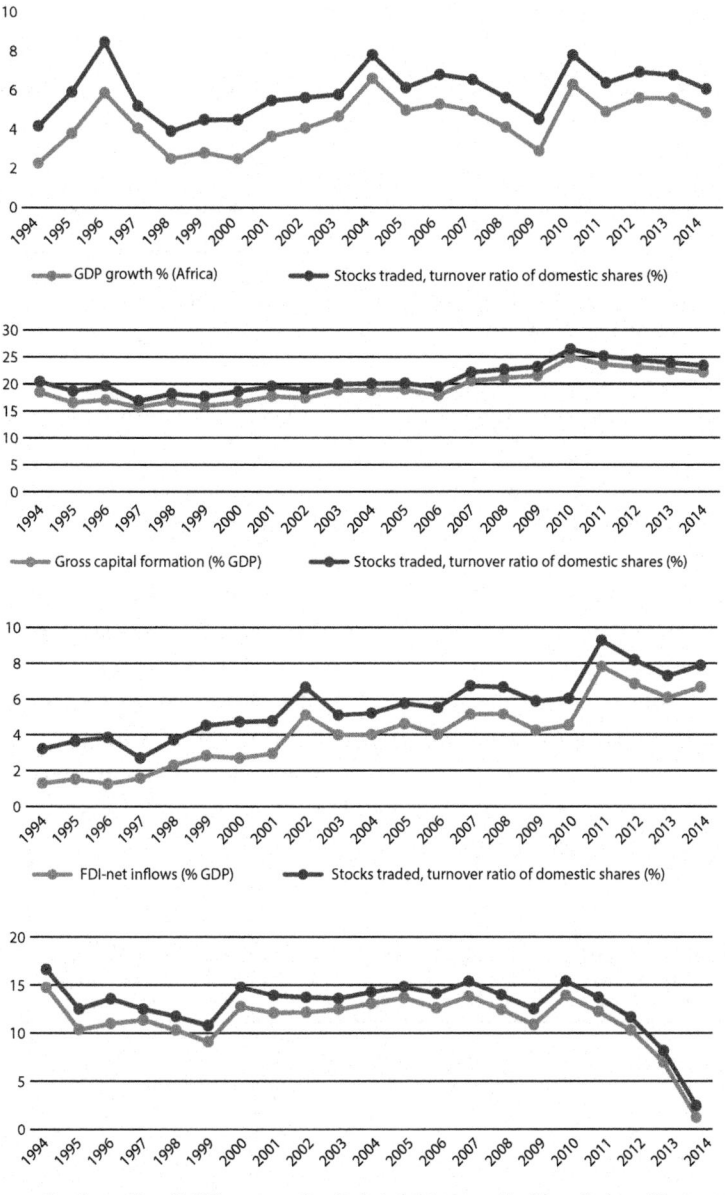

Fig. 8.2 Graphs of economic development indicators and a measure of stock market performance (proxied by stocks traded). All variables are continental averages

Table 8.4 Summary statistics: annual averages (1994–2014)

	Mean	Maximum	Minimum	Skewness	Stdev
FDI-net inflows	4.03	7.81	1.26	0.19	1.91
Gross capital formation	19.38	24.90	15.72	0.48	2.78
GDP growth	4.42	6.63	2.30	−0.14	1.29
Gross savings	11.32	14.74	1.28	−2.09	2.91
Market capitalization	15.69	26.24	6.79	0.22	5.97
Stocks traded	1.55	2.58	1.11	1.03	0.37

Notes: FDI-net inflows, Gross capital formation, Gross savings, are in percent of GDP. Market capitalization, GDP growth, and stocks traded are in percentages. Stdev = standard deviation.

liquidity levels and inefficiencies of the markets. In terms of skewness, both GDP growth and gross savings shows higher tendencies of declining growth since. The degree of variability (measured by standard deviation) of all variables appear moderate except the 5% standard deviation recorded for market capitalization.

Table 8.5 shows correlations of both measures of stock market performance and economic development. Principally, two correlations are worth noting. First, stocks traded are negatively correlated with all the measures of economic development. Market capitalization is, however, highly positively correlated with FDI-net inflows (0.79) and gross capital formation (0.73). Thus, increased foreign capital flows to Africa may induce higher capital formation with a consequential effect on stock market development.

Table 8.5 Correlations – annual averages (1994–2014)

	FDI	GCF	GDP	GS	MKT. CAP	ST
FDI		0.79	0.46	−0.29	0.79	−0.55
GCF			0.49	−0.16	0.73	−0.36
GDP				−0.04	0.14	−0.28
GS					−0.42	0.19
MKT. CAP						−0.39
ST						

Notes: FDI = FDI-net inflows, GCF = Gross capital formation, GS = Gross savings, are in percent of GDP. MKT.CAP = Market capitalization, GDP = GDP growth, and ST = stocks traded are in percentages.

8.4.2 Granger Causality

In Table 8.6, results of Granger Causality tests are shown for a system of economic development measured by *FDI-net inflows, gross capital formation, gross savings, and GDP growth*, on one hand; and stock market development measured by *market capitalization and stocks traded*. *A-priori*, stationarity test with augmented Dickey-Fuller (ADF) and Philips-Peron (PP) are conducted and all series are observed to be first differenced stationary (*results are available upon request*). Lag length of two is selected based on the Alkaike Information Criterion (AIC) as it provides the appropriate horizon over which the predictive ability of each variable is optimized. The results reflect a test of the null of no Granger Causality for the period 1994–2014.

The result from Table 8.6 fails to reject the null hypothesis of no Granger causality among the measures of stock market performance and economic development. Thus, though some nexuses may be established between stock market development and economic growth in Africa, the direction of flow of the cause and effect is not known. Implicitly, the

Table 8.6 Granger causality results: annual averages (1994–2014)

Null hypothesis	F-statistic
MKT. CAP ⟶ FDI	2.66
FDI ⟶ MKT. CAP	3.52
MKT. CAP ⟶ GCF	2.96
GCF ⟶ MKT. CAP	3.47
ST ⟶ GCF	0.04
GCF ⟶ ST	1.14
MKT. CAP ⟶ GDP	0.38
GDP ⟶ MKT. CAP	2.28
ST ⟶ GDP	0.40
GDP ⟶ ST	3.51
MKT. CAP ⟶ GS	1.51
GS ⟶ MKT. CAP	1.28
ST ⟶ GS	1.11
GS ⟶ ST	0.94
ST ⟶ FDI	0.05
FDI ⟶ ST	1.62

See notes under Table 8.5.

supply-leading and demand-following hypothesis, as well as the mutually causal theories, is not supported by these results. It stands to reason therefore that the effect of either stock market development on economic growth or the reverse in Africa may occur through some other economic and/or financial factors playing intermediary roles.

8.4.3 GMM Estimations

As a prelude to the GMM estimations, Fig. 8.3 gives a preliminary view on the linkages between stock market development and economic growth in a panel of six countries from 1993 to 2013 (using annual averages). The figure shows that generally higher levels of the measures of economic development (gross savings, gross capital formation, FDI-net inflows, and GDP growth) are associated with lower levels of market capitalization (a proxy for stock market development), and vice versa. This finding contradicts the popular view that stock market development stimulates economic growth (see Enisan and Olufisayo 2009). Perhaps, the results are so for Africa because of the low liquidity levels and efficiency, as well as small sizes of the continent's stock markets.

Next, we estimate a system Generalized Methods of Moments (GMM) in the Arellano-Bond one-step dynamic panel data estimation with 144 observations to determine the effect of economic development on the performance of stock markets. Initial test for over-identification of restriction support the validity of the instruments because we could not reject first- and second-order serial correlation. We find the p-values for both AR(1) and AR(2) to be high on the back of low z-values (*results are available upon request to the authors*). The results which are presented in Table 8.7 have market capitalization as the dependent variable.

Results from Table 8.7 indicate that the one-period lag of market capitalization, FDI-net inflows, and gross savings significantly influence current levels of stock market development (proxied by market capitalization of domestic listed firms) in Africa. For the economic growth indicators, whilst the effect of FDI-net inflows is positive, that of gross savings is negative. Thus, increasingly higher inflows of FDI into Africa have the potential of surging the wealth of local investors, and the wealth

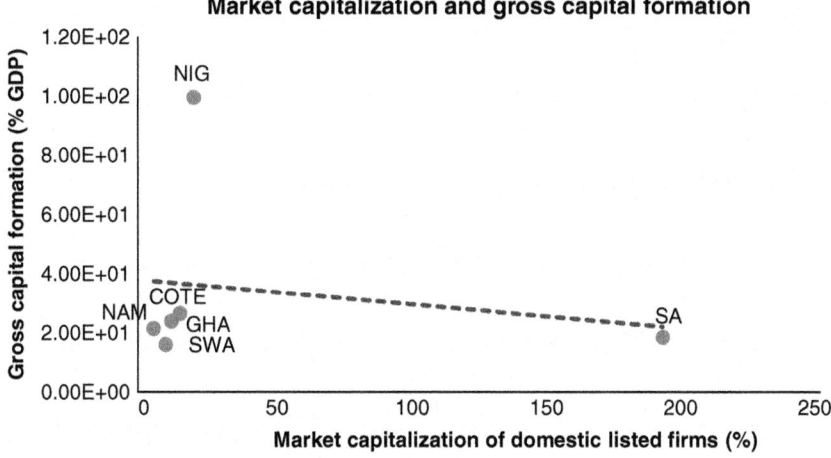

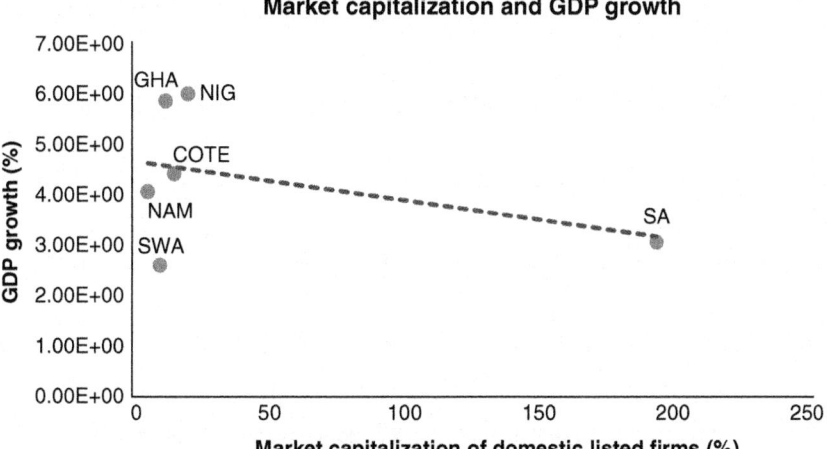

Fig. 8.3 Panel scatter plots of stock market performance indicator and measures of economic growth (annual averages: 1993–2013)

effect engenders the interest of investors in equity markets in the continent to spur the growth of the markets. Standard economic theory postulates that the flow of foreign capital to a recipient country increases its stock of capital and technological knowledge, leading to better economic performance. Capital flows could also provide additional

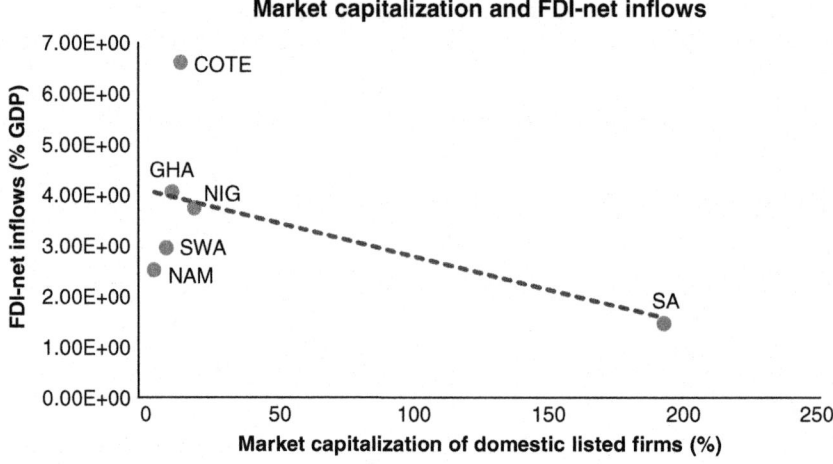

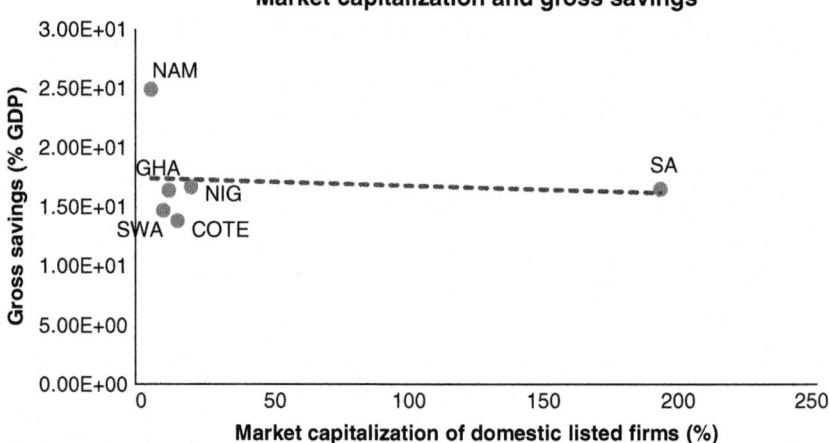

Fig. 8.3 (continued)

capital to local savings, promote capital accumulation, and market efficiency (Choong et al. 2010).

Since 2000 official remittances to Africa increased six-fold and were projected to reach USD64.6 billion in 2015 with Egypt and Nigeria receiving the bulk of flows. At the same time, increasing Greenfield

Table 8.7 GMM estimation results – dependent variable = market capitalization

Regressor	Co-efficient	Standard error	P-value
Mark. Cap (–1)	0.517	0.127	0.000*
GCF	0.282	0.329	0.392
GDP	0.014	0.109	0.898
FDI	0.316	0.073	0.000*
GS	–0.218	0.010	0.029**
Constant	20.906	10.374	0.044**

Notes: All variables are as previously defined; and *, **, respectively denote statistical significance at 1% and 5% levels.

investments from China and India are expected to increase foreign investment in the continent. The resultant effects of these are improvements in the overall economic growth and developments in the financial sector. Correspondingly, development characteristics of equity markets in Africa have witnessed significant improvements, perhaps partly on account of higher FDI inflows (see Table 8.1).

8.5   Conclusion

We examined the relationship between economic growth and stock market development in Africa using both trend analysis and regression estimations. At first, we present an overview of stock markets development in Africa from 2005 to 2011 focussing on some key development characteristics such as turn-over ratio, market capitalization, liquidity, and number of listed companies. We further analysed the institutional, operational, and infrastructural development characteristics of African stock markets as at end of 2014. The statistical properties of stock markets in Africa are examined. Then comes the review of both theoretical and empirical literature on the nexus between stock markets development and economic growth, as well as the determinants of stock market development. In all, two measures of stock market development (i.e. turn-over ratios of domestic shares and market capitalizations (%) of domestic listed firms) and four indicators of economic growth (i.e. GDP growth (%), FDI-net inflows (% of GDP), gross savings (% of GDP), and gross capital formation (% of GDP)) are used for analysis.

The analysis which involves examination of trends, correlation and causality measures, as well as dynamic panel data estimations, suggest that while Africa's economic growth may be stimulated by a number of factors, developments in the capital markets (stocks) could also have its own influence to exert either positively or negatively. Despite this, we do not find any lead/lag relationship between economic growth and stock markets development in Africa.

References

African Securities Exchanges Association. (2014). ASEA 2014 year book, available at www.africansea.org/ASEA/Default.aspx.

Agbetsiafia, D. (2004). The finance growth nexus: Evidence from Sub-Saharan Africa. *Savings and Development*, 28(3), 271–288.

Agbloyor, E. K., Abor, J. Y., Adjasi, C. K. D., & Yawson, A. (2014). Private capital flows and economic growth in Africa: The role of domestic financial markets. *Journal of International Financial Markets, Institutions, & Money*, 30, 137–152.

Ahmed, A. D., & Mmolainyane, K. K. (2014). Financial integration, capital market development and economic performance: Evidence from Botswana. *Economic Modelling*, 42, 1–14.

Akinboade, O. A. (1998). Financial development and economic growth in Botswana: A test for causality. *Savings and Development*, 3, 331–347.

Apergis, N., Filippidis, I., & Economidou, C. (2007). Financial deepening and economic growth linkages: A panel data analysis. *Review of World Economics*, 143(1), 179–198.

Arestis, P., & Demetriades, P. (1997). Financial development and economic growth: Assessing the evidence. *Economic Journal*, 107, 783–799.

Arestis, P., Demetriades, P. O., & Luintel, K. B. (2001). Financial development and economic growth: The role of stock markets. *Journal of Money, Credit, and Banking*, 33, 16–41.

Atindehou, R. B., Guyeie, J. P., & Amenounve, E. K. (2005). Financial intermediation and economic growth: Evidence from Western Africa. *Applied Financial Economics*, 15, 777–790.

Atje, R., & Jovanovic, B. (1993). Stock markets and development. *European Economic Review*, 37, 632–640.

Bagehot, W. (1873). *Lombard street*. Homewood, IL: Irwin.

Barajas, A., Chami, R., & Yousefi, S. R., (2013). The finance and growth nexus examined: Do all countries benefit equally? IMF Working Papers No: WP/13/130 (May).

Bayraktar, N. (2014). Measuring relative development level of stock markets: Capacity and effort of countries. *Borsa Istanbul Review*, *14*, 74–95.

Beck, T., & Demirguc-Kunt, A. (2009). Financial institutions and markets across countries and over time – data and analysis. World Bank Policy Research Working Paper Series (No. 4943).

Beck, T., & Levine, R. (2002). Stock markets, banks, and growth: Panel evidence. Working Paper 9082, National Bureu of Economic and Research, Cambridge, MA, 02138.

Beck, T., Demirguc-Kunt, A., & Levine, R. (2000). A new database on financial development and structure. *World Bank Economic Review*, *14*, 597–605.

Bekaert, G., & Harvey, C. R. (2014). Emerging equity markets in a globalizing world. Available at SSRN: http://ssrn.com/abstract=2344817

Bencivenga, V. R., Bruce, D. S., & Ross, M. S. (1995). Equity markets, transactions costs, and capital accumulation: An illustration. *The World Bank Economic Review*, *10*(2), 241–265.

Billmeier, A., & Massa, I. (2009). What drives stock market development in emerging markets – Institutions, remittances, or natural resources?. *Emerging Markets Review*, *10*(1), 23–35.

Bittencourt, M. (2012). Financial development and economic growth in Latin America: Is Schumpeter right? *Journal of Policy Modelling*, *34*, 341–355.

Blackburn, K., Bose, N., & Capasso, S. (2005). Financial development, financing choice and economic growth. *Review of Development Economics*, *9*(2), 135–149.

Caporale, G. M., Howells, P. G., & Soliman, A. M. (2004). Stock market development and economic growth: The causal linkage. *Journal of Economic Development*, *29*(1), 33–50.

Carp, L. (2012). Can the stock market development boost economic growth: Empirical evidence from emerging markets in central and Eastern Europe. *Prodecia Economics and Finance*, *3*, 438–444.

Castenada, G. (2006). Economic growth and concentrated ownership in stock markets. *Journal of Economic Behaviour and Organization*, *59*, 249–286.

Chaiechi, T. (2012). Financial development shocks and contemporaneous feedback effect on key macroeconomic indicators: A post Keynesian time series analysis. *Economic Modelling*, *29*(2), 487–501.

Choong, C.-K., Baharumshah, A. Z., Yuzop, Z., & Habibullah, M. S. (2010). Private capital flows, stock market and economic growth in developed and developing countries: A comparative analysis. *Japan and the World Economy*, *22*(2), 107–117.

Cihak, M., Demirguc-Kunt, A., Feyen, E., & Levine, R. (2012). Financial development in 205 economies, 1960 to 2010. In *Presented at the conference on financial deepening, Macro-stability, and growth*. Jointly organized by the World Bank and the International Monetary Fund, Washington, DC (24 September 2012). Available: http://faculty.haas.berkeley.edu/ross_levine/papers/Benchmarking%202013-03-29.pdf

De Gregorio, J., & Guidotti, P. (1995). Financial development and economic growth. *World Development*, *23*(3), 1433–1448.

Demetriades, P. O., & Hussein, K. A. (1996). Does financial development cause economic growth? Time-series evidence from 16 countries. *Journal of Development Economics*, *51*(2), 387–411.

Demirgui-Kunt, A., & Levine, R. (1996). Stock market development and financial intermediaries: Stylized facts. *The World Bank Economic Review*, *10*(2), 291–321.

Devereux, M., & Smith, G. (1994). International risk sharing and economic growth. *International Economic Review*, *35*, 535–550.

Eita, J. H., & Jordaan, A. C. (2010). A causality analysis between financial development and economic growth for Botswana. *African Finance Journal*, *12*(1), 72–89.

Enisan, A. A., & Olufisayo, A. O. (2009). Stock market development and economic growth: Evidence from seven Sub-Saharan African countries. *Journal of Economics and Business*, *61*(2), 162–171.

Fernandez, D., & Galetovic, A., (1994). Schumpeter might be right-but why? Explaining the relation between finance, development and growth. Working Paper, School of Advanced International Studies, Johns Hopkins University, 1994.

Fisher, I. (1907). *The rate of interest*. New York: Macmillan.

Florackis, C., Giorgioni, G., Kostakis, A., & Milas, C. (2014). On stock market illiquidity and real-time GDP growth. *Journal of International Money and Finance*, *44*, 210–229.

Goldsmith, Raymond, W. (1969). *Financial structure and development*. New Haven, CT: Yale University Press.

Graff, M. (1999). Financial development and economic growth – a new empirical analysis. *Dresden discussion paper series in Economics*, Nr. 5/99 Technische Universitat Dresden.

Greenwood, J., & Smith, B. D. (1997). Financial markets in development and the development of financial markets. *Journal of Economic Dynamics and Control, 21,* 145–182.

Gurley, J. G., & Shaw, E. S. (1955). Financial aspects of economic development. *American Economic Review, 45,* 515–538.

Gurley, J. G., & Shaw, E. S. (1960). *Money in a theory of finance.* Washington, DC: Brooking Institution.

Harris, R. (1997). Stock markets and development: A re-assessment. *European Economic Review, 41,* 139–146.

Hicks, J. A. (1969). *A theory of economic history.* Oxford, UK: Clarendon Press.

Jung, W. S. (1986). Financial development and economic growth: International evidence. *Economic Development and Cultural Change, 34*(2), 333–346.

King, R., & Levine, R. (1993). Finance and growth: Schumpeter might be right. *Quarterly Journal of Economics, 108,* 717–737.

Levine, R. (1997). Financial development and economic growth: Views and agenda. *Journal of Economic Literature, 35,* 688–726.

Levine, R. (2005). Finance and growth: Theory, mechanism and evidence. In P. Aghion & S. N. Durlauf (Eds.), *Handbook of economic growth* (pp. 865–934). North-Holland: Elsevier.

Levine, R., & Zervos, S. (1998). Stock market, banks and economic growth. *American Economic Review, 88,* 537–558.

Liang, Q., & Teng, J. (2006). Financial development and economic growth: Evidence from China. *China Economic Review, 17*(4), 395–411.

Lucas, R. E J. (1988). On the mechanics of economic development. *Journal of Monetary Economics, 22,* 3–42.

Mayer, C. (1988). New issues in corporate finance. *European Economic Review, 32,* 1167–1188.

McKinnon, R. I. (1973). *Money and capital in economic development.* Washington, DC: Brookings Institution.

Menyah, K., Nazlioglu, S., & Wolde-Rufael, Y. (2014). Financial development, trade openness and economic growth in African countries: New insights from a panel causality approach. *Economic Modelling, 37,* 386–394.

Meshach, A. J. (2007). Effects of financial integration on financial development and economic performance of the SACU countries. ECA/ADB AFRICAN Economic Conference 15–17 November 2007, Addis Ababa.

Moin, S. (2007). New frontier markets tempt investors. *African Review of Business and Technology, 1,* 1–7.

Morck, R., Shleifer, A., & Vushny, R. W. (1990). The stock market and investments: Is the market a slideshow? *Brookings Papers on Economic Activity, 2,* 157–215.

Ndako, U. B. (2010). Stock markets, banks and economic growth: Time series evidence from South Africa. *The African Finance Journal, 12*(2), 72–92.

Ngare, E., Nyamongo, E. M., & Misati, R. N. (2014). Stock market development and economic growth in Africa. *Journal of Economics and Business, 74,* 24–39.

Nieuwerburgh, S. V., Buelens, F., & Cuyvers, L. (2006). Stock market development and economic growth in Belgium. *Explorations in Economic History, 43*(1), 13–38.

Ntim, C. G., Oppong, K. K., Danbolt, F., & Dewotor, F. S. (2011). Testing the weak-form efficiency in African stock markets. *Managerial Finance, 37,* 195–218.

Obstfeld, M. (1994). Risk-taking, global diversification, and growth. *American Economic Review, 84,* 1310–1329.

Odhiambo, N. M. (2007). Financial development in Kenya: A dynamic test of the financeled growth hypotheses. *Economic Issues, 13*(2), 21–36.

Odhiambo, N. M. (2010). Finance-investment-growth nexus in South Africa: An ARDL bounds-testing procedure. *Economic Change and Restructuring, 43,* 205–219.

Pagano, M. (1993). The flotation of companies on the stock market, a coordination failure model. *European Economic Review, 37,* 1101–1125.

Quartey, P., & Prah, F. (2008). Financial development and economic growth in Ghana: Is there a causal link?. *African Finance Journal, 10*(1), 28–54.

Robinson, J. (1952). The generalisation of the general theory. In *The rate of interest and other essays.* London: MacMillan.

Rousseau, P. L., & Vuthipadadom, D. (2005). Finance, investment, and growth: Time series evidence from 10 Asian economies. *Journal of Macroeconomics, 27*(1), 87–106.

Saci, K., Giorgioni, G., & Holden, K. (2009). Does financial development affect growth? *Applied Economics, 41,* 1701–1707.

Saint-Paul, G. (1992). Technological choice, financial markets and economic development. *European Economic Review, 36,* 763–781.

Schumpeter, J. (1911). *The theory of economic development, 1934, 1964.* New York.

Senbet, L., & Otchere, I. (2008). *Beyond banking: Developing markets-African stock markets.* Tunisia: IMF Seminar.

Shaw, E. S. (1973). *Financial deepening in economic development*. New York: Oxford University Press.

Smith, G., Jefferis, K., & Ryoo, H.-J. (2002). African stock markets: Multiple variance ratio tests of random walks. *Applied Financial Economics, 12*, 475–484.

Stiglitz, J. E. (1985). Credit markets and the control of capital. *Journal of Money, Credit and Banking, 17*, 133–152.

Tang, D. (2006). The effect of financial development on economic growth: Evidence from the APEC countries, 1981–2000. *Applied Economics, 38*, 1889–1904.

Tiwari, A. K., Mutascu, M. I., Albulescu, C. T., & Kyophilavong, P. (2015). Frequency causality analysis of stock market and economic activity in India. *International Review of Economics and Finance, 39*, 224–238.

UNDP. (2003). *African stock markets handbook*. New York: United Nations Development Programme.

Zang, H., & Kim, Y. C. (2007). Does financial development precede growth? Robinson and Lucas may be right. *Applied Economic Letters, 14*(1), 15–19.

Zhang, J., Wang, L., & Wang, S. (2012). Financial development and economic growth: Recent evidence from China. *Journal of Comparative Economics, 40*, 393–412.

Gideon Boako is a doctoral research (PhD) candidate and Graduate Teaching Assistant in Finance at the University of the Witwatersrand Business School (Johannesburg, South Africa). He is currently a research associate to the Chair of African Philanthropy at the Wits Business School, Johannesburg. He obtained his Master of Philosophy and Master of Business Administration degrees in Finance at the Kwame Nkrumah University of Science and Technology School of Business (KSB-Ghana). Currently, he lectures Full Time at the Garden City University College (Ghana), and holds part time lectureship position at the KSB. Gideon is an associate editor of the *Ghanaian Journal of Economics (GJE)*. He has decent publications in top-tier peer-reviewed journals such as the *International Review of Financial Analysis, Applied Economics Letters, Finance Research Letters*, and *South African Journal of Economics*, and has attended academic conferences of international repute.

Paul Alagidede is Professor of Finance and the Area Head of Accounting and Finance at the University of the Witwatersrand Business School. He has a PhD degree in Economics from Loughborough University. Paul is the founding editor-in-chief of the *African Review of Economics and Finance* and the *Ghanaian Journal of Economics* as well as the executive director of the African Finance and Economics Consult. He is a visiting professor to a number of universities and research institutes around the world.

9

Conclusion

Gianluigi Giorgioni

9.1 Introduction

This chapter will draw some conclusion from each of the chapters of the book and will try to pick threads of opportunities and challenges in the context of a post-financial crisis situation.

The overriding conclusions are to recognise the limits of finance; to apply an eclectic approach where principles surely matter, but ideology should not play an excessively important role; to be able to link the macro-literature to the micro (and vice versa); and to reassess the role of the state.

G. Giorgioni (✉)
Economics and Finance, University of Liverpool Management School, Liverpool, UK
e-mail: G.Giorgioni@liverpool.ac.uk

© The Author(s) 2017

241

G. Giorgioni (ed.), *Development Finance*, Palgrave Studies in Impact Finance, DOI 10.1057/978-1-137-58032-0_9

9.2   Issues and Challenges: An Assessment of the Empirical Evidence

In terms of the limits of what finance can achieve the chapter by Gianluigi Giorgioni and the chapter by Gideon Boako and Paul Alagidede have reviewed the literature on the nexus between finance and growth. Both chapters agree that the nexus between financial development and economic growth is quite complex with mixed empirical evidence. The chapter by Giorgioni also highlights the fact that the impact of finance depends upon the type of finance (project-based financing being more impactful than finance to households including collateralised asset-based finance like mortgages) and the size of the financial sector, as there is some evidence of a threshold beyond which the impact of bank credit turns negative as reported by Arcand et al. (2015) (see also related paper reaching very similar conclusions such as Arcand et al. 2012, Cecchetti and Kharroubi 2012 and Law and Singh 2014). The ramifications at micro-level are that stock markets might have a stronger impact upon economic growth than banks. However, when Gideon Boako and Paul Alagidede looked closely at the relationship between stock markets and growth in a sample of sub-Saharan African countries, their results were not particularly strong. Also Giorgioni and Kok (2016) empirically assess the relationship between financial development and economic growth by distinguishing whether a country has a developed, emerging or 'frontier' stock market. Their results also provide evidence that the banking sector has an overall negative impact on economic growth, although the results do not provide evidence that this effect is linked to any specific threshold.

In the context of developing countries it is clear that the costs of monitoring, screening and enforcing payments of loans act as a sort of a very high hurdle to be cleared for financial institutions to lend to very small borrowers. From the literature it is clear that creditworthiness per se is not an issue as shown by Johnston and Morduch (2008) and that the lack of legal titles is not the problem as envisaged in some quarters. Or in other words, the size of the loan (and implicitly of the business activity that it will fund) prevails as an issue for financial institutions more than the lack of assets that can be used as collateral and/or the lack of legal titles of ownership (see Galiani and Shargrodsky 2010).

The size of the business venture is also the link with the literature on mis-allocation. Mis-allocation can explain the perceived disparity in TFPs between developed and developing countries and the wider dispersions of marginal rates of returns to capital in developing countries. One possible remedy to the disparity among countries and the wider dispersion within developing countries could be eased by the removal of a number of market frictions, in particular credit constraints (Banerjee and Duflo 2005, Banerjee and Moll (2010). However, it is apparent from the review of the literature that the evidence that financial restrictions affect mis-allocation is not conclusive (Midrigan and Xu 2014), while differences in the size of firms seems to be an important variable in explaining disparities of TFPs (Buera et al. 2011). This finding appears to be an ideal example for a more pragmatic approach as the literature on mis-allocation (and the impact of financial frictions on it) is clearly embedded in a neoclassical approach. Incidentally, this very same approach had provided the foundations upon which the whole micro-credit industry laid and recent criticisms of the intervention by micro-credit institutions indicate that it may not be the provider of a quick solution (see Bateman and Chang 2012 and Banerjie et al. 2015). The reader can also be directed to the chapter of this book focused on the impact of micro-credit upon poverty written by Supriya Garikipati. Recent critiques of the micro-credit experience have established that the size of firms matters and simply lending to very small business (some of them even operating below the minimum efficiency level of production and effectively unable to grow beyond this level) would only lead to an increase in the number of these micro-firms without helping countries to develop medium-sized firms in order to overcome the so-called 'missing middle problem' (see Hsieh and Olken 2014) faced by many developing countries. At a pragmatic level, this issue of structural small size of firms should be recognised and should receive the attention it deserves.

One possible solution is a more pragmatic acceptance of the role of the state in the financial sector, although, as it is discussed in the chapter by Rashmi Arora, the relationship between state intervention and financial development is clearly full of nuances.

The chapter has also examined the literature on the impact of interventions to reduce financial illiteracy and the literature focused on the impact legal titles upon access to finance. The section on financial illiteracy has clearly indicated that timely and ad hoc interventions are more likely to be more beneficial. The literature has also highlighted a number of methodological issues such as endogeneity and omitted variables that might affect the results of some of the empirical papers.

The chapter has also examined the literature on legal titles. The conclusion was that legal titles on their own do not appear to lead, directly, to either more access to finance or improved economic welfare. The main reason is that other variables, such as the size of the loan and/or the desirability of the assets used as collateral, are playing a more important role for potential lenders. However, legal titles do impact economic welfare through the channel of increased investment in the property and in human capital, probably as a consequence of the stability brought about by the legal title of ownership.

9.3 Government Intervention and Financial Sector Development

The role played by governments in the financial sector and their impact on financial development and economic growth have remained contentious. Historically, the high peak of government interventions in the financial sector was from the 1950s until the early 1990s, although the seeds for a re-think of the intervention of governments were sown in the early 1970s with publications critical of the so-called 'financial repression' and the attendant poor performance of public banks in several countries.

Several developing countries introduced reforms of the financial sector with the objectives of improving the allocative efficiency of the financial institutions and financial markets. However, one of the consequences of the recent global financial crisis was to re-start debates on the government's role in the financial sector.

Based on the analysis of the extant literature, the chapter by Rashmi Arora is unable to reach a conclusion on whether the resurgent intervention of governments in the financial sector has a positive or negative impact. Some strong agreement appears to be found on the recognition of a positive role played by public sector banks during the financial crisis, specifically for their positive countercyclical role, in terms of lending when private-owned banks had stopped to do so (Laeven and Valencia (2013); for the evidence that government recapitalisation of financial institutions had a significant impact on growth performance of financially dependent firms through increase in the supply of credit and for the useful role governments can play in the supervision and regulation of the financial sector (see Beck 2013, Freixas and Mayer 2011 and Demirguc-Kunt 2014). The mere acknowledgement that government interventions can be positive can signal a big ideological shift from the more anti-state intervention that had prevailed in previous years (see for instance World Bank 2001). It must be emphasised that the findings on the positive countercyclical role of public banks during times of crisis do not necessarily extend to 'normal times'. Cho (2010) argues that the role of state intervention is for prevention, containment and resolution of financial crises. It is also clear from the comparison of growth experience of the Asian tigers with the experience of sub-Saharan African countries that governments can play an important role in the process of development, especially in the early stages of economic development.

9.4 Overseas Aid as an Instrument of Development Finance

In this chapter Paul Mosley provides a critical but nuanced assessment of the literature on the effectiveness of aid over the period from the 1950s until now. The literature (and the policies based on the empirical findings of the literature) have considerably changed over the years and alongside these changes in policies also came a shifting in the effectiveness of aid.

This literature provides a prime example of the positive feedback between academic literature (empirical and theoretical) and practitioners' policies. The results from the empirical assessments of the effectiveness, at macro-level based on cross-sectional data, of overseas aid have oscillated from the positive effect estimated by Papanek (1972, 1973) to the more negative effects estimated in the 1980s leading to the notion of a micro-macro paradox in light of the high social rate of return estimated by the World Bank on its projects.

However, the effectiveness of aid, at least in the short-term, was re-established by the papers by Burnside and Dollar (2000) and Hansen and Tarp (2001), with or without policy conditions attached by the IMF and the World Bank.

In two successive papers, Rajan and Subramaniam (2008) and (2009) produced empirical evidence and the theoretical explanation for their findings, that aid flows have no significant and measurable impact on growth in the long-term once injections of aid were lagged (not only five-year and ten-year lags, as had been normal, but now 20, 30 and even 40 year lags). The explanations of their negative (or rather neutral) results are due to negative long-term effects of aid on governance (following the analysis of Bräutigam and Knack (2004) who produced empirical evidence of a negative correlation between the size of aid flows and institutional quality) and to 'Dutch disease' effects.

More recently Mosley (2015) find that aid continues to be a significant influence on growth.Clemens et al. (2012) differentiate between types of aid according to the impact which they seek to achieve and replicate the Burnside and Dollar (2000) and Rajan and Subramaniam (2008) models with the original data. The main finding is that once the definition of aid is restricted to early impact aid (i.e. they exclude humanitarian assistance or disaster relief vaccination campaign or school feeding project)', even the Rajan-Subramaniam model exhibits a positive impact of aid (thus redefined) on growth. The final and most ambitious recent attempt to rehabilitate overseas aid is that by Arndt et al. (2015) where they re-estimate a similar sort of 'new growth theory' model to that estimated by Hansen and Tarp in 2001 and find that has a significant impact not only on growth of GDP but also on headcount poverty, years of schooling and the infant mortality rate.

9.5   Migrant Remittances and Beyond: The Development Implications of Human Capital Mobility and Accompanying Financial Flows

The chapter by Ralitza Dimova reviews the theoretical and empirical literature on remittances providing a very nuanced and rich assessment of the implications of international migration and remittances for the economic development prospects of the economies of the countries affected by the outflows and inflows of migrants. The net effect of migration and remittances is highly dependent on the overall level of skills of both the country of origin and the country of arrival of the migrants and the level of skills of the migrants themselves. A large outflow of homogeneous and low-skill workers could increase, in theory, the equilibrium wages potentially pulling a poor developing country out of a poverty trap. However, the empirical evidence of this effect is more mixed. This lack of empirical evidence on the impact of large outflows of unskilled workers must also be seen in the context of the stronger evidence that, in fact, it is the more skilled workers who actually emigrate from developing countries. The net effect of outflows of skilled workers, at both theoretical and empirical, is also quite complex to determine. Clearly the loss of human capital in a less-developed economy can have quite a detrimental effect. However, this effect could be compensated by either the brain gain effect due to emulation effect or the enhanced inflow of capital and technology on account of networking and information sharing by skilled migrants located abroad, especially in high-skilled countries.

Undeniably, remittance flows towards developing countries tend to dwarf the size and effect of alternative cross-border financial flows in terms of their resilience, flexibility and stability, proving to be countercyclical in cases of crises and of major disasters.

The ultimate economic impact on the receiving economies is, however, dependent upon the end use of them (either consumption or investment) and the identity of the ultimate beneficiary. The latter is clearly influenced by the motives for sending remittances. Therefore, the overall implications of migration are heterogeneous and context specific making the task of drawing policy implication more difficult. Ralitza Dimova proves this point especially for the case of forced migration and for the case of remittances from and to refugees and displaced people where drawing the right balance between aid and economic integration is one of the key policy dilemmas.

Migrants can also bring back home cultural norms and values or new political orientation that may have an important impact upon the country of origin as documented by Bertoli (2015) and Bertoli and Marchetta (2015), who find that the temporary migrants in the Gulf countries tend to bring back home more conservative norms that involve greater fertility or Mahmoud et al. (2013) who find that emigration from Moldova in the late 1990s affected strongly the political preferences and electoral outcomes in the country, leading to the fall of the last ruling Communist government in Europe.

9.6   Multinational Enterprises and Economic Development in Host Countries: What We Know and What We Don't Know

The chapter by Rajneesh Narula and André Pineli evaluated in detail the literature on MNEs and their impact upon development. The mechanisms through which FDI has an impact upon development are relatively well-understood. Therefore, attracting MNEs could be a useful development strategy for developing countries, although there remain a number of practical challenges in achieving FDI-assisted development. Narula and Dunning (2000) indicated that engagement with MNEs may enhance structural change. However, governments should take a more pro-active stance aimed at changing the comparative advantage by, for instance, upgrading skills and education, rather than a more passive approach that tend to reinforce static location advantages of the country.

The successful catching-up policies of Japan, Taiwan and South Korea and possibly China in more recent years policies included restrictive FDI policies, prioritising technology transfer agreements, licensing and reverse engineering as vehicles to internalise foreign knowledge (Narula and Dunning 2010). Clearly the key ingredients were the knowledge transfers and linkages, and the capacity of domestic firms to absorb, internalise and upgrade their knowledge assets by taking advantage of the spillovers.

Therefore, to successfully implement an FDI-assisted development policy, developing countries must create an environment conductive to fully exploit the potential benefits resulting from the presence of foreign MNEs, including enhancing the local embeddedness of the MNEs. It is clear that a sound FDI policy must not be exclusively concerned with attracting capital investment, but give emphasis to policy that enhance the capacity to absorb the knowledge spillovers by domestic firms, while helping connecting to the value chains set up by MNEs. This may be done through a variety of interventions, from investment in human capital and technological capabilities to the promotion of industrial clusters to facilitate knowledge flows. The potential for linkages and spillovers is also influenced by the MNE's investment motivations, the affiliates' mandate and autonomy. Therefore, attention should be paid to attracting the 'right' type of MNEs. In a sense the quality of FDI a country receives is at least as important as the quantity.

Rajneesh Narula and André Pineli also observe that incentives and subsidies to attract MNEs are less important for long-term achievements than developing and upgrading the quality and extent of a country's absorptive capacity through improvements in its knowledge infrastructure and should be seen as a short-term solution and can only be justified if their costs are not outweighing than the overall expected benefits from the foreign investment.

Rajneesh Narula and André Pineli also make an important point related to the way linkages and spillovers are actually measured. The usual means of measuring them are increasingly outdated, and do not allow us to capture the structure of modern cross-border value chains. Countries increasingly specialise in specific tasks, instead of products. MNE affiliates also reflect these new realities, with growing specialisation and strong competition between subsidiaries of the same MNE. The dependency upon registered equity investments to construct the measures of foreign presence overlooks the increasing separation between control and ownership by MNEs.

MNEs can no longer be viewed as a synonym to FDI (Narula and Dunning 2010; UNCTAD 2011; Collinson et al. 2016), that is, MNEs are increasingly able to control the value chain in the absence of ownership. The truncated miniature replica that constituted the dominant pattern of the typical MNE affiliate is now a relic of the past (Pearce 2001). MNEs currently use a multitude of arrangements to access the desired location advantages of other countries, ranging from traditional FDI to outsourcing, with a myriad of partial internalisation schemes in the middle. It is hard to be specific on the extent to which non-equity modes of internationalisation are replacing FDI (or whether they are in addition to) because reliable data do not as yet exist. However, if traditional FDI measurements suffer from data inconsistency and problems of classification, these 'new' modes of governance are even harder to quantify.

9.7   The Impact of Microfinance on Poverty Alleviation: Making Sense of the Evidence

The chapter by Supriya Garikipati on the impact of microfinance on poverty (measured as income, consumption, expenditure, profits and assets) suggest that there is no visible impact of microfinance on profits and incomes and hence on poverty.

In terms of income, a clear conclusion that emerges from the literature is that the impact of microfinance is stronger on households that are above the poverty line. This supports the theoretical expectation that microfinance will have a positive impact if borrowers have viable investments and the necessary business skills. The better-off amongst the poor are more likely to have these conditions compared to the very poor.

Moreover, the impact on income is mixed, with numerous studies not finding any significant impact (Abou-Ali et al. (2009), Cotler and

Woodruff (2008), Takahashi et al. (2010), Imai and Azam (2012), Kaboski and Townsend (2012) and Nghiem et al. (2012)) and some event finding a negative association (Attanasio et al. 2011). The studies that find a positive impact also emphasise that it is conditional on the presence of other conditions.

The lesson that emerges is that impact on income cannot be taken for granted and there may be associated conditions that need attention.

The literature also report a positive impact of microfinance on consumption and expenditure – especially in the short run (Khandker 2005, Cuong 2008, Gertler et al. 2009, Attanasio et al. 2011, Berhane and Gardebroek 2011, Imai and Azam 2012 and Kaboski and Townsend 2012).

Business profits are also positively affected by microcredit, especially when borrowers have the essential business skills, longevity of membership and flexible repayment terms, although Banerjee et al. (2009) and Attanasio et al. (2011) are two studies that do not support the result on positive impact on profits.

Finally, most of the literature suggests a positive association between microfinance and long-term asset accumulation, although the impact is modest at best and may have little economic significance.

Overall the chapter provides some evidence that the benefits for the very poor are mixed and not guaranteed, while better-off individuals or households are in a much better position to benefit from microfinance initiatives.

The impact on consumption and expenditure, especially in the short run is positive, but the impact on income growth and asset creation is more uncertain. On the whole the impact is modest in size and in economic meaning bringing into question the poverty alleviation capacity of microfinance. Therefore, the gains from microfinance in terms of poverty alleviation are small and a policy solely relying on credit at market interest rate to take away poverty is unlikely to succeed.

It could be suggested to link repayments to actual business profit (like a profit and loss sharing agreement) and to link microcredit to other interventions such as training as there is some evidence that credit-only programmes do worse that credit-plus programmes (see Duvendack et al. 2011; Kabeer 2017; Dupas and Robinson 2013).

Finally, the need for longitudinal studies cannot be overemphasised to capture the complex long-term impact of microfinance.

9.8   The Stock Market Development and Economic Growth Puzzle: Empirical Evidence from Africa

Gideon Boako and Paul Alagidede examined the relationship between economic growth and stock market development in Africa. They observe that excluding the period before 1996 where percentage GDP growth and market capitalisation appear to move in sync, a negative relationship is observed for the two variables from 1997 to 2014. GDP growth is observed to increase (bend upwards) whilst market capitalisation decreases (bend downwards). However, the growth pattern of the two variables is not uniform as some cyclical sharp declines (rises) are observed for GDP growth (market capitalisations) for the periods 2004–2005 and 2010 respectively.

It is instructive to note that relative to other regions, stock market development in sub-Saharan Africa does not compare very well. First of all, most of the market capitalisation is concentrated in South Africa. Second, the total number of listed companies on all exchanges in sub-Saharan Africa barely changed unlike in East Asia Pacific and South Asia. Third, a similar pattern is observed for turn-over ratios (values of traded shares as a percentage of market capitalisation) where the turn-over in sub-Saharan Africa is one-third of the turn-over in the other regions an indication that the markets are not liquid. The above statistics suggests that, except South Africa, sub-Saharan African stock markets are generally small in size, immature, and have low levels of liquidity.

Although Gideon Boako and Paul Alagidede established some nexus between stock market development and economic growth in sub-Saharan Africa, the direction of flow of the cause and effect is not known. Implicitly, the supply-leading and demand-following hypothesis, as well as the mutually causal theories, is not supported by these results. These results confirm earlier finding, at national level, by Enisan and Olufisayo (2009) for Cote D'Ivoire, Kenya, Morocco, and Zimbabwe, although they had found a positive impact of the South African ad Egyptian markets upon growth, and Meshach (2007) for Botswana, although a more recent paper by Ahmed and Mmolainyane (2014) find a direct and robust significant association between financial integration and economic growth in Botswana from 1974 to 2009.

However, cross-sectional studies focused on Africa provide very mixed evidence with Agbetsiafia (2004) and Ndako (2010) reporting a positive influence of stock markets upon economic growth, while Atindehou et al. (2005) find evidence of weak causal relationship for 12 African countries studied.

Quartey and Prah (2008) for Ghana and Odhiambo (2007) for Kenya and South Africa, but not for Tanzania, find evidence in support of the demand-following hypothesis (i.e. that economic growth is an important determinant of financial development.

References

Abou-Ali, H., El-Azony, H., El-Laithy, H., Haughton, J., & Khandker, S. R. (2009). Evaluating the impact of Egyptian social fund for development programs. The World Bank, Policy Research Working Paper Series 4993.

Agbetsiafia, D. (2004). The finance growth nexus: Evidence from Sub-Saharan Africa. *Savings and Development, 28*(3), 271–288.

Ahmed, A. D., & Mmolainyane, K. K. (2014). Financial integration, capital market development and economic performance: Evidence from Botswana. *Economic Modelling, 42*, 1–14.

Arcand, J.-L., Berkes, E., & Panizza, U. (2012). *Too much finance?* International Monetary Fund. Washington, DC: *Working Paper, N, 161* (2012).

Arcand, J. L., Berkes, E., & Panizza, U. (2015). Too much finance? *Journal of Economic Growth, 20*(2), 105–148.

Arndt, C., Jones, S., & Tarp, F. (2015). Assessing foreign aid's contribution to growth and development. *World Development, 69*, 6–18.

Atindehou, R. B., Guyeie, J. P., & Amenounve, E. K. (2005). Financial intermediation and economic growth: Evidence from Western Africa. *Applied Financial Economics, 15*, 777–790.

Attanasio, O., Augsburg, B., Haas, R., Fitzsimons, E., & Harmgart, H. (2011). Group lending or individual lending? Evidence from a randomised field experiment in Mongolia. Institute for Fiscal Studies, IFS Working Papers: W11/20.

Banerjee, A. V., & Duflo, E. (2005). Growth theory through the lens of development economics. *Handbook of Economic Growth, 1*, 473–552.

Banerjee, A. V., & Moll, B. (2010). Why does misallocation persist? *American Economic Journal: Macroeconomics, 2*(1), 189–206.

Banerjee, A., Duflo, E., Glennerster, R., & Kinnan, C. (2009). The miracle of microfinance? Evidence from a randomized evaluation. Department of Economics Massachusetts Institute of Technology MIT Working Paper, 1–40.

Banerjee, A., Duflo, E., Glennerster, R., & Kinnan, C. (2015). The miracle of microfinance? Evidence from a randomized evaluation. *American Economic Journal: Applied Economics, 7*(1), 22–53.

Bateman, M., & Chang, H. J. 2012. Microfinance and the illusion of development: From hubris to nemesis in thirty years. *World Economic Review*, (1).

Beck, T. (2013). Finance, growth and fragility: The role of government. *The International Journal of Banking, Accounting and Finance, 5*(1/2), 49–77.

Berhane, G., & Gardebroek, C. (2011). Does microfinance reduce rural poverty? Evidence based on household panel data from Northern Ethiopia. *American Journal of Agricultural Economics, 93*(1), 43–55.

Bertoli, S. (2015). Does return migration influence fertility at home? *IZA World of Labor, 2015*, 204.

Bertoli, S., & Marchetta, F. (2015). Bringing it all back home: Return migration and fertility choices. *World Development, N, 65*, 27–40.

Bräutigam, D. A., & Knack, S. (2004). Foreign aid, institutions, and governance in sub-Saharan Africa. *Economic Development and Cultural Change, 52*(2), 255–285.

Buera, F. J., Kaboski, J. P., & Shin, Y. (2011). Finance and development: A tale of two sectors. *The American Economic Review, 101*(5), 1964–2002.

Burnside, C., & Dollar, D. (2000). Aid, policies and growth. *American Economic Review, 90*, 847–869.

Cecchetti, S. G., & Kharroubi, E. (2012). Reassessing the impact of finance on growth, bank for international settlements.

Cho, Y. J. (2010). The role of state intervention in the financial sector: Crisis prevention, containment, and resolution. ADBI Working Paper Series. Tokyo, Japan: Asian Development Bank Institute.

Clemens, M., Radelet, S., Bhavnani, R., & Bazzi, S. (2012). Counting chickens when they hatch: Timing and the effects of aid on growth. *Economic Journal*, *122*, 590–618.

Collinson, S., Narula, R., & Rugman, A. (2016). *International business*. London: Pearson.

Cotler, P., & Woodruff, C. (2008). The impact of short-term credit on microenterprises: Evidence from the Fincomun-Bimbo program in Mexico. *Economic Development & Cultural Change, 56*(4), 829–849.

Cuong, N. V. (2008). Is a governmental micro-credit program for the poor really pro-poor? Evidence from Vietnam. *The Developing Economies, 46*(2), 151–187.

Demirguc-Kunt, A. (2014). Presidential address: Financial inclusion. *The Atlantic Economic Journal (2014), 42*, 349–356. DOI: 10.1007/s11293-014-9429-z.

Dupas, P., & Robinson, J. (2013). Savings constraints and microenterprise development: Evidence from a field experiment in Kenya. *American Economic Journal: Applied Economics, 5*(1), 163–192.

Duvendack, M., Palmer-Jones, R., Copestake, J., Hooper, L., Loke, Y., & Rao, N. (2011). *What is the evidence of the impact of microfinance on the well-being of poor people?* London: EPPICentre.

Enisan, A. A., & Olufisayo, A. O. (2009). Stock market development and economic growth: Evidence from seven Sub-Saharan African countries. *Journal of Economics and Business, 61*(2), 162–171.

Freixas, X., & Mayer, C. (2011). Banking, finance, and the role of the state. *Oxford Review of Economic Policy, 27*(3), 397–410.

Galiani, S., & Schargrodsky, E. (2010). Property rights for the poor: Effects of land titling. *Journal of Public Economics, 94*(9), 700–729.

Gertler, P., Levine, D. I., & Moretti, E. (2009). Do microfinance programs help families insure consumption against illness? *Health Economics, 18*(3), 257–273.

Giorgioni, G., & Kok, S. K. (2016). Empirical assessment of the finance and growth nexus in frontier markets. In G. Andrikopoulos Kallinterakis (Eds.), *Handbook of Frontier Markets*. London: Elsevier.

Hansen, H., & Tarp, F. (2001). Aid and growth regressions. *Journal of Development Economics, 64* (September), 547–570.

Hsieh, C. T., & Olken, B. A. (2014). The missing 'missing middle'. *The Journal of Economic Perspectives, 28*(3), 89–108.

Imai, K. S., & Azam, M. D. S. (2012). Does microfinance reduce poverty in Bangladesh? New evidence from household panel data. *Journal of Development Studies, 48*(5), 633–653.

Johnston, D., & Morduch, J. (2008). The unbanked: Evidence from Indonesia. *The World Bank Economic Review, 22*(3), 517–537.

Kabeer, N. (2017). Economic pathways to women's empowerment and active citizenship: What does the evidence from Bangladesh tell us?. *The Journal of Development Studies, 53*(5), 649–663.

Kaboski, J. P., & Townsend, R. M. (2012). The impact of credit on village economies. *American Economic Journal. Applied Economics, 4*(2), 98–133.

Khandker, S. R. (2005). Microfinance and poverty: Evidence using panel data from Bangladesh. *World Bank Economic Review, 19*(2), 263–286.

Laeven, L., & Valencia, F. (2013). The real effects of financial sector interventions during crises. *Journal of Money, Credit and Banking, 45*(1), 147–177.

Law, S. H., & Singh, N. (2014). Does too much finance harm economic growth? *Journal of Banking & Finance, 41*, 36–44.

Meshach, A. J., (2007). Effects of financial integration on financial development and economic performance of the SACU countries. ECA/ADB AFRICAN Economic Conference, 15–17 November 2007, Addis Ababa.

Midrigan, V., & Xu, D. Y. (2014). Finance and misallocation: Evidence from plant-level data. *The American Economic Review, 104*(2), 422–458.

Mosley, P. (2015). Fiscal composition and aid-effectiveness. *World Development, 69* (May), 106–115.

Narula, R., & Dunning, J. (2000). Industrial development, globalization and multinational enterprises: New realities for developing countries. *Oxford Development Studies, 28*(2), 141–167.

Narula, R., & Dunning, J. (2010). Multinational enterprises, development and globalization: Some clarifications and a research agenda. *Oxford Development Studies, 38*(3), 263–287.

Ndako, U. B. (2010). Stock markets, banks and economic growth: Time series evidence from South Africa. *The African Finance Journal, 12*(2), 72–92.

Nghiem, S., Coelli, T., & Rao, P. (2012). Assessing the welfare effects of microfinance in Vietnam: Empirical results from a quasi-experimental survey. *Journal of Development Studies, 48*(5), 619–632.

Odhiambo, N. M. (2007). Financial development in Kenya: A dynamic test of the finance-led growth hypotheses. *Economic Issues, 13*(2), 21–36.

Omar Mahmoud, T., Rapoport, H., Steinmayr, A., & Trebesch, C. (2013). The effect of labor migration on the diffusion of democracy: Evidence from a former soviet republic. IZA Discussion Paper No. 7980.

Papanek, G. (1972). The effect of aid and other resource transfers on savings and growth in less developed countries. *Economic Journal, 82,* 863–874.

Papanek, G. (1973). Aid, private investment, savings and growth in less developed countries. *Journal of Political Economy, 81,* 120–131.

Pearce, R. (2001). Multinationals and industrialisation: The bases of 'inward investment' policy. *International Journal of the Economics of Business, 8*(1), 51–73.

Quartey, P., & Prah, F. (2008). Financial development and economic growth in Ghana: Is there a causal link? *African Finance Journal, 10*(1), 28–54.

Rajan, R., & Subramaniam, A. (2008). Aid and growth: What does the cross-section evidence really show? *Review of Economics and Statistics, 90,* 643–665.

Rajan, R., & Subramaniam, A. (2009). *Aid, Dutch disease and manufacturing growth.* Washington, DC: Center for Global Development, Working Paper 196.

Takahashi, K., Higashikata, T., & Tsukada, K. (2010). The short-term poverty impact of small-scale, collateral-free microcredit in Indonesia: A matching estimator approach. *Developing Economies, 48*(1), 128–155.

UNCTAD – United Nations Conference on Trade and Development. (2011). World Investment Report (2011). *Non-equity modes of international production and development.* United Nations: New York and Geneva.

World Bank. (2001). *Finance for growth: Policy choices in a volatile world.* Washington, DC: World Bank.

Gianluigi Giorgioni is a lecturer in economics and finance at University of Liverpool Management School (ULMS). His research interests focus on the impact of different sources of finance upon economic growth and development, currency unions in developing countries (CFA Franc Zone) and Islamic finance.

Index

© The Author(s) 2017
G. Giorgioni (ed.), *Development Finance*, Palgrave Studies in Impact Finance, DOI 10.1057/978-1-137-58032-0